W9-AOV-237

MONDAY

MORNING

QUARTERBACK

Other Books by JONATHAN YARDLEY

Ring: A Biography of Ring Lardner

Our Kind of People: The Story of an American Family

Out of Step: Notes from a Purple Decade

States of Mind: A Personal Journey through the Mid-Atlantic

Misfit: The Strange Life of Frederick Exley

MONDAY MORNING QUARTERBACK

JONATHAN YARDLEY

ROWMAN & LITTLEFIELD PUBLISHERS, INC.
Lanham • Boulder • New York • Oxford

ROWMAN & LITTLEFIELD PUBLISHERS, INC.

Published in the United States of America
by Rowman & Littlefield Publishers, Inc.
4720 Boston Way, Lanham, Maryland 20706

12 Hid's Copse Road
Cumnor Hill, Oxford OX2 9JJ, England

British Library Cataloguing in Publication Information Available

Library of Congress Cataloging-in-Publication Data
Yardley, Jonathan.
  Monday morning quarterback : notes from the 90s / Jonathan
Yardley.
    p. cm.
  ISBN 0-8476-9204-3 (alk. paper)
    1. United States—Civilization—1970– 2. Popular culture—
United States—History—20th century. 3. United States—
Intellectual life—20th century. 4. United States—Politics and
government—1989– 5. United States—Social conditions—1980–
6. Yardley, Jonathan. I. Title.
  E169.12.Y36 1998
  973.91—dc21   98-7243
                                                                CIP

Printed in the United States of America

♾ ™ The paper used in this publication meets the minimum
requirements of American National Standard for Information
Sciences—Permanence of Paper for Printed Library Materials, ANSI
Z39.48–1984.

∽o∾

For

Julian and Elinor Hartt

∽o∾

CONTENTS

꩜

INTRODUCTION

∾

One of my favorite stories, no doubt apocryphal, is told of a venerable newspaper editor—a Virginian, a Richmonder to boot—who was asked how he liked to relax of an evening. "I pour myself a glass of whiskey," he said, "and repair to my bed, where I sip whiskey and read my old editorials."

Hence the collection and publication of one's old newspaper columns. Don't for a moment believe that what's written today is forgotten tomorrow, at least not by the person who wrote it. Newspaper people may say, self-deprecatingly, that their work is the raw material of fish wrappings, but in our secret hearts we treasure it and fancy it to have immense powers of longevity. How else to explain the dusty compilations of journalistic ephemera that rest, untouched, on the most remote shelves of libraries and used-book stores?

Herewith yet another, though of course—in a fit of the naive optimism that is every writer's curse—I imagine a grander fate for it. I call it *Monday Morning Quarterback* because my column for the Style section of the *Washington Post* is published on Monday and because second-guessing is second nature to the newspaper homilist, which is exactly what I am. I come from a long line of preachers and teachers. The line ends with my generation, not a single member of which follows those honorable callings, but the habit is bred in the bone, as was once pointed out to me by a friend who said that preaching—and perhaps even teaching—is the essence of my Monday reflections.

This is quite correct. The nearly six dozen pieces here are the testament of a quite unashamedly old-fashioned man who is trying, with only limited success, to make sense of a senseless world and is doing so from the pulpit that a generous and tolerant newspaper has given him. It is true that old crocks have been grousing in a similar manner for as long as there have been old crocks, but since the world will always offer something to complain about, someone's got to do the complaining. I volunteered in the fall of 1957, when I expressed an opinion in the pages of the *Daily Tar Heel*, at the University of North Carolina, and I haven't stopped since.

Seven years ago, under the title *Out of Step*, I published my first collection of Monday columns. In choosing the pieces for this one I have made every effort to avoid retracing ground already explored in that earlier book, but a certain amount of repetition is inevitable. The controversies about which I write change from year to year, but the convictions that I bring to bear on them remain the same. Whatever else I may be, I am not a relativist. I believe what I believe, and I weigh every passing event against it.

Precious little, alas, meets with my unqualified approval. There is much to laugh about in Broadway's longest-running show, the human comedy, and not much about which to cheer. The older I get and the longer I sit in the audience, the more I am convinced that laughter—as opposed to anger, or ideology, or partisan rancor—is the only appropriate response to this circus, which is why most of the pieces here are light-hearted in tone. Many were written to amuse myself and in the hope that they might amuse readers; senses of humor being such as they are, that is for each reader to decide.

It certainly is true, though, that beneath the laughter lie dismay and sorrow. There is much about the modern world that pleases and even delights me—its technology most of all, and its extraordinary means of instant communications—but there is far more that I find repellent. With the power in our grasp to achieve brilliance, we dash without a moment's reflection to the shoddy, the meretricious, the self-serving, the shallow. This in substantial measure is the subject matter of Part One, with its four sections devoted to the writing and publishing of books, the press and the media, the academy and ideological fashion, and politics.

The last requires a moment's explanation. My reputation,

such of it as I may have, derives from book-reviewing as well as commentary on cultural and social matters, but my deep interest in politics and not-inconsiderable journalistic engagement with it date back to the 1950s. For about two decades politics was my chief professional preoccupation, mainly the politics of North Carolina—it is sufficiently byzantine to be an education in itself—but also of the nation. When I joined the *Washington Post* in 1981, I was shy about commenting on politics in a newspaper the staff of which includes many of the best informed and wisest of political journalists, but in time that shyness evaporated. There were subjects about which I had things to say, and I said them. Several of the pieces in which I did so are included here; they are not about the nuts and bolts of politics, in which I no longer have any interest at all, but about what politics tells us about ourselves and our country.

As a boy in the 1950s I followed the presidential races between Dwight Eisenhower and Adlai Stevenson with intense interest. I admired Stevenson greatly, for his civility, his wit and his eloquence, and remained loyal to his genteel liberalism for many years. In North Carolina in the 1960s I also became deeply involved in the civil rights movement, not as a participant—I firmly believe that journalists can do their work properly only on the sidelines—but as an editorialist who wrote sympathetically about the sit-ins and other demonstrations against segregation in its many forms. I felt then, as I feel now, that the cause of civil rights was utterly unconnected to ideology or partisanship, but to live in the upper South in those days and to embrace that cause was to be a "liberal." It never occurred to me that I was, or might ever be, anything else.

Gradually my interests—and my politics—began to change. In the mid-1960s I worked as an editorialist for the *Greensboro Daily News* and took on the part-time job of book editor. I began to feel that writing editorials was pointless—most of what I wrote seemed to vanish into a vacuum—and at the same time my literary interests grew steadily stronger. I began writing book reviews not merely for my own paper but for others as well and for national magazines. By the mid-1970s I had abandoned the editorial page and become a full-time book reviewer. I had also, though I was only dimly aware of it at the time, begun to undergo a transformation in my political convictions.

To say that I flipflopped from left to right is inaccurate, because I was never a genuine leftist; I come from a family tradition of social and cultural conservatism, and I have always been faithful to this, albeit at times in my fashion. So it can come as no surprise that events of the 1960s and 1970s left me deeply shaken. Though I opposed the war in Vietnam and endorsed many of the ends, if not the means, of the Great Society, I was appalled by the wholesale repudiation of authority and tradition not merely by the pampered young of the middle class but by the adults—professors, university administrators, journalists, intellectuals, politicians—who followed in their train. I was, as it happened, at Harvard on a postgraduate fellowship when Harvard Yard was "trashed"; this, with all its repercussions, eventually became the shaping event in my adult life.

Now, three decades later, my politics are not easily defined. I am, in the words of my friend and colleague David Nicholson, "an unregenerate integrationist," which still, in the minds of many, makes me a "liberal." I detested the presidencies of Ronald Reagan and George Bush, which in those same minds also makes me a "liberal," but I even more ardently detest that of Bill Clinton, which makes me a . . . go figure. I believe in a just society and in a small government, and I do not believe that those convictions are mutually exclusive.

On matters of culture and society, I remain true to the faith of my fathers. The let-it-all-hang-out mood of the Sixties was not without its alluring aspects, especially for one who at the time was still young and under hormonal overload, but their appeal to me quickly disappeared. I am a person of reticence and restraint, old Wasp qualities that I, against the drift of fashion, continue to honor. I welcome the New, but expect it to prove its worth before acknowledging its place beside the Old. I find little of value or interest in the Flavors of the Month that academics, intellectuals and too many of my fellow journalists fall all over each other to embrace. If at times this leads me into an excess of scorn not merely for the Flavor of the Month but also for those who so eagerly lap it up, well, 'tis a pity, but one over which I have never lost a moment's sleep.

There is, in the columns collected in Part Two of this volume, respite from such matters. These are pieces of a more personal nature, and, though at times my spine can be seen to stiffen in them, a more subdued and reflective character. The chapter on sports is a chronicle of my gradual and reluctant disengagement from major league baseball. The shorter selection of tributes to people whose deaths diminished my world is self-explanatory. As for the last, it is something of a grab bag; many of the pieces therein actually are, as the chapter title indicates, about me, my little world and what interests me about it, while a few others are odds and ends for which I feel affection and which fit into no other clear category.

With one exception, the pieces are arranged chronologically; it made sense to run the ones about Baltimore's football raid on Cleveland consecutively, and I have done so. I have tried to keep repetitiveness to a minimum, but, as I said a few paragraphs earlier, some is unavoidable. Having beaten that particular dead horse to a fare-thee-well, I have included not one column about federal subsidy of the arts and humanities, and I have kept my moans and groans about the schools of creative writing to the absolute minimum. Readers who do me the kindness of hearing me out each Monday doubtless will regard both of these omissions as great blessings.

∽◌∾

Every writer should be so fortunate as to have one person in mind as he works: his ideal reader, whose standards and tastes he respects above all others', whose praise he treasures above all others'. My fortune is good beyond measure, because my ideal reader is Marie Arana-Ward. Her support, counsel, encouragement and love are indescribably precious gifts.

As the 1990s began my editor at Style was, as from my first day at the *Post*, my old and dear friend Ellen Edwards. When

Ellen moved on to reporting and then to motherhood, her place was taken by Rose Jacobius, for which I quickly became immensely grateful. I am also indebted to Style's Sunday staff, whose editors pass final judgment on my columns and whose advice often improves them far more than I ever could on my own. Over the years these have included Mary Alma Welch, Tom Kavanagh, and David DeNicolo. Heartfelt thanks to all of them. I would be remiss did I not also express my gratitude to Mary Hadar, David Von Drehle, Leonard Downie, Robert Kaiser, Donald Graham, Nina King and David Nicholson and, most particularly, Marie Arana-Ward.

During the years these pieces were written I was married to Sue Hartt. She shouldered the burden of reading my daily journalism and occasional attempts at something higher for nearly a quarter-century. Her patience, forbearance and good humor were, when one considers what she had to put up with, entirely astonishing. My first collection of columns was dedicated to her. This one is dedicated to her father and stepmother, whose place in my life and heart is incalculably large.

Jonathan Yardley
Baltimore
February 19, 1998

PART ONE

ONE

⧽o⧼

THE
LIT'RY LIFE

⧽o⧼

IN THE RED

◆

January 13, 1992

The birth of a publishing house is usually to be celebrated, all the more so since it occurs so rarely and since the hopes of all participants tend to be at once so lofty and so fragile. But it's pretty hard to work up much of a hurrah for the rough beast that got itself born in Manhattan last week; it is called New Press, but there's really nothing new about it at all—unless smugness and presumption were manufactured for the first time at the hour of its birth.

The New Press is the brainchild of Andre Schiffrin, who ran the firm of Pantheon for nearly three decades but was shown the door in 1990 by its parent corporation, Random House, when he declined to pare back his publishing program or his staff. At the time a mighty effort was made by Schiffrin and his friends to represent his dismissal as yet another instance of corporate cold-bloodedness, not to mention—because Schiffrin's political fancies run to the left of center—ideological censorship, but in truth there was a good deal more to the case than that.

The truth was that Schiffrin and his overpopulated staff were running Pantheon toward, if not into, the ground. Precise figures on Pantheon's deficit have been difficult to come by, but estimates have ranged from $400,000 a year to (more likely) $3 million or more. Schiffrin and his claque did not dispute the shortfall but argued that (a) Random House could afford to cover it with the profits from other divisions and (b) Random House was *obliged* to cover it because of the exquisitely high moral tone of the Pantheon list.

To their immense credit, the people who make such decisions at Random House were having none of it. Schiffrin was let go, and after his toadies set up a great public lamentation on his behalf, several dozen high executives of the firm published a letter in which was said, among many other things: "There is no reason why Pantheon shouldn't live by the same fiscal rules as the rest of us at Random House and throughout the industry."

Thus the matter seemed, early in the spring of 1990, to have ended. The leadership of Pantheon changed but the firm's essential character—intellectual, Continental, leftish—remained the same. Various of Schiffrin's editors and authors trooped off to other houses, but as that happens all the time in publishing, for reasons having nothing to do with ideology and everything to do with greed, scarcely an eyebrow was raised. It was back to business as usual.

Except, that is, for Schiffrin, who was out of a job. From time to time rumors circulated about his imminent resurfacing, but for nearly two years there was no definitive word. In the normal world this might seem in any event a matter of interest to Schiffrin and no one else, but that fails to account for the utter abnormality of the publishing industry, wherein the subject of other people's jobs passes from fascination to obsession to mania. Thus it was that at the meeting in New York of the American Booksellers Association, in June of last year, the word "Andre" tinkled in the air much as the word "God" echoes through a convention of Jesuits.

Last week the skies at last parted and the truth became known. Schiffrin had spent the two years currying support among those who dole out money at such philanthropic enterprises as the Rockefeller Brothers Fund, the MacArthur Foundation and the (!) Andy Warhol Foundation for the Visual Arts. About a dozen such organizations have agreed to underwrite New Press, which Schiffrin said at a press conference in its honor will "create a new structure for publishing in much the same way that PBS created an alternative to commercial television." New Press will be independent and nonprofit, indeed is projected to run at a loss; after five years Schiffrin hopes that revenues from sales will cover 80 per cent of expenses, leaving his friends at the foundations to pick up the balance.

It is of course always immensely amusing to see the foundations get taken to the cleaners, and Schiffrin deserves the highest marks for doing so in such elegant fashion; it is far less amusing that the City University of New York, a publicly financed institution, is providing free office space for the patently ideological operations of New Press. As for the idea that, as Schiffrin put it, "there is a gap between the commercial houses and the university presses, and we think we can fill it," that is either self-delusion or twaddle pure and simple; ditto for the notion that there exists in trade publishing a de facto "market censorship" operating to assure that books of exquisitely high moral tone "don't make their way through to the public."

How is New Press going to fill these gaps and rectify these ghastly injustices? Well, its first list, to be published this spring, includes *Race: How Blacks and Whites Think and Feel About the American Obsession*, by Studs Terkel, several of whose previous books have been best-sellers; *AIDS Agenda: Emerging Issues in Civil Rights*, produced by the establishmentarian American Civil Liberties Union; and *Early Black Photographers 1840–1940*, drawn from the eminently distinguished Schomberg Center for Research in Black Culture.

Consider by way of contrast the spring catalogue of Pantheon, which arrived the same day as news of the birth of New Press was published. Its 20 titles include *One Nation Under the Gun*, by Rick Hornung, an account of the Mohawk uprising in Canada; *Singing the Master: The Emergence of African American Culture in the Plantation South*, by Roger D. Abrahams; *The Stories of John Edgar Wideman*, a collection by the prominent and outspoken black novelist; and *Coming Out: An Anthology of International Gay and Lesbian Writing*.

It's difficult to imagine a snugger fit than these two lists; they go together like a horse and carriage, except that maybe the Pantheon list is just a shade more lefty than the New Press list.

The notion that "market censorship"—for which read "conspiracy"—keeps books of leftist or any other political coloration out of print is fantasy, pure and simple, though doubtless a useful fantasy if you're trying to cajole a few foundations into forking over a few million dollars. As one who receives in each day's mail the latest books from a broad variety of American publishers, I (and my aching back) can testify to nothing so much as the incredible range of opinion those books embrace. Left, right, middle; nutty left, kooky right, soporific middle—you can get anything you want at this particular restaurant, just so long as you're willing to pay for it.

That's the only real difference between Andre Schiffrin and most other publishers: the latter recognize their responsibility, to corporate owners and stockholders, to earn a fair return. As the 1990 letter by Random House executives put it, "unlike Pantheon, we have preserved our independence and the independence of our authors by supporting the integrity of our publishing programs with fiscal responsibility." Shiffrin's record, at Pantheon and now at New Press, clearly indicates that he believes himself to have risen above that duty.

So be it. If Schiffrin can talk the foundations into subsidizing his fantasies about how the marketplace, in the best of all possible worlds, ought to operate, more power to him; if he manages to publish a few good books along the way, more power to him still. But do the rest of us a favor: Don't try to sell us the fiction that the moral life of publishing is being elevated by this undertaking. The hunch here is that the real trouble with publishing these past two years hasn't been that worthwhile, controversial books haven't been published; it's that they haven't been published by Andre Schiffrin. This is the problem that New Press seems to exist largely, if not solely, to rectify.

DAISY CHAIN

∽o∾

June 22, 1992

Esquire is at it again. Five years after inflicting upon its readers a "Guide to the Literary Universe," the self-styled "Magazine for Men" is back with what it chooses to call "A Down-to-Earth Guide to Where Budding Writers Come From." This fey, cluttered document is in all respects depressing, and in none more so than this: It is absolutely, conclusively and terminally accurate, in essence if not all particulars.

No, it's not supposed to be taken seriously, or at least not *that* seriously. It was done in fun, no doubt, and is meant to be received as such—and try telling that to the assistant professor of creative writing at Yahoo State who cannot for the life of him find his name anywhere herein. But whatever the motives behind its formulation, this latest "Guide" paints a faithful portrait of the American literary scene in this, the final decade of the 20th century. It is all the more faithful when one considers the source: Though *Esquire*, with unwonted modesty, absents itself from the "Guide," it is in fact a most sedulous participant in precisely the literary culture it depicts.

Five years ago *Esquire*'s "Guide" was both cynical and frivolous. It was, as was noted in this space at the time, "not so much a ranking of writers and publishers as one of hustlers and promoters," all of them occupants of "a sordid place where money, publicity and notoriety are held dear while art and character are valueless." This, it will be recalled, was the high moment of the Brat Pack novelists, as well as the editors and agents and other

9

hangers-on who profited off them; *Esquire*, which was right in the middle of the pack, celebrated them with all due ceremony. But the Brat Pack is history now, its few minutes of allotted time having long since elapsed. These are the 1990s, a kinder and gentler age, so *Esquire*'s stormy cosmos of 1987—it even had a "Red Hot Center"—has been replaced by a leafy, verdant garden wherein grow the tender shoots of American literature. It is inexpressibly sweet and insufferably cozy.

A garden is how *Esquire* chooses to represent it, but a daisy chain would be more to the point. The literary world that this two-page drawing all too tellingly portrays is a tiny, closed circle the chief constituents of which are publishing houses and the fiction editors they employ; general-circulation magazines and literary journals, most of the latter doggedly obscure; and—this above all—university writing programs and the writers/professors/gurus who hold sway therein.

Esquire does not explain how this circle operates—its "Guide" is accompanied by scant text or apologia, only the drawing and the lists it features—but one need possess no brilliant powers of deduction in order to fathom its workings. The aspiring writer enrolls at a university and attaches herself to a guru in the writing program; he steers her stories into one of the little magazines, and after enough have appeared he moves her along to an editor at a publishing house with whom he has a relationship of mutual convenience; the aspirant's first book appears, she is hired as a teacher of creative writing at her alma mater or some other institution, and soon enough begins playing her own little part in the eternal clockwise movement of the chain.

Around and around it goes, where it all ends, everybody knows: in the publication of books that are of importance and interest only to those who participate in the chain. Spend some time prowling around through the various lists *Esquire* provides, and you're likely to be struck by nothing so much as this: All but a handful of the individuals included are utterly unknown to all but a handful of Americans outside the chain. This is true not merely of the editors and publishers, whose work is mostly done behind the scenes, but also of the writers/professors/gurus; these great gods of late-20th-century American literature are to all intents and purposes unheard-of outside the tiny precincts in which they exercise their titanic powers.

It is this tight insularity that distinguishes the literary culture of today from its forebears. There is nothing new about the incestuous politics it plays. One need only read George Gissing's penetrating, prescient novel, *New Grub Street*, published in 1891, to understand that so long as there has been a literary profession there has been literary politics. It is no less instructive to read the biography of—for example—the sainted F. Scott Fitzgerald and thus to be instructed about the delight he took in playing at literary patron and mentor; long before the writing schools came along to institutionalize the procedure, Famous Writers were hard at work embellishing their own reputations by furthering the careers of others.

Thus it was and thus it will always be. But if Gissing's was an incestuous little world, it was also one in which a writer had to earn his keep by practicing his trade, by being out and about in the real world he attempted to portray in his fiction; ditto for the world of Fitzgerald, who largely supported his insatiable self and his equally insatiable wife off stories sold to commercial magazines and whose circle was as much social and artistic as it was literary.

The practitioners of "high" literature in the shank years of this century have no such concerns. They are the beneficiaries of stipends, or sinecures, paid out of university treasuries; if few of them get rich, neither do any of them get poor. They are as comfy as can be. They preen before their adoring disciples, give readings of "works-in-progress" to throngs of two dozen or more at wine-and-cheese receptions, publish in magazines that circulate in the low four figures, issue from time to time their slender volumes of anemic stories—and fancy themselves to be at the very center of the literary universe.

An unintended consequence of this serene, hermetic existence is that nothing of weight or distinction is written by those who live it. Not merely are the writers/professors/gurus cited by *Esquire* near-universally unknown, they are the authors of work so pallid and irrelevant as to mock the idea of serious literary fiction and poetry—authors, that is, when they actually depart from the pleasant distractions of writing-school life long enough to do any writing of their own. To be sure a few among them possess stylistic and imaginative gifts, and the books of a very few sometimes achieve notice outside the daisy chain, but these are rare and atypical exceptions. The salient fact about the writing done by these people is that it simply and conclusively *does not matter*.

Perhaps this is itself of no consequence. The protestations and prayers of publishers and booksellers to the contrary notwithstanding, literature doesn't occupy the central cultural position that it did in the pre-technological age. Perhaps we wouldn't listen to our novelists and poets even if they did have anything pertinent or enlightening to tell us; after all, what is a mere purveyor of words by contrast with the high priests and priestesses of mass popular culture?

But what *Esquire* is here to tell us, albeit inadvertently, is that the "mighty oaks" and "green thumbs" and "perennials" who populate its garden haven't the slightest interest in talking to us. It isn't depicted in *Esquire*'s drawing, but there is a wall around this garden behind which its inhabitants choose to hide. Inside the garden all is cozy and snug, because the wall shields the garden's occupants from the hard, complicated and indifferent world outside. That they choose to stay behind it is easy enough to understand, human nature being such as it is; it is equally easy to understand why scarcely a soul on the outside knows, or cares, what they do there.

THE CULTURE OF SELF

∽०∾

March 15, 1993

Looking down upon these United States from the literary pique he occupies, Philip Roth surveys the passing scene and finds it, you will scarcely be surprised to learn, not at all to his liking. "I don't think there's a decline of the novel," he told the *New York Times* last week in the course of promoting his most recent book, "so much as the decline of the readership. There's been a drastic decline, even a disappearance, of a serious readership." He continued:

> By readers, I don't mean people who pick up a book, once in a while. By readers, I mean people who when they are at work think that after dinner tonight and after the kids are in bed, I'm going to read for two hours. That's what I mean. Number Two, these people do it three or four nights a week for two and a half, three hours, and while they do it they don't watch television or answer the phone.
>
> So if that's what readers are, how many of them are there? We are down to a gulag archipelago of readers. Of the sort of readers I've described, there are 176 of them in Nashville, 432 in Atlanta, 4,011 in Chicago, 3,017 in Los Angeles and 7,000 in New York. It adds up to 60,000 people. I assure you there are no more. We would be foolish to add a zero. Maybe there are 120,000. But that's it, and that is bizarre.

Is the preternaturally witty Roth having sport with us once again? Yes and no. The exact figures he quotes are subject to argument—there are, as it happens, 183 readers in Nashville—but the essence of his argument is beyond dispute. Though the proposition that we ever were a nation of readers—readers, that is, of serious fiction and poetry—is dubious at best, there can be no doubt that we now are nothing of the sort. Where once serious fiction played at least a marginal role in our cultural and social life—it was not so long ago, for example, that writers such as William Faulkner and John Cheever could be found adorning the covers of national news magazines—it can now fairly be said to play no role at all. But whether this is to be blamed on a "decline of the readership" as opposed to a "decline of the novel" is, at the very least, debatable.

Roth mentioned, in passing, "the pressures in the society," by which presumably he meant television, technology, mass pop culture, instant communications and all the other ingredients that, stirred together, make our world seem far too crowded and busy to allow time and space for a pastime so leisurely as reading. This is all too true. The person who spends all day in front of a computer or plowing through law books or crunching great big numbers can be forgiven if, at day's end, he or she prefers to collapse in front of the video machinery rather than cuddle up with, say, *Operation Shylock*, the book on behalf of which Roth for the moment now condescends to speak with mere journalists.

This is an "inescapable" fact of contemporary American life, to borrow Roth's word, and it must be reckoned with in any effort to understand what has happened to reading in America. Roth was quite correct to note that "there is a change in the mental landscape having to do with concentration," but the problem goes deeper than a growing reluctance among Americans to devote serious, concentrated attention to matters other than work and personal affairs.

The real problem is that Americans now want and expect to be amused, and to receive that amusement in a passive way. In recent weeks I have been told by three distinguished professors of the humanities, speaking separately and independently, that what they now encounter among students is the expectation not of learning but of entertainment. A generation that finds Bud Light ads amusing and that takes Steven Spielberg movies seriously has neither time nor interest for reading and reflection; as that generation goes, so goes the country itself, in large measure because it was taught to love amusement by its parents—by my own generation, that is, and Roth's.

Yet to blame the "decline of the readership," however accurate that may be, gets only to part of the problem. To deny that there has been a concomitant "decline of the novel" is either plain ignorance or willful disregard of the self-evident facts. Central among these is that what represents itself as serious, literary fiction no longer speaks to a serious general readership—which does, in fact, exist, whatever its size may be—in language to which that readership can respond or about matters in which it is interested.

One need look no farther than Philip Roth himself for proof of this. Three decades ago he gave every indication of becoming the supreme novelist of his generation. I remember as vividly as if it were yesterday coming across his collection of stories, *Goodbye, Columbus,* two or three years after its publication in 1959, and feeling at once that I had found someone who spoke to me as I was at that moment in my life, a very young man still feeling his way into the world of adulthood.

That feeling was reinforced by *Letting Go,* Roth's first novel, which for all its shapeless and excessive length was admirably ambitious, and by his second, *When She Was Good,* in which Roth had the courage to try speaking in a voice not his own about an experience not his own. Then of course there was *Portnoy's Complaint,* the stupendous and revolutionary comic novel that brought any number of old phobias and obsessions out of the dusty closets in which they had so long been hidden. With *Portnoy* its author became that rarest of American creatures, a genuinely famous writer, one who had left the rarified (and largely irrelevant) world of the literati in order to speak to the culture as a whole.

But after *Portnoy* Roth went into an odd retreat. At the very moment that he made what can only be called a breakthrough, he chose to retreat into himself. Or, perhaps more accurately, into the Self. The egocentrism that had lurked beneath the surface of all his early books—except, perhaps, *When She Was Good*—was transported in the wake of *Portnoy* to center stage. Never mind Roth's insistent protests that what he was writing was scarcely autobiography—"I made it all up," he told the *Times* last week—and never mind all the tiresome debates his novels stirred up about the blurred line between fact and fiction. The single most important aspect of all the fiction Roth has written since *Portnoy* is the Self at its center; it is this Self, and this Self alone, in which Roth is interested.

This preoccupation with the ego (not to mention the libido) may be exaggerated in Roth's case, but it is symptomatic of contemporary American literary fiction. Nothing is now rarer on the American literary landscape than a writer—Ernest J. Gaines, Anne Tyler, Peter Taylor—who writes about society as much as Self, who gets outside the prison of self-preoccupation and fixes his gaze on the larger world. Not merely has that prison claimed the vast majority of contemporary American novelists, but it has isolated them from the vast majority of readers, whose interest in the solipsism of others can only be sustained for so long.

It is for this reason, far more than because of any "decline of the readership," that the fiction of Philip Roth has failed since *Portnoy* to find a following much larger than, say, the figure of 60,000 he so casually mentioned. The "inescapable" if inconvenient fact is that Americans in large numbers *will* read novels of some seriousness if they reach outward rather than retreat inward; the success of ambitious if flawed books by Tom Wolfe and Scott Turow is testimony to that, as is the large readership that Anne Tyler's novels consistently enjoy.

This isn't to deny that the serious readership in America is small and getting smaller. It is to say that the blame rests on writers as well as on readers. "Some people believe in God," Roth told the *Times*, "and I believe in the reader." Balderdash. He believes in nothing except Philip Roth, and he expects us to join him prostrate before the altar. Can anyone really be surprised that the church is just about empty?

ONCE IS ENOUGH

✍

April 25, 1994

In last week's obituaries for Ralph Ellison two themes were predominant: admiration bordering on adulation for *Invisible Man*, his masterpiece, and regret mixed with bewilderment over his failure to publish another full-length work of fiction. Though no one was so foolish as to say that Ellison had somehow let us down by publishing only one novel, there was a prevailing sense that his life ended incomplete, that *Invisible Man*, however great, was not enough.

This complaint had in fact been made frequently and widely long before Ellison's death. American readers, whether titled professors or mere initiates, could not quite comprehend the phenomenon of a writer who came from almost nowhere to present us with a work of art at once magnificent and unique and who then failed, or declined, to give us another. Over the years the triumph that was and is *Invisible Man* gradually diminished in the eyes of many because it stood alone rather than with many volumes in a lifetime's work.

Obviously the complaint has more to do with our expectations than with Ellison's achievement, but its sources are easy to identify and not without legitimacy. For one thing it is hard for us to look at a single piece of art and comprehend it as a life's work; we see the long shelves filled by Faulkner and Dreiser, by contrast with which *Invisible Man*, flanked only by two collections of essays, seems small and unfinished. For another, it is natural that, having been given immense pleasure and enlightenment by

Invisible Man, we should long for more of the same from its creator. For yet another, we assume that a writer whose first book reaches such heights has even greater accomplishments within his reach, and we are eager to see precisely what form they might take.

All of these hopes and expectations are entirely reasonable, but what we don't know is whether they are counterproductive, whether their very existence creates additional obstacles over which a writer must climb on his way to other works. American culture is a carnivorous creature, gobbling up writers and artists in its insatiable appetite for more, more, more of whatever it was that they first gave us. We can only guess at how much they pay for this.

It is important to realize that Ellison's was in this sense a very American story. The one-book great writer, or the one-book not-so-great writer, is among our most common and characteristic literary phenomena. The phrase "one-book writer" is so often employed that it should be listed in our dictionaries of literary terms. Usually it is used pejoratively, as in, "He's just a one-book writer," or, "She only has one book in her." The implicit if unfounded assumption is that the person who can write only one good book is not a writer to be reckoned with.

A writer can write more than one book and still be a one-book writer. Frederick Exley published three novels, but only the first, *A Fan's Notes*, really counts; the second and third were pale attempts to repeat what he had so splendidly done the first time around. *The Red Badge of Courage* is Stephen Crane's one book, though he published others, just as *Pale Horse, Pale Rider* is Katherine Anne Porter's and *The Moviegoer* is Walker Percy's and *The Awakening* is Kate Chopin's.

This is not without explanation. It is by no means coincidental that most of the aforementioned books, as well as *Invisible Man*, are heavily autobiographical. Their principal inspiration and raw material are the inner and outer lives of the men and women who wrote them, but those are also their principal limitations. Autobiography is not a bottomless resource, as the fiction of Philip Roth so pointedly if inadvertently reminds us. The autobiographical novelist, having said all or close to all in that first great explosion of creative self-exploration, is left either to cover the same territory over and over again or to go on to other matters. American writers, who come to maturity in a literary culture that venerates Freud and Joyce, rarely choose the second path.

Beyond that, the larger American culture often exercises a distracting or debilitating influence. A literary success such as Ellison enjoyed with *Invisible Man* raises a hullabaloo that, in and of itself, gets in the way of further work. In Ellison's case the hullabaloo was all the more distracting because, as the author of what was immediately recognized as the greatest work of fiction to emerge from black America, he found himself invited to an endless round of conferences and panel discussions and board meetings. Being by all accounts both congenial and gentlemanly, Ellison apparently found it hard to say no; he seems to have taken pleasure in these occasions and the people to whom they introduced him, but they took him away from his desk.

Not merely that, but when expectations are raised to unwonted heights, they can become powerful deterrents to further work. "The success of the novel imposed a burden on Mr. Ellison," William Grimes reported in the *New York Times* last week. "It set an almost impossible artistic standard to live up to." This is by no means a trivial matter. It did not take long for *Invisible Man* to become embedded in the American literary canon and to survive all of that canon's subsequent revisions. Long before its author had entered middle age, *Invisible Man* had become an American classic. The burden of attempting to match it, much less improve upon it, must have been daunting indeed.

We know that Ellison tried. Unlike Thomas Heggen and Ross Lockridge, who so despaired of equalling the great successes of their first books that they committed suicide, Ellison soldiered bravely on. He wrote many fine essays, collected in *Shadow and Act* and *Going to the Territory*, and by all reliable accounts he worked intently on the massive manuscript of a second novel. Surely among the saddest of American literary stories is that of how he lost hundreds of pages of manuscript in a fire, a loss that left him dispirited for years but from which he eventually recovered and then returned to work.

Possibly this manuscript will be edited and published posthumously. We must pray that this happens only if those closest to Ellison judge the manuscript worthy of his own exacting standards. We have already had too many posthumous novels cobbled together out of bits and pieces in order to cash in on their authors' renown; we must not add Ralph Ellison to the list of authors thus victimized. Instead we must tell ourselves that had he never written another word, to have written *Invisible Man* was an accomplishment not merely of a lifetime but for the ages. Nothing—absolutely nothing—can diminish it.

MR. AMIS'S TEETH

∾∘∾

February 6, 1995

The most famous teeth since George Washington's are to be found not in a medical or dental museum but in the steel-trap jaws of one of England's most celebrated, not to mention self-celebrated, youngish novelists. This we learn from transatlantic reports about what bids fair to be the literary tempest to end all literary tempests, or so at least one must be permitted to hope.

Being British it is a tempest in a teapot. Being literary it is mortally savage. It calls to mind the hoary apothegm that academic rivalries are so vicious because the stakes are so small. Ditto for the lit'ry folk, who can work themselves into lathers over matters that the big dogs who bark in the real world would decline even to sniff at, much less raise a leg over.

The matter in dispute last week centered upon Martin Amis, an elfin creature who has parlayed the fame of his father, Kingsley, and his own quite considerable literary skills into a leading position in the post-Thatcherite world of English letters. Amis is the author of several deft if brittle pieces of apprentice work, one novel (*Money*) of genuinely grown-up stature, and a great many essays notable more or less equally for wit, intelligence and nastiness.

All of this, combined with a peculiarly British proclivity for awarding authors the kind of public éclat that Americans bestow upon talk-show hosts and post-adolescent basketball players, has made Amis something of an *enfant terrible*, even though he has by now crossed the line into his forties and the utter untrustworthiness attendant thereto. This means not merely that his name crops up with tiresome frequency in the press but also that— taking a cue from his American counterparts—he has become afflicted with delusions of grandeur.

Or, to put it as his literary rival A.S. Byatt has, "*folie de grandeur.*" This thrust was made in response to reports that Amis had demanded the princely sum of 500,000 pounds—$794,500 American—for his new novel, a tale of the literary life called *The Information.* Byatt went ballistic. She fumed that Amis "must believe that his name is so extraordinary" and that his demand amounted to "a kind of male turkey cocking," and then went for the jugular, or, to be quite precise about it, the molar: "I always earn out my advances and I don't see why I should subsidize his greed, simply because he has a divorce to pay for and has just had all his teeth redone."

It was at this point that the conflict escalated from mere literary chirping to thermonuclear war. According to Sarah Lyall of the *New York Times*, the "conventional wisdom" was that Byatt "had violated the unwritten compact of solidarity among authors and had badly misstepped on the issue of Mr. Amis's teeth," upon which, according to his friends, "he had indeed endured painful and costly dental treatments, dictated not by vanity, but by acute medical necessity." Amis himself, whether due to a siege of bashfulness or to medico-dental exigency, "wouldn't comment."

That was only the beginning. Byatt retired from the field of combat, bloodied perhaps but having scored a direct hit on the opposition. Then others moved to the fore. At this point the proceedings become so populous and confused that only full-time spectators at literary contact sports can identify all the players and the ploys for which they are noted. Suffice it to say that Amis quite out of the blue dumped his agent, Pat Kavanagh, the wife of one of his good friends, the novelist Julian Barnes, and betook himself to the stable of Andrew Wylie, the New York agent who, were he an ice-hockey player, would be permanently assigned to the penalty box on grounds of rough play.

To give the man his due, Wylie went right to work and before anyone knew it had extracted from HarperCollins, according to Lyall, "somewhere between $731,000 and $795,000 . . . , a sum, interestingly enough, not substantially different from what Ms. Kavanagh had negotiated earlier." That got HarperCollins the novel in Britain but not the United States, where rights to two Amis novels were purchased some time back by Harmony Books, a Random House imprint. The first of these, published a few years ago, was *Time's Arrow*, which fell to earth I know not where. Inasmuch as Random House paid $400,000 for the package, *The Information* had better out-sell Danielle Steele if it hopes to get its money back.

The obvious point is that although this may seem to be much ado about mucho dinero, in fact the stakes are high only by the picayune standards of the literary world. For his authorial labors of a couple of years or more Amis may net a couple hundred grand after taxes and dentist's bills, but a second-string second baseman for a second-division ballclub makes that much in half a season, it's a half an hour's box-office receipts for a moderately successful movie, it's what Barbra Streisand makes for a few minutes' crooning.

In the big scheme of things it's pocket change—true high rollers drop that much of an evening at Atlantic City and never look back—but in the lit'ry world it's not just feuding money, it's blood money. Not merely will A.S. Byatt and Martin Amis most likely never again exchange a cordial word, but ditto for Amis and Pat Kavanagh, perhaps Amis and Julian Barnes as well. Doubtless the world will continue to spin merrily along even if all this indeed comes to pass, but what a pity that so many darling people should nickel and dime themselves into enemy camps.

More's the pity since money is supposed to be such an *American* vice. You know, Americans "talk about money in that sharky American style, as if money were the only gauge of anything, the only measure." You know: "Heat, money, sex and fever—this is it, this is New York, this is first class, this is the sharp end." This is—that was—Martin Amis in 1985, in *Money*, the title and themes of which seem just about ready to come back to haunt him. It was also Amis who gave to a collection of his essays about America the title *The Moronic Inferno*, leaving us to wonder how, in its new age of greed, England is now different.

Leaving us to wonder as well: Whatever happened to socialized dentistry?

THE AGE OF CONFESSION

✌︎

May 20, 1996

By any sensible reckoning last week's Second Coming of Marion Barry was appalling, a public *mea non culpa* that was intended to stir empathy but succeeded only in producing nausea. Its professed theme was *I'm O.K., You're O.K.*, but its true import was—to borrow the title of Wendy Kaminer's send-up of pop psychology—*I'm Dysfunctional, You're Dysfunctional.*

That the mayor of the capital of these United States should feel no compunction about appearing before microphones and cameras to deliver a confession both intimate and self-serving should have provoked general astonishment, but it aroused little more than a yawn. In some measure this is explained by the particulars of the case; Barry's act has played too long, with the result that we are both weary of it and incapable of surprise at whatever turns it may take. But the broader explanation is that we now live in the Age of Confession, in which the overt expression of real or imagined inner pain is not merely permissible but mandatory.

Additional proof of this dreary reality appeared only a day before Barry's news conference. The *New York Times Magazine* for May 12 published a special issue called "True Confessions: The Age of the Literary Memoir," wherein were published a dozen reminiscences many of which turned as rapidly as possible into accounts of childhoods spent in families of decidedly dysfunctional character. These were proceeded by a brief essay in which James Atlas proclaimed "the triumph of memoir" in "a virtual library of dysfunctional revelation," and followed by a briefer one in which Mary Karr announced her "working definition for a dysfunctional family: any family with more than one person in it."

None of this is quite so new as these publicists would have us believe. "All happy families resemble each other, each unhappy family is unhappy in its own way": Tolstoy knew that uncommon unhappiness makes for more arresting storytelling than ordinary happiness, and so has virtually every other storyteller since that ancient art first began to take shape. The difference now is that the story has become less important than the storyteller; narrative, whether fiction or nonfiction, now serves not to enrich the reader but to have therapeutic effects upon the writer.

Therapy is all well and good, but making a public proceeding out of it is unseemly. As practiced these days in this country, public confession has as much to do with voyeurism as with healing. It intends to draw in the reader or observer through the shock of intimate confession, and it contends as well in a competition in which everyone tries to walk away with the blue ribbon for worst childhood, most alcoholic father, most possessive mother, most abusive Little League coach. In the end it is not a damnation of dysfunction but a celebration of it.

This may say any number of things about our culture, but one of them most certainly is not that a new golden age of literature is upon us. Rather than a stark departure from what has become the literary norm, the "triumph of memoir" turns out to be merely a continuation of and variation upon all the worst characteristics and excesses of that norm. The only real difference is that young writers who recently were encouraged to spill their private beans in autobiographical fiction are now encouraged to do so in nonfictional narratives. This is neither change nor progress.

James Atlas apparently feels otherwise. He regards the memoir as "surprisingly robust" these days: "A sure sign: the catalogues of universities now offer courses in memoir and the literature of self. Perhaps an even surer sign: literary agents making their annual pilgrimages to the famous writing program at the University of Iowa and signing up memoirists for six-figure deals.

(They used to sign up novelists.) With auguries like these, who can doubt the memoir is here to stay—if not forever, then for a good long while?"

What's so good about that? Me, I find it terminally repellent. The absorption of memoir into the academic sausage grinder should be cause for lamentation rather than applause. Nothing can be better calculated to snuff the life out of any literary genre than the clammy process by which it is reduced to both subject of academic study and object of academic production. When the professors crowd around, it's time to crank up the hearse and start digging the hole.

Not all in the professoriat are guilty. By weird coincidence, on the same day that the *New York Times Magazine* celebrated the literature of dysfunction, Joan Mellen of the Temple University English Department published a heartfelt complaint in the *Baltimore Sun* about contemporary literary fiction, which she described as "narrowly focused on personal lives." Young writers, she said, "wallow in a dead-end of questions of ethnic identity and sexual betrayal, and a timid reliance on the suffocatingly personal, as if the experience of the individual, in or out of a family, were the entire canvas available to the novelist."

Those words apply with equal force to the new fiction and the new memoir. Both genres have degenerated into vehicles for self-infatuation, the gloomier and more angst-haunted the better. Like the bubbleheads who line up to confess for Montel and Oprah, young writers of ostensibly literary aspirations mean to let it all hang out. Their methods are not in fact literary, for extraordinarily little craft is exercised in the telling of their tales; they are so isolated in their tiny private universes that they believe all they need do is speak and the world will stand transfixed.

This is only possible, though, when confession is combined with narrative force and literary artistry. It is unfortunate to see Mary Karr transforming herself into spokeswoman for what the headline on her essay called "Dysfunctional Nation," but it remains true that her memoir of a peculiar childhood, *The Liar's Club*, is a work of genuine originality and merit, if not quite the "classic of American literature" James Atlas prematurely declares it to be. Ultimately what matters most about that book, aside from its literary quality, is not the dysfunction but Karr's ability to rise above it; unlike so many others, she does not deal in dysfunction for its own sake.

The success *The Liar's Club* has enjoyed is gratifying, but it is also dangerous. All those agents and editors descending on the writing factory at Iowa are looking for nothing but sales. They want books, in today's book-promotion jargon, "in the tradition of *The Liar's Club*," and they don't care a whit whether those books are original; they'd prefer *Liar's Club* clones, and they can count on the writing-school gurus to prod their disciples into producing them—after, that is, the gurus produce their own true confessions. The fiction factory has turned into the memoir factory, but it's grinding out the same old baloney.

WRITIN' MAN BLUES

✒

August 26, 1996

Duty calls, Pleasure beckons. To the left of my word processor lies Duty, demanding that attention be paid and torture suffered. To its right lies Pleasure, promising joys beyond calculation and rewards too delicious to contemplate. In the middle sits yours truly, child of the Protestant Work Ethic, closet hedonist. What is a poor boy to do?

Duty came in the mail several weeks ago, interrupting a pleasant holiday with an unpleasant thud on the front porch. It is the fifty-fourth issue of *Granta*, the terminally self-important Anglo-American literary magazine. This issue is called "The Best of Young American Novelists," and contains the work of twenty persons alleged to have attained such lofty status, chosen by four eminent judges from nominees submitted by eighteen rather less eminent judges of regional competitions.

Pleasure, I paid for myself, $43.98 to be exact, at a discount house off the Baltimore Beltway. It is *Down Every Road*, a four-compact-disk compendium of the work of the nonpareil Merle Haggard as recorded by Capital Records between 1962 and 1994. It contains a grand—"grand" is the only word that will suffice—total of one hundred songs, and there is not a bummer in the bunch. I have already listened to it more times than I can count; now I would like to listen to it, as Count Basie used to say, one more once.

So there you have it: the agony of reading contemporary American "literary" fiction on the one hand and the ecstasy of listening to five hours of songs by one of the great figures of contemporary popular music on the other. If you think there's no connection between the two beyond the polar-opposite emotions they arouse in me, read on.

Truth to tell I have made a noble effort to read my way through *Granta 54*, but there's an inescapable problem: the writing inside. Reading *Granta 54* means reading yet more work by yet more products of a literary culture that is now about two steps from the grave it has dug for itself. Open it to almost any page and you'll find a writer wallowing in autobiographical self-infatuation, incapable of lifting his or her eyes away from that infinitely fascinating navel long enough to gaze at the larger and more important world outside. Yes, the level of technical skill is fairly high, but none of these writers has anything of interest to say—to me, at least—with all those finely turned sentences and perfect little paragraphs.

The enterprise itself is flawed from the outset. Almost without exception, the judges of this competition—and make no mistake about it, competition is just what it is—are ranking gurus of the academic writing departments. One shudders to think of the secret agendas that were pursued as tender young writers were nominated and rejected, nominated and approved. Like the writing-school culture itself, *Granta 54* is a daisy-chain operation, complete with back-scratching and quid pro quos. The one saving grace is that the only place it is likely to be read with anything approximating the eagerness *Granta*'s editors expect is in—where else?—the writing schools themselves.

This is where Merle Haggard comes in. Along about my fifth or sixth pass through *Down Every Road* I chanced across an article about it, and more generally about Haggard, in the August issue of the *Atlantic*. That magazine is almost as smug as *Granta*, but it does have its moments. This piece, by a music journalist previously unknown to me named Tony Scherman, is one of them. It is at once a properly and persuasively admiring assessment of Haggard, and a vivid thumbnail sketch of a man who has never hesitated to say what he thinks. That's gotten him in trouble from time to time with the politically correct—viz., "Okie from Muskogee," "The Fightin' Side of Me"—and now it's likely to stir up the animals down in Nashville.

The reason is that Haggard doesn't like much of anything the younger practitioners of country music are doing these days. He told Scherman why in words that ought to be cast in bronze and set on a tablet:

> These songs they got on the radio now, my wife says it sounds like they're singin' about air. What more can they do to the sonofabitch? They've got it down to a science. They've got grooming classes where they can turn out Elvis Presleys—one a day, I think. They gather up at nine-thirty in the morning, they go off in little groups and come back with these prefabricated songs about things that never happened, and it sounds that way. It's so refined, it's so perfect, it's so in tune, and there's no feel, no God-dang soul to it, there's no story, there's no melody, and I just wish I could say somethin' else, but that's my opinion.

The first time I read those words, I was knocked right out of my socks. There, in one paragraph, was everything I'd been trying to say about contemporary American fiction for a decade and a half, but said with a voice of experience I cannot hope to possess. The things that are wrong with country music today are exactly the same things that are wrong with literary fiction today: a total absence of real-life experience, empty technical facility, a follow-the-leader mentality, a preoccupation with self and an indifference to story-telling. Any time Haggard wants work as a literary critic—God knows why he would—this space is his for the asking.

The problem about which he spoke isn't restricted to country music or literary fiction; it's widespread in American culture. Individuality has been replaced by mentorship in which imitation is not merely encouraged but honored, and each genre has become a hothouse more interested in talking to itself than in embracing new audiences. Moviemakers produce films full of references to other movies, novelists write books about novelists, country musicians sing about being country musicians. Obviously the life of the artist is a legitimate subject, but when it becomes the only subject, the ultimate effect is to alienate the artist from the audience.

That's already happened in American literature, a process compounded and hastened by all the external forces that are driving people away from books and into other forms of intellectual pleasure, edification and instruction. Apparently it is happening in country music as well, though the sales enjoyed by today's look-alike musicians suggest the end is not yet nigh. Sooner or later, though, it will come. I just wish I could say something else, but that's my opinion.

PUCKER UP

᳂

March 10, 1997

The e-mail piled up fast in the aftermath of a tart review last week of *The Kiss*, the memoir that has lit'ry Manhattan and its satellites abuzz. Apart from one genuinely idiotic letter in which it was suggested that my dislike for the book arose from some instance of sexual abuse in my past, the mail was overwhelmingly of one mind: How has American culture sunk so low as to take a book such as this seriously, and why are so few people willing to speak out not merely against such trash but against those who condone and abet it?

Heaven knows, *The Kiss* is unadulterated junk. My objections to it arise, mercifully, not from any skeletons skulking in my closet but from its utter lack of literary merit and its transparent meretriciousness. It deserves to be dismissed not because of any larger developments in American society and culture of which it may be symptomatic, but for the simple—and important—reason that it is a bad book. Given Katherine Harrison's dreary prose and catatonic self-absorption, her book would be just as dreadful if the kissers in question had been her and her teddy bear rather than her and her daddy.

But there can be no question that the book is symptomatic as well. Within the tiny world of such literary culture as we still can claim, it is the logical if thoroughly distasteful culmination of a process that has made exhibitionistic narcissism the coin of the realm. This has its origins in various serious developments of the 1920s, chiefly the fiction of James Joyce and the psychology of

Sigmund Freud, but as it has been explored by writers of ever greater mediocrity its seriousness has long since vanished.

Thus we have a process of regression that marches steadily downhill from *Ulysses* to *Portnoy's Complaint* to *The Kiss*. That is a considerable oversimplification of what has been, in fact, a complicated business, but in essence it is true: We have gone from a literature of the self that embraced larger worlds to one in which the self is not merely all but is a marketable commodity, the more outrageous the more marketable. The guise of fiction is no longer necessary or, in purely commercial terms, desirable; the writer willing to etherize herself upon the table of public scrutiny is the one most likely to achieve notoriety and the rewards that now accompany it.

This is as true in pop culture as in the literary hothouse. The present spectacle of the establishment press falling all over itself to legitimize Howard Stern as a representative figure of the age is evidence enough of that. To wit, in the current issue of the *New Yorker*—it used to set much of the cultural agenda by its editorial decisions, but now merely responds to publicity handouts like all the rest of the press—is an article by David Remnick that uses the occasion of Stern's new movie, *Private Parts*, to certify him as "mainstream."

Remnick is an able journalist and his profile of Stern is not without its amusing and perceptive aspects. But in so uncritically accepting Stern on his own terms, it accedes in the lowest-common-denominator redefinition of American cultural standards. For there can be no question that, however droll Stern may occasionally be in an *Animal House* way, he is surpassingly and terminally vulgar: crass, coarse and common. If there are those who find him funny, so be it; if they want to worship at his altar in a movie theater, so be that as well. But don't wrap him in layers of exegesis the net effect of which is to transform him into an Everyman for our times.

The oddity is that while the intelligentsia rush to embrace market-driven exhibitionists such as Harrison and Stern, the larger and less definable American culture in which the booboisie is said to rule seems far less comfortable with them and their ilk.

In a country as immense as ours, it doesn't take all that many people to make someone rich and famous, but this doesn't prevent searchers after larger meaning from reading more import into these passing phenomena than the evidence can sustain. Are Harrison and Stern *really* the new avatars of America?

There's little reason to think so. Middle America, for want of a better term, remains now as it has always been inherently conservative, not so much in ideological or political terms as in its reluctance to march to the latest tunes played by Manhattan and Hollywood. It would be as dangerous and foolish to read too much into a few days' e-mail as it is to exaggerate the importance of Harrison and Stern, but there can be little question that *The Kiss* will find scant attention and even less admiration outside the media centers or that *Private Parts*, though its audience will be far larger, will be anything more lasting than this spring's hot movie—hot, that is, in certain relatively narrow circles.

Some time back Daniel Patrick Moynihan, writing in the *American Scholar*, argued accurately and influentially that we have been "defining deviancy down"—lowering our standards of what constitutes criminal or anti-social behavior—as a coward's way of dealing with the increase in such behavior. Subsequently it has been argued that a parallel "dumbing down" has taken place in American culture, a process in which marketplace democracy has resulted in a lowest-common-denominator culture.

There is much truth to this, as no observer of current American culture needs to be reminded. But the more important truth may be that the real "dumbing down" is taking place among the ostensible guardians of our civilization: those academicians and journalists who, infatuated with sensation and Flavor of the Month and the potential rewards therefrom, have abandoned all standards, have in fact created a standards-free cultural marketplace. Harrison and Stern are cynical, Lord knows, but it is highly doubtful that they are any more so than the publishers and filmmakers and critics and writers now trumpeting their significance.

These are, as no one knows better than the person who wrote them, the words of a mossback, or an old fogy, or an antique. In writing them I risk, indeed invite, the scorn of those who are, as they would have us believe, pushing envelopes. But what is it that they are really pushing? Is it the outer edge of art or merely the limits of public tolerance? There is no evidence of the former in the "work," if it can be called that, of either Katherine Harrison or Howard Stern. There is, on the other hand, plenty of evidence that both know how to curry the favor of self-selected cultural style setters who can't tell genuine art or good taste from schlock or vulgarity, and who in any case clearly prefer the latter.

Papa's Complaint

〜⚬〜

July 21, 1997

Icons, icons, icons. We had so many icons around the house last week, you could hardly get from one room to the next. Thanks to the *New York Times* and the *Baltimore Sun*, Woolworth's was an "icon." In the *Washington Post*, Hechinger's— *Hechinger's!*—was an "icon." In the *Wall Street Journal*, "the black, family-owned funeral home" was an "icon." Again in the *Washington Post*, Ernest Hemingway was an "icon."

It's the new twist on Andy Warhol's axiom. Where a few years back everybody got to be famous for fifteen minutes, now everybody—and everything—gets to be an icon for fifteen minutes. In the case of Ernest Hemingway, maybe longer. Why, Hemingway was an icon before anyone had heard of icons. He was Papa: stormy, husky, brawling, writer of the big shoulders. Back when I was a pup every boy who could put pencil to paper dreamed of being Papa, and more than a few spent the rest of their lives trying, mostly to absolutely dreadful effect.

Then, maybe a couple of decades ago, Papa stopped being Papa, or at least many of us stopped thinking of him that way. People took a second look at his prose and saw there was less there than met the eye. People took a second look at *The Old Man and the Sea* and saw that it was possibly, just possibly, the worst novel ever written by anyone masquerading as a major writer. People took a second look at the macho style—the booze, the boats, the broads—and saw that not far beneath it lay a man desperately trying to overcompensate for an uncertain sexual identity.

So in some of the places where literary and pop-cultural reputations are made, Papa took a beating. But apparently word of this never made its way to the subtropics, for in Key West they just kept right on worshiping Ernest Hemingway as though he were, for once and for all and forever, Papa. They held festivals in his honor, wore T-shirts and other raiment sporting his bearded image, and held contests to choose those who most closely resembled him.

So they do, more or less, unto this day. More or less, that is, because the right to conduct public Papa-worship for veneration and profit has become a bone of some of the more ludicrous contention to hit the headlines in recent years. The three sons of Papa—John, Patrick and Gregory—have suddenly decided that, in the words of one who represents them, only "an authorized licensee" can "market Hemingway memorabilia in any form" or "charge admission" to the Hemingway Home museum in Key West.

In order to protect what the brothers Hemingway now perceive as their interest in their father's name and image—his iconography, as we say these days—they have engaged the services of Fashion Licensing of America and its president, Marla Metzner. She has, this newspaper reported last week, "plans to 'market Hemingway as a very upscale lifestyle brand,' " and she has already set about bringing this to fruition, through her offices and those of the brothers' company, Hemingway Ltd.

The first step toward that end can only be described as a stroke of genius. Keepers of the Hemingway flame—Hemingway iconodulists—will recall that the writer, deeply depressed, took his life in 1961 by firing a shotgun into his head. So what was the very first Hemingway Ltd. licensed product? Yes: a Hemingway shotgun.

Hard on the heels of that, Hemingway Ltd. came up with another "upscale lifestyle brand," a Mont Blanc pen selling for a cool $600. (Whether the full text of *The Sun Also Rises* is programmed into the pen has not, as yet, been disclosed.) Presumably we will not have long to wait for the Hemingway Safari ($47,500 per person, only at Nieman Marcus), the Hemingway Sport Utility Vehicle ($175,000, from Land Rover) and the Hemingway Finca Grande (800 feet of Caribbean waterfront, helipad, library fully stocked with 1920s first editions: $7.4 million at Sotheby's). Not every Hemingway is with the program. Lorian Hemingway, a niece of the master, says of those involved with Hemingway Ltd.: "I don't want to be so incautious or careless that I ascribe greed to it, but frankly, that's what I think it is. Ever since they have gotten this trademark they have tried various ways to pull money out of it, like the insane licensing of a Hemingway shotgun. And now to patch up that image, they've licensed . . . a Mont Blanc pen. Personally, I think that is more of an insult to Hemingway than a bunch of people going around in hats and T-shirts."

Considering how quick her uncle was to take offense, she's probably right. He may have thought that the rich weren't really different, they just had more money, but he had a distinctly limited tolerance for people who tried to buy what they couldn't earn. The spectacle of some Wall Streeter prowling the Idaho countryside with his Hemingway shotgun would have infuriated or amused him. Perhaps both. So too the more intimate picture of that same bond trader trying to write the Great American Novel with his $600 Hemingway Mont Blanc.

What's even more preposterous about the Hemingway brothers' moneygrubbing is the price they're making Key West pay for it. Say what you will of that tiny island, with its shameless mixture of local color and rank commercialism, there can be no doubt that its funkiness and its delight in its association with Hemingway are genuine. The Hemingway Days Festival, with its look-alike contest at Sloppy Joe's bar and its arm-wrestling competition and its other bibulous celebrations, probably comes closer to the heart of the writer—when he was off-duty, easing back, having fun—than anything that happened last week at the brothers' International Hemingway Festival; this was held at Sanibel and Captiva, upmarket islands Hemingway never visited, and featured, according to the *New York Times*, "a literary conference, golf and a children's arts camp."

Sounds like Papa, doesn't it? Whatever one may think of the man and/or his work—me, I don't think much of either—he deserves to be given his due, and his due wasn't golf or a children's arts camp, much less a literary conference. Once those egg-heads and airheads got to nattering away up there in the panel discussion, Papa would have knocked back a pint of rum and shouted them off the premises. He had his pretensions and his affections and his insecurities, but the drinks and the fishing and the carousing were as much of his essence as all those perfect little sentences that just screamed for a bit of the fat he so sedulously scraped away from them. Whoever and whatever he was, he wasn't a $600 pen or an afternoon's lit'ry chitchat. He wasn't an icon, either.

GOOD OL' BOY

༄

October 20, 1997

The Faulkner centennial has come and gone. The 5-K run has been run, the T-shirts have been sold, the fireworks have fired off and fizzled out, the bluegrass and country concerts have closed and so has the arts-and-crafts festival, "featuring ceramics, pottery, raku ware, weaving, wood carving, oil painting, water colors, porcelain, handmade old world dolls, basketweaving and others." All of which may well leave you, as it most certainly leaves me, wondering: What in the name of Montgomery Ward Snopes does any of this have to do with William Faulkner?

The answer is simple: absolutely nothing. Faulkner might or might not have been appalled by the silliness that took place in honor of his birthday—truth to tell he probably wouldn't have given a damn—but he certainly would have been puzzled, not merely by the pertinence of "Fun Run" ("A 1/2-mile run for children 10 and under") to the author of *Absalom, Absalom!* and *As I Lay Dying* but by the astonishing metamorphosis in his native state of Mississippi that all this folderol reflects.

Not that the Faulkner carnival was limited to Mississippi. The University of Mississippi's Faulkner Web page (http://www.mcsr.olemiss.edu/egjbp/faulkner/faulkner.html) and its many links suggest that scarcely a crossroads in Ol' Dixie managed to get through the summer and early autumn without a Faulkner hoedown or hog wallow. Over in Charlottesville, where Faulkner in his dotage resided among the First Families of Virginia, the whoopin' and the hollerin' haven't stopped yet, with a screening of the film adaptation of *Intruder in the Dust* scheduled for the Virginia Film Festival.

But if the festivities were spread far and wide, Mississippi was the focal point from first to last. This obviously was appropriate, since Faulkner was born in New Albany (that's where the "Fun Run" was held) and spent most of his adulthood a few miles away in Oxford, seat of the university and, these days, of the Center for the Study of Southern Culture, which gets much of the credit and much of the blame for what's happening lately in the land of grits and molasses.

Credit goes to the center for helping to drag Mississippi out of its dark, discredited past. Under the direction of William Ferris, who is now chairman-designate of the National Endowment for the Humanities, the center has cast a wide net, bringing into academia the work of Southern writers, musicians and artists who previously had been regarded as unworthy of scholarly attention. Many of these were or are black, and their long-overdue recognition is entirely, indisputably laudable.

As for blame, it goes to the center—and to Ferris—for turning much of the South's indigenous culture into a marketable commodity that looks for all the world like Dixie Chic. Inspired by the center, a growing industry now exists in the South for cultural enterprises the dominant characteristic of which is a regional self-consciousness that too often borders on the merely cute. Little magazines of aggressively Southern charm are popping up faster than anyone can read them; a Website cloyingly called Y'all features a "Wrassling" bout between "The General" Robert E. Lee and "Wild Bill" Faulkner; the academic study of Southern "popular culture" is spewing out dissertations and other ephemera at an extraordinary, not to mention appalling, rate.

What all of this means for William Faulkner at age one hundred is that he is the wallflower at his own party. Oh, there have been toasts and salutations aplenty, not to mention the usual indigestible scholarly papers, one of which was called "Tick Tocks, Whirs and Broken Gears: Time and Identity in Faulkner." But mostly the celebrations seemed to applaud the celebrants rather than the guest of honor. The chief one, in New Albany, claimed to "honor the creative spirit of Mississippi and celebrate the people, places and events that shaped one native son," but the connection between Faulkner and, say, bluegrass, R&B and soul music is, at best, exceedingly difficult to discern.

The net effect of all this is to trivialize Faulkner, to drag him down to the level of those partying on his birthday rather than to admire him from afar on the pedestal where he belongs. This isn't to suggest that overtly ulterior motives were behind the planning of these festivals; of the sincerity of most of those involved there can be little doubt. But when the greatest of all American novelists becomes an excuse for hawking a "Centennial T-shirt" ($10) and a "Faulkner Centennial Mug" ($10) and—yes!—a "Centennial Celebration Cookbook" ($19.95), what we are talking about is not exactly a literary occasion.

"Living in the South, we are all post-Faulknerians," according to Diane Roberts in a most engaging article, in the current issue of the *Oxford American*, about her long fixation on Faulkner: "He shaped the way we see the woods and hills, he reminds us powerfully (though we may not need it) of the weight of the past, he reinvented the Southern Gothic so thoroughly that we can never look straight at a ruined plantation house again. Southern artists from James Dickey to Billy Bob Thornton have absorbed him like humidity."

Yes and no. The South's image of itself—or at least the literary South's image of itself—unquestionably has been shaped more by Faulkner than by anyone else; he remains, in the railroad imagery employed by Flannery O'Connor, the "Dixie Express," racing down the track even unto this day. But the "humidity" is losing its moisture. The "weight of the past," so central to Faulkner's work, is more imagined than felt in a region no longer haunted by guilt and defeat but, like the rest of fin de siècle America, looking to cash in on whatever merchandise it can move.

So: Welcome to the bazaar, Mr. Faulkner. Over in the CD bin you'll find "Invasion of the Cooters," featuring " 'Faulkner's Revenge,' a 12-minute backwoods homage to William Faulkner." In the art shop there's William Dabney's "commemorative print" (signed, limited edition, $125) honoring your "Postage Stamp of

Native Soil." In the bookstore you may stumble across a few cop-ies of your own work, but mostly you'll drown in Faulknerian lit-crit, much of it of the odiously fashionable variety, reducing Dilsey and Temple Drake and Quentin Compson to the Holy Trinity of race, gender and class.

Like Diane Roberts, I for many years "lived and breathed William Faulkner." I knew his work almost by heart and thought the entire universe revolved around it. Also like Diane Roberts, I've managed to shake the obsession and move on to other things. It's comforting, though, to know that he'll still be around should the impulse strike again. He'll be right there in the Dixie Depart-ment, smack upside Billy Bob Thornton and Jerry Lee Lewis.

THE ODD COUPLE

❧

November 24, 1997

Difficult though it may be to believe, it has been fully a quarter-century since the *New York Times Magazine* inflicted upon its readers a piece of unexampled drivel entitled "An 18-Year-Old Looks Back on Life." Written by Joyce Maynard, a college student, the article was an exercise in self-indulgence and self-promotion that, in succeeding on both counts, anticipated the self-indulgence and self-promotion that have become the distinguishing characteristics of American journalism in these fin de siècle years.

For at least one reader of the *Times Magazine*, "An 18-Year-Old Looks at Life" apparently was something of an aphrodisiac. Stirring from his long, notorious silence, J.D. Salinger sent La Maynard his felicitations and regards. One thing led to another—as, alas, it so often does—and soon enough the cherubic student paid the celebrated writer a visit at his house in New Hampshire. There she stayed for fully nine months, doing heaven knows what, until the spring of 1973, when, according to a story in the *Times* last week, "their nine-month relationship ended."

Gone but not forgotten. Last week's report was occasioned by the news that Maynard is now under contract, with a hitherto blameless publisher called Picador USA, to write a memoir. She told the *Times*'s reporter, Dinitia Smith, that this "would describe her relationship with the famously reclusive writer J.D. Salinger, the author of *The Catcher in the Rye*, breaking a 25-year silence about the affair."

"The affair." So *that's* what they did. It said so in the *New York Times*, so it must be true. So too, apparently, is the following, in Maynard's very own words describing her feelings about Salinger: "I viewed him as my mentor and teacher and the person I trusted most in the world. He was the first man I ever loved. My purpose is not to divulge his story. I'm sticking to my own story."

This, even in an age of confessional memoir gone berserk, will be a high-wire act well worth watching. How, pray tell, does one write about one's "relationship"—oh, what the hell, call it an "affair"—with someone else without, in the process, writing about that someone else? If you've been troubled ever since your sophomore year at college by all those late-night bull sessions about the sound of one hand clapping, or a tree falling in the forest with no creature within earshot of its fall, try to imagine a memoir about the agony and the ecstasy of one person . . . ah, but this is a family newspaper, so let your imagination do the walking.

To put it in more literary terms, try to picture a work of fiction in which the story of Lolita is told in full but the story of Humbert Humbert is barely hinted at, much less revealed in all its sordid splendor. As Vladimir Nabokov well knew, the juicy part of that tale is not Humbert's nymphet but Humbert himself, with his oddities and his longings and his wry observations about America's infinite capacity for vulgarity. Nabokov, a literary artist of surpassing genius—and, it might be added, taste—knew where to direct his microscope.

No one familiar with Maynard's previously published work—of which, unfortunately, there has been much—will suspect her of either genius or taste. Nor will any such reader have to be told upon whom *her* microscope will be focused. As Ms. Smith of the *Times* dryly observed, "She has made her career in journalism writing about her own life." She was barely out of her teens before she had written and published her first memoir—to quote Patsy Cline: imagine *that*—and she has spent the intervening two-plus decades adding to this literature of self-preoccupation, as well as getting herself married (not to J.D. Salinger, more's the pity), having three children and getting herself divorced, all of this, of course, adding grist to her mill.

She is writing her memoir-in-progress, Maynard told the *Times*, because, when her daughter became eighteen years old in 1996, "I watched her struggling with becoming a young woman in the world. I remembered who I used to be." But why remember? Just read the clips. It's all there, in newspaper stories and magazine articles and books: the endless tale of the most fascinating, compelling, riveting, enchanting person whom it has been Joyce Maynard's privilege to meet.

So now she will add to the record by telling not quite all about the, uh, *thing* she once had with J.D. Salinger. To be sure, as she confessed to the *Times*, "I don't for a moment think he would want me to write this," but what is Salinger's privacy by contrast with her own endlessly urgent need to share with the rest of us the infinite importance of being . . . herself? No doubt even as these words are written you are lashing yourself into your chair, lest you soar into the ether from the mad anticipation and bliss stirred by the news that Maynard is at it again.

You may, on the other hand, find yourself struggling to comprehend self-infatuation so vast and reckless that the victim of it cannot imagine a detail of her life so minute or trivial as to be of no interest to everyone else on this planet. Joyce Maynard may not be able to claim the renown or the wealth enjoyed by Barbra Streisand—it's not for want of trying!—but when it comes to election to the Ego Hall of Fame, between those two it's a toss-up.

This being so, Salinger really should have known, as he admitted the diminutive Maynard into his lair back in 1972, that what he had on his hands was a tiny time bomb. This device is now scheduled to ignite on the eve of the Millennium; "the winter of 1999," according to the *Times*, is the hour planned for publication of this book, apparently as yet untitled, though you can bet that whatever title it ends up with will be, in the mold of everything else Maynard has written, terminally cute.

The one scene the book will not contain is the one that this reader would most like to have observed. It presumably took place sometime last Friday in the quaint New Hampshire town of Cornish, when Salinger—"Jerry," to the once-adoring Joyce—turned to page A33 of his *New York Times* and found the news of his quondam cupcake's impending indiscretion. Two thoughts must have flashed through his mind: (a) "I'd better write my side of the story," and (b) "I'd better call my lawyer."

To quote Frank Sinatra: Ring-a-ding-ding!

❦

MEDIA MADNESS

❦

Scoop Goes to College

✎

January 11, 1991

"**H**ello, Sweetheart." That's what I said when the gal in the newsroom picked up the phone one day last week. Her name is Della but we call her Sweetheart. That's just the way we are. Newspaper guys. Bunch of cards. Laugh a minute. We call her "gal," too. That's just the way we are. Witty. Devil-may-care. Sexist pigs.

I was out on assignment. Hadn't seen the office for days. My beat is books and writers. It's a tough beat. Reason I was on the road: A bunch of authors in New York were picketing a publisher. It was bringing out a new edition of *Peter Rabbit*. Animal-rights crowd was up in arms. Upper West Side seething with unrest. Next thing, blood in the streets. I had to be there. When a big story breaks, you can't keep Scoop away.

That's what Sweetheart calls me. "Oh, hello, Scoop." That's what she said when she picked up the phone. "You again, huh? What's happening this time? Norman Mailer having triplets? Heh heh heh." That's the way she is, that Sweetheart. Hell of a gal. Talks out of the side of her mouth, just like the guys. That's why we all love her.

"Okay, Sweetheart," I said. "Cut the comedy. Hot news waits for no man. Get me rewrite." Just like that she stopped fooling around. Made the connection quick as you please. It rang a couple of times, then answered.

"English Department," some gal said. What? I was non-plussed. That's what we call it in the newspaper game: nonplussed. It's a Ben Hecht kind of word: classy. Last time you read it was probably in "The Conning Tower." F.P.A. The *New York World*. Swope. Pulitzer. Hearst. Good old days. Runyon. Winchell. Broun. They were all nonplussed. That's why we loved them.

Well. I was so nonplussed I lost my cool. What I said to this gal was, "*English Department?*" Just like that. In italics. A cool newspaper guy *never* talks in italics, but I did it. Hell, I just did it *again*.

So there I was. Half out of breath. Feeling like a damned fool with all those italics tumbling out of me. But the gal on the line was cool as a cuke. "Yes, English Department," is what she said.

"But I want rewrite!" I said, barely keeping the italics out of it. "This is Scoop! I've got a story that's hotter'n a prairie dog in heat! I don't want any English Department! I want *rewrite!*"

"Scoop," she said, getting familiar a little quick for my taste, "Scoop, you've *got* rewrite. Haven't you been reading the papers lately, Scoop?" I had to admit I hadn't. The pressure of events had been too great. I was behind on my reading. "Okay, Sis," I said, "fill me in on it."

"No," she said, "go read the *New York Times* yourself. The story's inside the A section. Headline reads, 'Yale Weighs Challenge to Newspaper's Owner.' Read it and call me back."

So I found the story and I read it. "Yale University is weighing whether to challenge the ownership of the *St. Petersburg Times*," it said, "in a move that could make the *Times* the property of Yale." It went on to talk about confusion over a will, and the Internal Revenue Service, and the Poynter Institute for Media Studies. Yale, the story said, claimed an "obligation to investigate the possibility" that under the will, the paper belonged not to the Poynter Institute but to Yale.

I read it and then I read it again. Damned if it made any sense to me. So I called the office and went through the same rigamarole. "Hello, Sweetheart. Get me rewrite." "Hello, Scoop. Just a sec." "English Department."

"This is Scoop," I said. "So what do Yale and the Poynter

Institute and the *Saint Pete Times* have to do with me?" And that's when she told me. That's when the ---- hit the ---.

What she told me was that the *Saint Pete* business was all a ruse, a ploy, a trick. A wily stratagem: That's what Ben Hecht would have called it. A diversionary tactic: That's what S.L.A. (Slam) Marshall would have called it. Yale may have been making public moves to take over the *Saint Pete Times*, but behind the scenes Yale was closing in on the *Washington Post*.

Whatever Yale wants, Yale gets. "So you see, Scoop, you're working for Yale now. The School of Economics has taken over the business section, the Poly-Sci Department is running the national desk, and you—lucky you!—get the English Department."

For the second time in a single day I was nonplussed. I had to stall for time. "Uh, what's your name, Sis?" I asked. "I am Clothilde Haight-Ashbury," she answered, "and I will thank you not to call me Sis. My friends call me Mother Jones, though whether *you* will ever be any friend of mine is certainly open to question."

Hmm. This clearly called for a more diplomatic approach. I went into my Richard Harding Davis mode. "Madam," I said as politely as possible, fearful though I was that "Madam" might be taken as an insult, "Madam, I wish to give no offense. All this is news to me: a bolt from the blue, to coin a phrase. Please elucidate the particulars, begging your pardon."

"I will be happy to do so. Now that Yale University is sole proprietor of the *Washington Post*, you report not to Book World or Style but to the English Department. You no longer have an editor, but a chairman. Pardon me: a chairperson. At the moment this person is at the annual convention of the Modern Language Association, delivering a paper called 'Wilted Flowers: Images of Detumescence in the Fugitive Poetry of Lady Grisel Baillie,' so for the moment the department is closed."

"But what about my story?" I asked, fairly foaming at the mouth. "What about the Peter Rabbit Riot? This news is hotter'n a Texas barbecue festival! Roll the presses!"

"Oh, calm down," is what this creature said. "You're on the academic schedule now," she said. "Publish or perish may be the name, but the game is publish every, oh, fifteen or sixteen years. A week off at Thanksgiving, a month at Christmas, two weeks in the spring, three months in the summer—hey, Scoop, welcome to the real world. Put the Peter Rabbit Riot on the back burner. Go spend the winter at the British Museum."

"But what about rewrite?" I asked. "Without rewrite, who's going to punch all the right cliches into my hard-boiled scoops? Who's going to make sure I misuse 'presently' and 'hopefully' and 'tragically'? Where are my editors?"

"Oh, we don't have editors any more, Scoop. We have English professors. I realize that you are what we at Yale call a 'mere journalist' and don't know about such things, but the Yale English Department just happens to be the mother church of semiotics and structuralism. At Yale we don't 'edit' you. We deconstruct you. By the time we're finished with your prose, the only people who will be able to read it are tenured Lacanist scholars holding Yale Ph.D.s. At last count there were twelve of them. By the year 2006 they will be ready for your exegesis of the Peter Rabbit Riot. So take your time. Relax. Give yourself a treat: Read a bit of Paul de Man or Jacques Derrida. You know: Light reading."

It was more than I could take. I hung up on her. I know it was hanging up on my career—on those rye-soaked nights at Bleeck's saloon and those 3 a.m. card games with the other news-hounds and those green eyeshades and galluses—but principle comes first with a guy like me. One farewell phone call, and then I was gone. "Hello, Sweetheart. . . ."

"*Sweetheart?* Where do you get this 'Sweetheart' business? You can call me Ms. Della, buster. I've got tenure now, and your --- is -----."

PRISONERS OF HYPE

∽∘∾

September 30, 1991

Last week was Media Week around our place. Ordinarily the house is mercifully—some might say monotonously—quiet: My wife goes off to work, the dogs and cats go to sleep, the phone seldom rings, and I'm left in peace to pursue the business of reading and writing. But once or twice a year Media Week comes along, and when it does, everything goes haywire.

The last time it happened, within the space of a few days *Time* called, *Newsweek* called, *People* called, *Nightline* called, and heaven knows how many others now forgotten called. Why? Because Kitty Kelley's book about Nancy Reagan was coming out, and the ladies and gentlemen of the press somehow knew that I had once had a run-in with some anonymous people calling themselves "The Friends of Kitty Kelley." Grist for the gossip mills was wanted, and I was called upon to provide it.

Last week's barrage of calls was less intense, but strong enough all the same to throw a couple of days out of kilter. *Today* called, then *People*, then a TV station in Baltimore, then a radio station in San Diego. Word had gotten out that this newspaper was steaming into print with an early review of *Scarlett: The Sequel to Margaret Mitchell's "Gone With the Wind"* and that I had written it; again, grist for the mills.

As someone who's ordinarily so far out of the media loop as to be in outer space, I find the rare invitation to come inside both fetching and amusing. Going on television is not so much fun as those who haven't done it seem to imagine, but on the other hand it makes you seem like a big deal inside the family for a couple of hours and you get a few calls from friends who haven't checked in for months, or years. So I go to the television studio or do the telephone interview for the radio station, and then disappear happily into the anonymity that is my usual lot.

Invariably, though, the thought occurs as I retreat back into my lair that what draws me out of it is nothing more elevated than the machinery of hype. As a professional reviewer of books I from time to time encounter some of uncommon merit, but not once in more than a quarter-century of these labors have my comments on such books been solicited by television or radio or magazines. It would have been my great pleasure, for example, to speak this year to the viewers of *Today* or the readers of *People* about the merits of *Black Ice*, by Lorene Cary, or *Ride a Cockhorse*, by Raymond Kennedy, but oddly enough in neither case did *Today* or *People*—or anyone else in Medialand—solicit my opinions.

Of course there's nothing odd about it at all. Good, serious books don't generate hype any more than good, serious recordings or movies do. The appetite of the media for publicizing and celebrating the shoddy and meretricious is inexhaustible, and all of us who labor therein are guilty in one measure or another; I'm quite well aware that, even though my review of *Scarlett* was unfavorable, I participated in the process of hype by the mere fact of making a concerted effort to get that review into print as early as possible.

This is not something that those of us who call ourselves journalists like to advertise. One of our most cherished myths is that we are aloof from the machinery of hype, that we are superior to those who practice the arts of promotion and publicity or, as they are known generically, PR. The newspaper reporter or editor who moves into PR is universally regarded as not merely a turncoat but a sellout; it is assumed that he or she has slunk away to become a member of some inferior species the only virtue of which is that it has the wherewithal to buy drinks and lunches for reporters and editors.

The plain truth is that the relationship between the press and those who seek its favors is intimate, symbiotic and mutually profitable. The case of *Scarlett* is a textbook example of how PR attempts to use the media and how, in turn, the media merrily permit themselves to be used.

Scarlett is PR pure and simple. It began not in the imagination of its author but in the calculations of those who manage the estate of Margaret Mitchell. They realized that the copyright on *Gone With the Wind* will expire early in the next century and determined that if further profit is to be made from it, now is the time. Accordingly they ignored Mitchell's stated desires and put the rights to a sequel up for auction. It was won by Warner Books, and Alexandra Ripley was hired, ex post facto, to manufacture the product. This she did, for a time against the resistance of editors at Warner who wanted a book even worse than the one she was prepared to write. The result was *Scarlett*.

It was not, as they say in business, a pre-sold product. Notwithstanding the persistence of public curiosity about the love lives of Scarlett O'Hara and Rhett Butler, Warner faced real obstacles in marketing the book, chief among them skepticism about Ripley's claim to Mitchell's mantle. It chose to overcome them with a frontal assault of hype. The manuscript was as closely held as an account in a Swiss bank, stirring speculation about its contents. No advance proofs were made available to reviewers; finished books went out only a couple of days early, and only to those who agreed not to publish their descriptions or opinions before Wednesday of last week.

What Warner did, in other words, was to orchestrate an exquisitely timed crescendo of publicity. Did any of us in the media resist its supplications? Did anyone "violate" its publication date in order to get the jump on the competition? Did anyone say the hell with Warner, we're not giving you any free publicity?

In every instance, to the best of my knowledge the answer is in the negative. Last Wednesday morning the newspapers and news shows were blanketed with features about Ripley and reports about the crush on the bookstores that her novel had caused. The stories all came out on time, just as Warner had planned, and they were almost universally positive to the point of puffery; only

a couple of the interviews with Ripley that I read were even remotely skeptical, and that was pretty much limited to the subtle
device of incrimination through direct quotation.

No doubt all of us thought that by singing in this choir we
somehow were reporting "the news," but in truth we were doing
nothing except chanting the lines the PR people had fed us; even
those of us who wrote unfavorable notices were singing on cue,
so our attentions helped whip up public curiosity about the book.
Scarlett wasn't news in the sense that, say, the latest round of spar-
ring with Saddam Hussein was news; it was publicity masquerading as news, and nothing more.

It was also business as usual. It happens every day. Press
releases, handouts, news conferences, briefings: these carefully
controlled forms of PR provide a steady diet without which the
media, as they now operate, would collapse from lack of nutrition.
The author on tour for a book, the movie star promoting a new
picture, the manufacturer unveiling a new product: this is unadulterated PR, but it is offered up as news.

To what extent the people who read or watch the results are
aware of this no doubt is unfathomable. What is more troubling
is the extent to which those of us who write it and broadcast it
have managed to persuade ourselves that we are somehow above
it all. The truth is that if PR exists to solicit free advertising, the
media exist to provide it; we have space and time to fill, and PR
does the job neatly. Every week is Media Week in a culture where
PR and journalism too often are indistinguishable.

SO MUCH FOR PRIVACY

୶୭

August 17, 1992

Imagine, distasteful though it may be to do so, that some years ago you became ensnared in an especially unpleasant domestic dispute, one that in time involved the attentions of the courts and the press. Eventually the case was resolved, if only after a fashion, and you attempted to get back to the ordinary business of your life. But today you open a newspaper and read, to your horror, that the case is to be the subject of a made-for-television "docudrama," one in which an actress will portray you and speak words allegedly said by you.

Your horror would be entirely justified. Your life allegedly belongs to you, not to the writers and producers of broadcast entertainment, yet because you were once involved in a case tried in public you have become, in effect, public property. You have no control over how you are portrayed, no protection—beyond the very thin shield offered by the libel laws—against misrepresentation of your words, your actions, your motives, your emotions. You are nothing to the people making this docudrama except raw material, ripe for exploitation.

If you think that this is merely an imagined horror, a worst-case scenario, think again. For corroborative evidence, have a look at last week's edition of the *Washington Post Magazine*, wherein Susan Cohen, a free-lance writer, published an extensive account of how the repellent Morgan-Foretich child-abuse case is being exploited by ABC Television and an independent director-producer, Linda Otto. Cohen's reportage is admirably unjudgmental and objective but leaves little doubt as to the central fact, which is that under the cover of what ABC slimily calls "our obligations to the public," the case is being milked for every ounce of its sensation value.

ABC claims that the case, which was put into limbo a couple of years ago when Elizabeth Morgan decided to stay in New Zealand with her daughter by her ex-husband Eric Foretich, is even unto this day "the subject of considerable public interest." Perhaps so, though it is scarcely interest of a clinical or legalistic sort. The story of Morgan and Foretich and their daughter Hilary is real-life melodrama, the stuff of cheap, lurid entertainment; it involves sex and child-abuse—or at least the accusation thereof—and clandestine movements and a mother languishing in jail. It would take an uncommonly imaginative and prurient scriptwriter to dream up so much dirt; no wonder ABC, which over the years has set such elevated standards, positively salivated at it.

To be sure ABC was scarcely alone. Since the case first became public five years ago, the legitimate press as well as the fabricators of television shows has had a field day with it. Newspapers are read mostly by middle- and upper-middle-class people, and this was a case of the middle-class; the newspapers squeezed as much out of it as they could. Ditto for the managers of television news, who like those in the print media were happy to let both Morgan and Foretich have free time and space to air their grievances in exchange for the pleasure of milking this particular cash cow down to the last drop.

But there is a difference between journalism and entertainment, though the libel laws seem not to acknowledge as much. However misguided or even sleazy journalism can be, it labors under a constitutional right to report and comment upon the news. No such right—or responsibility—is inherent in the business of entertainment, the purpose of which is to amuse. Yet according to Cohen, "The libel laws are the same for docudramas and journalistic accounts," and according to a lawyer with whom she spoke, in the eyes of the courts "it's a greater invasion of privacy when you've got a real person you're showing on the screen than when you've got an actor."

That's lunacy. Though everyone in journalism must be grateful for libel laws that permit an open climate for the expression of ideas and the reporting of facts, it is quite another thing to extend the protection of those laws to people whose only interest in "public" figures is to exploit them in voyeuristic entertainments. The same goes for the privacy laws: Why should a person have even fewer privacy rights when portrayed by an actor than he does as himself?

That certainly appears to be the case with Eric Foretich. The docudrama upon which Linda Otto is working is the result of negotiations between her and Elizabeth Morgan. Though Morgan is no longer involved in the project, there seems little question that the film, to be called *A Mother's Right: The Elizabeth Morgan Story*, will favor her side of the controversy and present matters accordingly. Foretich, understandably, is unhappy about this. "It's very simple for Linda Otto to get her money and her kudos," he told Cohen, "but what does it do to my life and to Hilary to be victimized by this woman who has her own agenda?"

Fortunately for Foretich, he seems to be as litigious as his ex-wife is self-publicizing. His lawyers have been after ABC and Otto constantly, demanding a fair portrayal of his side of the case; from what Cohen writes, it appears that what they'll end up with is a depiction somewhat less unfair than it might have been had they remained silent.

But questions of fairness and unfairness, though they are what the participants are squabbling about, really are quite secondary to the central issue, which is: What right do Linda Otto and ABC have to appropriate Eric Foretich, without his permission, as a character in a television entertainment? For that is exactly what *A Mother's Right* will be when it appears, as was implicitly acknowledged by an ABC executive who told Cohen: "A mother-daughter story is a very relatable kind of story. It's a fact-based story. If it's a story that's been out there, you've got a leg up."

Translation: *A Mother's Right* comes pre-sold, thanks to all the publicity the Morgan-Foretich case received. It gives ABC a "leg up" on all the other broadcasters who will be competing for viewers' attention during the couple of hours it is on the air. None of this has anything to do with "considerable legitimate public interest" or "our obligations to the public." It has everything to do with ABC's corporate venality, its thirst for ratings shares and advertising revenues.

Precisely why it is that the courts have collaborated in such exploitation is a mystery, but presumably it has much to do with the lack of any clear statutory guidance. On the evidence presented by Cohen and the various lawyers with whom she spoke, it seems that in the absence of any legislation to the contrary, the courts have concluded that (a) the docudrama is a form of journalism and (b) it enjoys the same rights that journalism does. They have concluded thus even though the docudrama uses the methods of drama and fiction instead of reportage and even though it invariably reworks—and thus distorts—the facts of the case, or story, being adapted.

It is a position that not merely slights the rights of the individuals involved but positively mocks them. Whatever the innocence or guilt of Eric Foretich in this case, the (still unresolved) charges filed against him by his ex-wife did not extinguish his right to privacy or to decide for himself whether others are entitled to profit off the events of his life. That the law as it now exists effectively denies him those rights should be a source of dismay and outrage, yet scarcely a soul has spoken out.

Perhaps this is because we have acquiesced in the attempt, made on both sides of the fence, to blur beyond distinction the line between news and entertainment. Perhaps we really do believe that a person loses all rights when he or she is forced, for a time, out of the cocoon of privacy and into the spotlight. But as you watch *A Mother's Right* and the character "Eric Foretich" depicted therein, ask yourself this: How would you like it if that character were you?

ON THE COUCH

✌︎◦︎⌇

August   24,   1992

Did you celebrate Family Values Week? If not, you missed the gala to end all galas. Family Values Week was the occasion for all the families we know and love to strut their familial stuff, each in its uniquely fetching way.

Thus it was that in London an in-law of the Windsor family put herself on public display *au naturel*, complete with foot-licking inamorato and paparazzi in waiting. In the House of Windsor, "family values" have to do with embracing the tired and lost of the world: lounge lizards, porn queens, fortune hunters, round-heeled debutantes, epicene courtiers and footloose matrons. The House of Windsor is many things, but its inbred behavior patterns prove nothing so much as that, in the immortal words of the late and universally lamented Polly Adler, a house is not a home.

In Houston, meantime, at the Republican Convention "family values" were as thick as flies, or fleas. George Herbert Walker "Who *[sic]* Do You Trust?" Bush was paterfamilias to a Grand Old Family that positively burst at the seams with what J. Danforth "Father Knows Best" Quayle called "the traditional values of middle America," which, on the evidence of Houston, would appear to be Hillary-stomping, homosexual-bashing and bellicose religiosity. But the real star of the show was Barbara Pierce "Grandma Moses" Bush, who wears the pants in this particular family and played every string on the "family values" Stradivarius as if she were the reincarnation of Jascha Heifetz.

Yet the most touching display of Family Values Week was

presented many miles to the northeast, in the most exclusive neighborhoods of Manhattan and suburban Connecticut, where the First Family of New York finally let a breathless public behind the drawn blinds of its singular existence. It was a media show such as has not been seen since Elizabeth Taylor last lost sixty pounds—or gained sixty pounds, or got married, or got divorced—and into the bargain it was a feeding frenzy for psychiatrists and psychologists and all the other ologists who slop at the trough of our national obsession with self.

One such is John Ray Jr., Ph.D., who practices in Widworth, Mass., and who rendered (from afar, of course) this verdict: "No doubt, he is horrible, he is abject, he is a shining example of moral leprosy, a mixture of ferocity and jocularity that betrays supreme misery perhaps, but is not conducive to attractiveness. He is ponderously capricious. Many of his casual opinions on the people and scenery of this country are ludicrous. A desperate honesty that throbs through his confession does not absolve him from sins of diabolical cunning. He is abnormal. He is not a gentleman."

Okay: Stop those calls and letters. You English majors know that's no psychiatrist but Vladimir Nabokov, masquerading in the Foreword to *Lolita* as a devotee of the gray eminence whom he liked to call "the Viennese Quack." But reading about the tangled web woven by Woody and Mia and Soon-Yi—not to mention Dylan and Moses and Satchel and heaven knows what other kinfolk in that benighted "family"—it was pretty hard not to think of Humbert Humbert and "the perilous magic of nymphets," wasn't it? If ever there was a case of life imitating art—"the wayward child, the egotistic mother, the panting maniac," as the aforementioned John Ray Jr., Ph.D., wrote of Nabokov's unholy trio—then this surely was it.

The incredible tangles of the web aroused a piteous chorus of journalistic bathos. "Say it ain't so, Woody," was the brokenhearted refrain from coast to coast as devotees of the sainted Woody's cinematic oeuvre tumbled over backwards trying to explain away his sudden descent into what looked for all the world like Nabokov's "parody of incest." Many trees were felled to accommodate these lamentations, not to mention the somber musings of the ologists.

Say it for the ologists: They aren't shy. Should you fall victim to a sneeze or an itch and call your physician for help, he would say, "Come on in and let me have a look." The ologists labor under no such qualms. Over-the-phone diagnosis is their stock in trade, especially where the woes of the rich, famous and lionized are concerned and double-especially if they have never had direct personal contact with the victims in question.

Thus it was that the *Washington Post* had no trouble rounding up a psychology professor at a remote college in (!) North Carolina who merrily proclaimed, "It's incestuous even if it's not incest," and opined of the wandering Woody, "He may have become someone who feels he has enough power or insularity to *really* break with convention in a way he only did humorously in films." It also rounded up the managing editor of something called—this is not a joke—*Common Boundary: Between Spirituality and Psychotherapy*, who reached as deep into her bag of tricks as she could go and announced that we live in an age where "all our idols . . . have these dark dissociated corners of the soul."

The *Baltimore Sun* outdid the *Post*, and then some. In the space of twenty column inches it managed to cite the sweet nothings of "a Brookline, Mass., psychologist who specializes in the psychology of men"; the chief of psychology at the Shepard and Enoch Pratt Hospital near Baltimore; "a Los Angeles psychologist who treats patients in the entertainment industry"; the director of the Center for Abuse Recovery and Empowerment at the Psychiatric Institute of Washington; "a Washington-based clinical psychologist specializing in families, adolescence and relationships"; and a Washington clinical psychologist who is a board member of—this is no joke, either—the Forum for Psychoanalytic Study of Film.

The *New York Times* preferred to heed the voice of the people, though its man-in-the-street examination of l'affaire Woody had a distinctly pop-psychological twist. One "writer and radio personality" told the *Times* that "Woody's work is a meaningful corroboration of *my* battle," while a novelist—the *Times* doesn't look for any old man in any old street—pitched in that Woody "It's all about pain, the recognition of pain, making our pain fun."

But it was left to Edward Koch, the former mayor of New York generally and Manhattan spiritually, to express what all of us were so desperately trying to articulate. "What he is," Koch told the *Times*, "he's the analysand, representing millions more. Let me put it this way. If I were building a statue to Dr. Freud, and I were going to put it in New York, and the statue was going to be Freud in his office, it would be Woody Allen on the couch."

Right: Live by the shrink, die by the shrink. As the *Post* reported, "Allen has been in strict Freudian analysis for most of his adult life." Spend a lifetime eating "neo-Freudian hash"—thanks, Professor Nabokov—and sooner or later you're likely to toss it all up. "Freudian voodooism"—thanks again—when practiced as sedulously as it seems to have been by this *auteur* of upper-middle-class self-adoration, is nothing except a ticket to trouble.

The whole family seems to have bought the ride. Mia and her many children, according to the *Post*, "have spent months in psychiatric care, . . . coping with the implications" of Woody's intrafamilial escapade. By the time all of them have been run through that particular mill, they should be set for life.

Ah, yes: "family values," Manhattan-style. George Bush and Dan Quayle may preach the gospel according to their own values and the Windsors may practice the royal variation on the theme, but up there in Herr Doktor's favorite city the people know what really keeps happy families all alike: "the scholastic rigmarole and standardized symbols of the psychoanalytic racket." Thanks again, Humbert Humbert.

BANALITY TRIUMPHANT

⮞⮜

March 7, 1994

Twenty years of *People* magazine? Saints preserve us! No, no, no. Since *People* went into business the celestial hierarchy has undergone a radical transformation, so let's say it the right way: Twenty years of *People* magazine? Celebrities preserve us!

We live in the "Age of Celebrity." How do we know that? We know because *People* tells us so, in the smarmily self-applauding managing editor's letter that introduces the twentieth-anniversary issue of *People*, a 316-page doorstopper for which, against all instincts to the better, I shelled out $3.95 plus tax last week. Looking back over the past two decades, the author of the letter, Landon Y. Jones, declares:

> All of us enter history at an arbitrary point, including magazines. *People* arrived in 1974 in a world wearied of war in Vietnam, the worst recession since the Depression, and journalism that brooded over interest rates at the expense of human interest. While newspapers and some magazines covered the doings of TV and movie stars, the most compelling and timeless aspects of human behavior often lay unexamined by careful journalists. So when the upstart new magazine began bringing breezy writing and high-standard reporting to the personal lives of famous people, the very idea of celebrating celebrity had a freshness all its own.

Thus we have the party line as it emits from the Time and Life Building. It is, to put it mildly, a dubious line. The image of journalists brooding "over interest rates at the expense of human interest" may be vivid, but it is factually false—since the first reporter set pencil to paper, the trade has always had a voracious appetite for the banal—and, obviously, self-serving. The implication that the people at *People* are "careful journalists" who do "high-standard reporting" is nothing less than hilarious; *People's* stock in trade is tear-jerking and puffery, written up as ordered by the PR flacks of Hollywood and television.

What *People* neglects to tell us is that the magazine's debut was received within the trade to general hoots of derision and to quite specific doubts that Henry Robinson Luce, the beetle-browed founding father of Time Inc., would have welcomed its birth. Luce did not for the most part publish serious magazines, *Fortune* being the most notable exception, but in his humorless way he was a serious man whose deepest interest was in precisely the kind of journalism so contemptuously dismissed in Landon Jones's missive to *People's* readers. To be sure he had a strong instinct for the bottom line and thus winked at many offenses against journalistic propriety committed by his editors, but as one of those editors says in a forthcoming book about Luce by Robert E. Hertzstein, Luce wanted to "edit up" rather than "down."

So it's difficult to imagine that Luce would have wanted his name, or Time's corporate name, on the masthead of a cheap bit of fluff such as *People*, but then since Luce's death in 1967 his magazines and their successors have gone in directions he would have had some difficulty fathoming, especially in the period since Time joined corporate hands with Warner. But in one sense Luce quite surely would have approved of *People* and its twentieth-anniversary issue. Luce was a great one for the blending of sweeping generalization and journalistic hubris, and he would have recognized the "Age of Celebrity" as handmaiden to "The American Century" that Luce himself so famously declared more than five decades ago in an issue of *Life*. The days when Time Inc. lived high on the hog may be long gone—the cart loaded with free booze no longer rolls down the corridor as deadlines approach—but the sense of institutional self-importance is as overweening as ever.

It's a mark both of Time and the times that the focus of this hubris is not a magazine such as *Life*, which tried to do serious things in an entertaining way, but one such as *People*, which succeeds in doing frivolous things in a trivial way. Not many journalists still insist on writing and editing "up" these days; they have been led in the downward direction by *People* and its various imitators, ranging from *USA Today* on the (relatively) high end to the supermarket tabloids on the low. Certainly *People* has been a trend-setter, as Landon Jones so proudly proclaims, but the trend is not one calculated to please anyone who believes that journalism has obligations higher than the vending of trashy celebrity and the accrual of profit.

A year after *People* made its debut Nora Ephron took a hard look at it in one of the splendid columns about the media that she was then writing for *Esquire*. She noted, correctly, that it was (as it still is) "essentially a magazine for people who don't like to read," that "*Time* and *Life* started out this way too, but both of them managed to rise above their original intentions." She ticked off various ways in which *People* made her grouchy, and then said:

> It seems a shame that so much of the reporting of the so-called human element in *People* is aimed at the lowest common denominator of the also-so-called human element, that all this coverage of humanity has to be at the expense of the issues and events and ideas involved. It seems even sadder that there seems to be no stopping it. *People* is the future, and it works, and that makes me grouchiest of all.

It makes Landon Jones ecstatic. We are now in "the Newsy 90s," he gleefully announces, and he leaves no doubt that we got there aboard the *People Express*. What does it mean to be in the Newsy 90s? It means that personality is all and content is nothing; "Style Without Substance" is the implicit motto of the magazine and of the decade whose journalism it has so insidiously corrupted. It means exploitation disguised as sympathy; just as *People* rode to fat sales on its bathetic photo essays about Ryan White, the boy who died of AIDS, so the TV news shows now shed crocodile tears over others variously afflicted, whether physically or socially or psychologically. It means too that what Ephron in another column called "the celebrity pool" has expanded to ludicrous dimensions "in order to fill the increasing number of column inches currently devoted to gossip."

Gossip being of course the real—and only—business in which the editors and writers of *People* are engaged. "High-standard reporting" indeed! If the people at *People* really believe that, they're fools; if they don't, they're cynics. Students of the long history of Time Inc. probably will agree that they're both.

This Is a 'Celebration'?

༺⚬༻

June 27, 1994

It is a revealing measure not merely of the parlous state of American literary fiction but also of the current editorial climate at the *New Yorker* that of the 196 pages in the magazine's "special" fiction issue only 46 are actually devoted to new fiction, and those 46 are liberally sprinkled with cartoons, advertisements and illustrations. Perhaps it is true, as the contents page declares, that "The New Yorker Celebrates Fiction," but its celebration is wary, halfhearted and unconvincing.

This double issue has been issued to great huzzahs of self-congratulation as well as a rather edgy publicity campaign, the edginess apparently traceable to a lack of conviction on the part of the *New Yorker*'s business managers that there is now much of a market for magazine fiction. That apprehension is well founded, but the huzzahs are not: The *New Yorker* is merely doing what *Esquire* has done for years and, its reputation notwithstanding, doing it not a bit better.

The conceit upon which *Esquire*'s fiction issues have been founded is that summer is the peak period for fiction reading. This may be true, as is suggested by the obstacle courses of Judith Krantz, John Grisham and Robert James Waller through which one must struggle in order to get from one's beach towel to the ocean, but there is little reason to believe that short stories such as those published by either *Esquire* or the *New Yorker* are high on anyone's summer reading priorities.

Certainly no reason is provided by the six published in the June 27–July 4 *New Yorker*. With the exception of amiable if second-echelon pieces by the Irish writer William Trevor and the hard-boiled novelist Elmore Leonard, these stories are limp, airless and unengaging. To be sure the fiction of Alice Munro is a taste that, to my eternal shame, I seem incapable of acquiring; those who love her work no doubt will love "The Albanian Virgin." But what are we to say of yet another exercise in archness by Nicholson Baker, or a miniature in the Kmart genre by Judy Troy, or a tedious monologue by David Foster Wallace?

Probably we are expected to say very little, for despite the assertion in a surpassingly smug editors' "Comment" that "stories get published here because stories please us," in these 196 pages fiction plays second fiddle in its own "celebration." Fearful, apparently, that an excess of fiction would drive their readers elsewhere, the editors have shoehorned these six stories in among a surfeit of nonfiction and clutter, much of it quite astonishingly self-applauding in nature.

The issue's tone is set by the aforementioned "Comment," wherein it is proclaimed that "the style of reporting pioneered and developed in this magazine over its nearly 70 years of existence draws heavily on the aesthetic techniques of fiction . . . and occasionally rises, or aspires to rise, to the level of literature." Having thus established its own pre-eminence, the *New Yorker* presses the theme throughout.

The first nonfiction piece is a profile by James B. Stewart of the novelist James Wilcox that is intended to describe the writing life as now lived in Manhattan. On a single page Stewart manages to tell us, in Wilcox's words, that "it was a thrill to get a real, typewritten letter from the *New Yorker*," even if it was a rejection; that, later, "being published in the *New Yorker* was a milestone for Wilcox—an affirmation, of sorts"; and that "the *New Yorker* story offered confirmation that Wilcox had talent."

Moving along a few dozen pages, after struggling through the Baker and the Troy and a predictable survey of the fiction best-seller lists, we find ourselves in the hands of Roger Angell. To the larger world he is known as the finest baseball writer of his day, but within the little club on West 43rd Street he is first and foremost an editor of fiction. It is in this capacity that he speaks to us now, in "Storyville." He means to be avuncular in this account of how fiction is chosen and edited at his magazine but succeeds primarily, alas, in being smug. Even those who believe as I do in the primacy of editors will be put off by this depiction of authors such as a "soft, musing" John Updike or a young Woody Allen gratefully receiving the *New Yorker*'s patient ministrations: "Allen's modest early submissions here so resembled the work of his literary hero S.J. Perelman that I had to remind him that we already had the original on hand; he saw the point and came up with the remedy, almost overnight."

Hard upon this comes a seven-page spread of photographs "of 14 fiction writers closely associated with the *New Yorker* taken by our staff photographer, Richard Avedon." However one may feel about these writers qua writers, in these pictures they emerge as mere objects of institutional narcissism. In the blink of an eye the *New Yorker* has progressed from burying its authors' bylines at the end of their stories, to giving them proper and prominent credit, to exploiting them as pinups. What this says is that the *New Yorker* is serious about them not as writers but as celebrities.

Onward, through various offerings including a resuscitated Jazz Age manifesto called "The Wild Party," with sexually explicit illustrations by Art Spiegelman. So much for the war between the sexes as once wittily depicted in these pages by James Thurber, to whose work and memory an eight-page exegesis by Adam Gopnik is devoted. There is a certain amount of sense in it and a certain amount of nonsense, but the ultimate effect is to put the crowning touch of self-celebration upon the *New Yorker* itself.

To say that Harold Ross and William Shawn would have recoiled at virtually everything in this issue is as pointless as it is true. Ross and Shawn are dead, dead, dead. Their day is done. So too is the heyday of fiction in the magazine to which they devoted their working lives. This has something to do with the age in which we live and something to do with the people who now run the magazine. Literary fiction is dying, the victim of mass indifference that is scarcely alleviated by its own narrow solipsism. As for the editors, they are apostles of the "new" journalism; apart from design and typography, most of what now appears in the *New Yorker* would be equally at home in *Esquire* or *Rolling Stone* or *Vanity Fair* or any other chic organ of that genre. In such a climate a fiction "special" is more a hollow gesture to the past than a genuine celebration.

Nannies in

High Dudgeon

～◦～

January 12, 1998

Late in his long and prominent career as a television journalist David Brinkley seems to have developed what the fastidious
would call an unseemly appetite for filthy lucre. That was one
conclusion to be drawn from his memoir, published a couple of
years ago. After writing in a genial manner about his life and career, Brinkley inexplicably veered off into a harangue—a rant, in
today's felicitous usage—about "blue-suit rimless-glasses bureaucrats on the tax-writing committees" and their "pure sensual pleasure of taking still more money away from business people who
make more money than they do, and who produce wealth rather
than consume it."

Reading that outburst, one could only sense that Brinkley's
real resentment involved the extraction of money from his own
pockets by tax-writing bureaucrats, that the tongue-in-cheek cur-
mudgeon of *The Huntley-Brinkley Report* had metamorphosed, in
the 1990s, into a bitter fatcat huffing and puffing about federal
highway robbers. It wasn't a particularly pretty sight, but it surely
was a familiar one; there's nothing quite like the acquisition of
substantial sums of money to turn yesterday's flower children into
today's plutocrats, and it happens all the time.

This being the case, how could anyone have been surprised
when Brinkley, having made what seems to have been universally

praised as a graceful, self-effacing departure from ABC News' *This Week* program, turned right around and signed up as corporate spokesman for something called Archer Daniels Midland, a regular sponsor of . . . *This Week*? One Sunday morning Brinkley was in the anchor's chair, exchanging portentous nothings with the bloated egos who assemble there each week; the next Sunday Brinkley was in an "infomercial" (surely the English language harbors no more odious coinage), nattering about the many virtues of Archer Daniels Midland.

So at least I read in last week's newspapers. It being my deep conviction that almost anything—lawn-mowing, house-painting, septic-tank-draining—is a better way to spend Sunday morning than listening to bigfoot Washington journalists mouth off at each other, I have never seen more than snippets of *This Week*, and those involuntarily. But even on limited evidence it is abundantly plain that it, and all the other dreadful programs like it, has far less to do with the serious discussion of public issues than with the projection of egos and, if they can be called that, "personalities."

These programs bear scant resemblance to "journalism" as the word was understood in the naivete of my youth. Perhaps in the 1950s and early 1960s, when Washington journalism was still under the proprietorship of stuffed shirts who assembled each week to *Face the Nation* or *Meet the Press*, there was a semblance of serious—nay, solemn and soporific—talk about the news. But even then the seeds were sown for today's Sunday morning talk shows, which like almost everything else in television are merely variations on the theme of entertainment, if, that is, that's what entertains you.

All of the above being so—and if it says so here, then you can bet your booties that it *must* be so—what is truly ludicrous about David Brinkley's Sunset Years conversion from "journalism" to hucksterism is not the conversion itself but the response it aroused in the media. One would have thought that Mother Teresa had risen from the dead and signed up with Larry Flynt. "Much of the news community is . . . aghast over David Brinkley's decision," Howard Kurtz reported in the *Washington Post* last

week, and then proceeded to quote a long honor roll of emi-
nentos—Daniel Schorr, Bernard Kalb, Walter (Uncle Wally!)
Cronkite—to that effect.

This was as nothing, though, by comparison with the olym-
pian scorn that had already descended on Brinkley from the op-
ed page of the *New York Times*. Ordinarily its columnist Maureen
Dowd is that newspaper's Vampira-in-residence, sinking her oh-
so-delicate fangs into anyone Inside-the-Beltway who arouses her
disdain. On this occasion, though, she presented herself as nanny
and scold, expressing her "outrage" at Brinkley's "sad transformation from revered to scuzzy," recalling with rueful affection
"the splendid reputation he had painstakingly built up with several generations of Americans over half a century" and then, ris-
ing to the full majesty of her wrath, signing off as follows: "David
Brinkley was the avatar of ABC in its brief moment as a Tiffany
news operation. Now he's just another celebrity at the jingling
till."

Oh, get off it! Not merely is that prose right out of Ad Age's
Cliche Central ("avatar," "Tiffany news operation," "jingling
till"), but it is impossible to imagine a less credible defender of
journalistic objectivity and reticence than a Washington bigfoot.
Dowd herself may keep within the limits of extracurricular buck-
chasing prescribed by her employer, but she is a prominent member of a local journalistic community that desperately seeks celebrity and the rewards attendant to it, a community that regards the
reporter or columnist as the equal, in candlepower, of any politico
or pop-cultural "icon."

This is a community in which the upwardly mobile yearn to
follow a straight line from reporter to commentator to television
talk-show regular to book-author to lecture-circuit superstar. It is
a community some members of which—free-agents unencum-
bered by conflict-of-interest rules—not merely think nothing of
accepting huge speaking fees from groups whose activities they
may someday report or comment upon, but who aggressively seek
such engagements through the—to borrow a word—scuzzy
speakers' bureaus whose services they retain.

For any member of this community to turn on David Brinkley because he's raking in a few advertising dollars is hypocritical on its face. That goes not merely for those cited above but for yours truly. My speaking income may be ridiculously small—a few hundred bucks a year—by contrast with what's raked in by regulars of *This Week* and other lecture-circuit launching pads, but I take what I can get. Though it was gratifying to read a recent report that Washington blowhards are no longer as popular out there in lectureland as they used to be, they're still chasing the dollars as avidly as ever. Precisely what difference there is between earning $30,000 or $40,000 haranguing the grommet manufacturers for 45 minutes and earning heaven knows how much crooning the virtues of Archer Daniels Midland for 60 seconds is so fine as to elude my grasp. That, need it be said, is because there is no difference at all.

∽o∾

POLITICALLY

CORRECT

∽o∾

E E K !

‍⁀⁓

S e p t e m b e r   2 4 ,   1 9 9 0

Here we go again, on a journey with our friend the freshman student Alice, back down the academic rabbit hole. Down, down, down. "Either the well was very deep, or she fell very slowly, for she had plenty of time as she went down to look about her, and to wonder what was going to happen next." Semiotics? Deconstruction? Faculty-club Marxism? Small wonder that as she fell Alice cried, "Curiouser and curiouser!"—she was "so much surprised that for the moment she quite forgot how to speak good English" and lapsed instead into profspeak.

When at last we landed with Alice at the bottom of the hole, what did we find? On a previous trip, you may recall, we were plopped into a classroom where the young scholars were studying the television program *M*A*S*H*, with an eye to its fathomless cultural and sociological ramifications. Another time we hit the floor and found ourselves next to a professor who was explicating the epistemological underpinnings of intercollegiate basketball. As for the last time down, it put us smack in the middle of the popular-culture department, where graduate students were deconstructing Pink Floyd and Yogi Berra.

But this time . . . ah, this was the grandest trip of all. This time as we tumbled down the hole, holding Alice's hand for dear life—"Down, down, down. Would the fall *never* come to an end?"—and praying for a safe landing, how could we possibly have known that our destination would be a suburb of Wonderland called—yes!—Comix World. We tumbled and tumbled, and when at last we awoke there we were, in the arms not of Morpheus but of Batman.

Downward we fell, only to find the drones of academia moving ever upward, like primeval creatures struggling up from the slime toward the earthly perfection that is humankind's highest vision. They've left *M*A*S*H* behind them, like some anachronistic dorsal fin, and shed themselves of Yogi Berra as if he were a vermiform appendix; now, with Utopia itself perhaps only a step or two away, they have come to Superman and Dick Tracy and Felix the Cat and—hosanna!—Donald Duck.

We found news of their progress reported in the official journal of Wonderland, the *Chronicle of Higher Education*, under the headline: "Looking for the Messages in Batman and Donald Duck: Researchers Turn to the Comics." Its reporter, Ellen K. Coughlin, wrote: "Ephemeral and seemingly trivial, comics are nevertheless attracting the attention of an increasing number of academic researchers, who regard the crudely drawn characters who speak with the aid of white balloons as serious forms of art, narrative and cultural expression."

In her travels through Comix World, Coughlin found many strange and wondrous creatures. One of them, called Thomas Inge, professor of humanities at Randolph-Macon College and "a specialist in the history of the comics," confessed to her that "among all forms of popular culture, we're at the bottom of the heap," but one of the great things about life in the rabbit hole— why else do they call it "Wonderland"?—is that all things are possible. Thus it is that Inge was able to say as well: "Things are falling together. We are now witnessing a birth of comics scholarship."

A great moment in the history of the cosmos, that: Let us pray that Stanley Kubrik or Steven Spielberg—better yet, both!— was there to put it on film. The birth of the universe, the birth of the messiah, the birth of a nation, the birth of comics scholarship . . . it all just sort of runs together in a seamless web, the universe triumphant.

So there we sat, on our tuffet, dumbfounded at the very thought of this incontrovertible evidence of the existence of God, when along came our old friend the White Rabbit, chairman of the English Department and head cheerleader and director of public relations for Wonderland. He was as always in a terrible hurry. "Come come!" he said. "You must come along! Ellen K. Coughlin is interviewing another of our strange and wondrous creatures!"

Indeed she was. His name was Joseph Witek, and she told us that he was an assistant professor of English at Stetson University. He was quick to speak. "Comics pose a fascinating semiotic problem," he said, as we gasped at this deft use of the academic vernacular. "People have been thinking about words and pictures together, and pictures as a form of language. This is a narrative form that has developed that approach for a long, long time."

Once again we were dumbfounded, as our minds cast back to the earliest days of comics, when illustrators plied their trade with foolscap and quills and Alley Oop roamed the land. We were musing thus—Alice said she particularly liked to think about the Katzenjammer Kids—when Ellen K. Coughlin broke in to put it all into historical perspective. She said:

> The early comic strips are prized for their artistic creativity and experimentation. George Herriman's "Krazy Kat" is held up as an early example of American Dadaism. Windsor McKay's "Little Nemo in Slumberland" is considered one of the most beautifully drawn strips ever. Milton Caniff's cinematic technique in "Terry and the Pirates" and "Steve Canyon" could be a primer in the use of framing, angles and lighting.

Speechless again! And soon to be all the more so, for the White Rabbit dashed back in and sped us right along, following pell-mell in the faithful Coughlin's footsteps as she raced to the next, and unquestionably the climactic, leg of her journey. There we found her talking to David Kunzle, a professor at the University of California at Los Angeles, a man of so many parts that they required elaborate enumeration. He is "an art historian who is interested in the 'social effects' of comic art"; he is "the author of two volumes on the historical precursors of the comic strip"; and—voila!—he "studies comics from a Marxist perspective."

Yes. Coughlin told us that Kunzle "has looked at the cultural messages in the Donald Duck comic books." Really? Yes, the scholar said, "They're very imperialist." Remember how Scrooge McDuck made his fortune in Middle East oil fields? The McDuck stories "reflect American foreign policy very clearly, from the Korean War to the Vietnam War." Wow. And then double wow when Kunzel applied the clincher. "The Disney corporation shudders to hear this," he told us, "and thinks it's just a crazed Marxist talking. But it's clearly true."

Up in the tree the Cheshire Cat looked down and grinned his famous grin. "Clearly true," he said, and laughed weirdly at the very thought of the Disney corporation brought shuddering to its knees by a mere citizen of Wonderland. His laugh got a little out of control, so at last Alice, who by now was rather worried, asked him, "What sort of people live about here?"

"In *that* direction," the Cat said, waving its right paw round, "lives a Hatter; and in *that* direction," waving the other paw, "lives a March Hare. Visit either you like; they're both mad."

"But I don't want to go among mad people," Alice remarked.

"Oh, you can't help that," said the Cat; "we're all mad here. I'm mad. You're mad."

"How do you know I'm mad?" said Alice.

"You must be," said the Cat, "or you wouldn't have come here."

Well. *That* gave Alice pause. She sat thinking about it for a while and then all of a sudden poof! and there she was, back at home. "Oh, I've had such a curious dream!" she said, and she told her sister, "as well as she could remember them, all these strange Adventures of hers that you have just been reading about." Strange, yes, but oh so wonderful.

FUDGING *OUR TOWN*

❧

December 3, 1990

The fortieth anniversary season of Arena Stage got off with a bang and now is muddling along with a whimper. Its spectacular performance of Berthold Brecht's *The Caucasian Chalk Circle* has been followed by a soggy one of Thornton Wilder's *Our Town*, which proves nothing so much as that even the best of theatrical companies—and Arena most certainly is among them—is capable of putting on a bad show.

In part this is no fault of Arena's. Now more than a half-century old, *Our Town* is showing both its age and the flaws that excessive familiarity invariably exposes. Seeing it for the first time in at least a quarter-century, I was taken aback by the corniness of so much of its language, the banality of its rhetoric and the clumsiness of its construction; it's a period piece pure and simple, and its continuing presence in the standard repertoire probably has more to do with nostalgia than with genuine dramatic merit.

But Arena has compounded the play's problems. For whatever reason its director, Douglas Wager, has chosen to emphasize the sappiest aspects of Wilder's play; he has been abetted in this misguided endeavor by much of the cast, in particular Robert Prosky's gratingly aw-shucks interpretation of the role of Stage Manager. But a more serious problem is Arena's attempt to turn *Our Town* into a vehicle for the new political correctness. In what can only be viewed as a wildly inappropriate example of "non-traditional casting," it has turned this melodrama about turn-of-the-century white New England Protestants into a multi-racial and multi-cultural extravaganza, in the process making it into something it simply is not.

It is an effort consistent with longstanding Arena policy as determined in large measure by Zelda Fichandler, the co-founder of the theater who is retiring at the end of the current season as its producing director. A tribute to her in the playbill now being distributed to Arena patrons reads in part:

> Her commitment has been instrumental in Arena's efforts to diversify its staff and to be more responsive to the significant minority populations that constitute its community. In keeping with her artistic vision to embrace cultural diversity, Zelda has led the theater in a far-reaching effort to increase multicultural representation on Arena's stages, in the audience, and among theater personnel.

This is an admirable policy, and it has had many admirable results. Few cultural institutions in the country have been so responsive to American heterogeneity as Arena Stage; not merely was it among the first to stage plays that try to deal honestly with racial and ethnic matters—it was at Arena that *The Great White Hope* made its famous debut—but it has been a pioneer in offering employment to members of minority groups, blacks in particular, not merely in visible places on stage but in behind-the-scenes jobs as well.

Its commitment to non-traditional casting is part of this, and its production of *The Caucasian Chalk Circle* showed precisely how effective such casting can be. Brecht's play may contain an ample measure of twaddle, but it is full of theatrical energy and it transcends, in setting and cast of characters, most cultural and racial considerations. Arena's production turned the play into a spectacularly diverse human tapestry, in so doing emphasizing its essentially fabulous nature and making it into a better play than it really is.

But *Our Town* is quite another matter. To be sure it is, like *The Caucasian Chalk Circle*, a fable, but it is one set in a very specific, very narrow time and place. If it speaks to the universal, as certainly it does, it speaks all the same through the medium of a

New Hampshire Yankee town, in the language of the people who inhabit such a town and in customs such as would have been encountered there from 1901 to 1913, the years embraced by the play. Clearly one of the play's themes is that even in a place as remote and provincial and homogenous as Grover's Corners, we can find a microcosm of the world or, if you like, the universe; but its homogeneity is essential to its character, indeed may well be essential to Wilder's message, and to fudge it is to fudge the play itself.

This is what Arena does. Of the twenty-six members of its cast (several play more than one role), seven are black and one is Hispanic. This means among other things that there are two pairs of interracial siblings—George and Rebecca Gibbs, Emily and Wally Webb—and that the role of Dr. Gibbs is performed by an actor whose accent calls to mind not a turn-of-the-century Yankee physician but Ricky Ricardo. It goes without saying that this is the result of honorable intentions; the effect, though, is merely jarring and distracting.

There are two reasons for this. The first and most obvious is that it bears no relationship to reality, either Wilder's or New Hampshire's. As recently as 1980 that state had a black population of less than one-half of 1 per cent, and a Hispanic population of .005 per cent; New Hampshire, that is to say, even now comes about as close to being lily-white as any of the American states, so to represent it otherwise may be noble but is also preposterous.

The second and in some respects more important reason is that in attempting to transcend race and ethnicity, this production inadvertently calls attention to both. The young actors playing Rebecca and Wally are attractive and able, but because they are black it simply defies credulity that they could be sister and brother to, respectively, George and Emily; the actor playing Dr. Gibbs does his best, but his Hispanic accent is wholly incongruous within a cast the other members of which are striving mightily to sound like New Hampshire Yankees.

The result is that the playgoer ends up making a conscious effort to put the cast's racial and ethnic identities out of mind, which gets in the way of the play and renders it, if not entirely implausible, in great measure so. To say this is not to denigrate non-traditional casting but to point out that there are some plays (and movies) in which it works and some in which it does not. Try to imagine the title role of *Purlie Victorious* played by a white actor, or the matriarch in *A Raisin in the Sun* by a white actress, and you get the point: The casts of certain plays have distinct racial or ethnic compositions, just as do certain families and communities in the world itself, and to represent them otherwise is to misrepresent them.

Non-traditional casting is a wonderful idea in principle and often in practice, as *The Caucasian Chalk Circle* so memorably demonstrated; as was noted in this space during the brief furor over the casting of *Miss Saigon*, the theater has the power to make us disbelieve what our own eyes tell us, a power that nontraditional casting depends upon for its effectiveness. But it is one thing to open acting opportunities where in the past they have been closed, and another to impose artificial racial or ethnic or sexual constraints on plays to which they are ill-suited.

Like everything else in this over-sensitized society of ours, non-traditional casting is a tricky business. I don't propose to have the final answer to it, and I guess that if I had to choose between clumsy efforts to lower racial barriers such as Arena's *Our Town* and no efforts at all, I'd choose *Our Town*. But the play now being performed at Arena Stage, however deep the bow it makes toward political correctness, is not the play that Thornton Wilder wrote; that should count for something, but these days it doesn't.

'WHITE MALE PARANOIA'

⁓⌘⁓

December 10, 1990

Lord knows it is true that, as one Catherine Schuler wrote in this newspaper's letters column last week, "the white male experience is not universally interesting." As one with more than a half-century of such experience under my belt, I am ready to testify that not merely is it "not universally interesting," it is often downright boring. Compound being white and male with being Anglo-Saxon and Protestant, even if as in my case lapsed Protestant, and you have all the ingredients for terminal tedium.

Still, it's the lot into which I've been cast, so however dreary it may be I try to make the most of it: go with the flow, as it were, even if the flow rarely musters much more than a trickle. Truth to tell, being white and male isn't something I spend a great deal of time thinking about, even though statistics tell me that I'm rapidly fading into the tapestry of American minority groups and even though word came to me not long ago of a lawyer's warning: "If you're a white male, forget it. That's the one group in our society that no longer has any legal rights at all."

Which is why you could have knocked me over with a feather when I read Schuler's letter, which was provoked by an excerpt in the *Washington Post*'s Outlook section from Alvin Kernan's new book, *The Death of Literature*. The letter began:

> Isn't it enough to subject readers to Jonathan Yardley's white male paranoia every week without adding a Yardley clone on Sundays? I refer to "Literature: R.I.P." by Alvin

Kernan. When are men like Messrs. Yardley and Kernan going to drop their defensive posturing and stop blaming women and minorities for the decline of Western culture? When are they going to acknowledge that the white male canon is just that: white and male. That doesn't necessarily mean the canon is worthless, but it does suggest that the criteria for selecting "classics" was *[sic]* devised by and favors *[sic]* white males.

For a couple more paragraphs Schuler, a professor of theater history at the University of Maryland, went on in the same vein. She said that "woman-hating has never kept a book from being included in the canon," and then attacked the *Post* itself for failing, as she sees it, to publish "a full discussion of curriculum transformation" for which, she said, "plenty of women and minorities can present a cogent argument."

No doubt that is true—just as it is doubtless true that the *Washington Post* would happily publish such a document should someone submit it—but Schuler's letter struck me as having a lot less to do with cogency than with spite. "White male paranoia," "defensive posturing," "woman-hating"—this isn't the stuff of reasonable debate, much less cogent argument, but rather that of ad hominem attack; as such it debases, rather than elevates, the points Schuler was attempting to make.

As such, further, it would not be worthy of comment, except that it is all too representative of the style debate is assuming these days in literary and academic circles. Rather than dealing with the issues—and I am quite ready to acknowledge that real issues do exist, many worthy of vigorous discussion—it shunts them aside in favor of slurs and misrepresentation. In this matter I can speak only for myself and not for Kernan, though I am delighted to be convicted of guilt by association if, as seems to be the case, published agreement with many of his arguments is sufficient cause for the accusation. Kernan says that literature is becoming irrelevant to American life and thus is dying a rapid death; among the reasons he cites for this is the prevalence within literature departments of a new scholarship that emphasizes not the literary quality of works under study but their political correctness, especially in regard to radical feminism and hothouse Marxism.

Mea culpa: I think Kernan is right. But just what does thinking this, and having the temerity to say it in public, have to do with "white male paranoia"? Nothing at all, and to say that it does is merely a cheap, easy shot. Rather than dealing with the merits or weaknesses of arguments made by the likes of Kernan and me—by no means all of us white males—the charge of "white male paranoia" dismisses them as mere prejudice, which is to say irrational and thus beneath discussion.

By what bizarre contortion of logic can a journalist who has publicly stated that such serious American literature as is now being written is almost entirely the work of women be dismissed as a victim of "white male paranoia"? How can this same journalist, who believes Ralph Ellison's *Invisible Man* to be the masterpiece of postwar American literature, be accused of "blaming women and minorities for the decline of Western civilization"? How does "woman-hating" connect with a journalist most of whose professional relationships, all of them happy, are with women?

As the journalist in question I can only say: Beats me. Schuler's accusations, like so many fired from her side of the Great Literary Divide, have nothing to do with the facts as I know them and everything to do with distortion. Not being privy to the mental processes of those who make such representations, I cannot say whether they are the result of willfulness or mere ignorance. But whatever the explanation for them, the net effect is the same: They tar the opposition with the brush of prejudice, narrowmindedness and paranoia.

It's loony. I could fill reams of column space praising the work of women writers from Jane Austen to Kate Chopin to Edith Wharton to Ellen Glasgow to Eudora Welty to Flannery O'Connor to Pauli Morrison to Susanna Moore—through the years I've done precisely that, over and over again—but let me slip just for a moment and wonder aloud whether conformity to feminist orthodoxy is a legitimate measure of literary distinction and . . .

bang! Down comes the gavel: Guilty as charged of "white male paranoia."

It's the same as being accused of "racism" if you have the temerity to take issue with the proponents of Afrocentric education. The charge is utterly false, but once made it sticks like the most tenacious glue, coloring and distorting everything that the accused party says or writes. The result is that a civilized discussion of difficult and interesting issues is made impossible, smothered as it is under a blanket of emotion and, inevitably, mistrust.

Certainly it's true that throughout most of the Western past literature and education were dominated by white males; so was just about everything else. This may well have been undesirable, but it is a fact of history which we deny only by fabricating a land of make-believe. With lamentably few exceptions, the great work of Western culture was done by white males; it constitutes the heart of our literary and artistic heritage, and to imagine otherwise is mere self-delusion. It is the work that must be taught from grammar school through university, if future generations are to understand the essence of their cultural birthright; to shove it into the background as worthless is breathtakingly irresponsible.

That is what I believe. It is a conviction, not a prejudice; to dismiss it as "white male paranoia" and "woman-hating" is, in the end, not debate—it's insult, the intellectual equivalent of a pie fight. Laurel and Hardy did it better.

A Slow Boat

to Albania

✎

December 24, 1990

All I want for Christmas is . . . yes, the hour is late and the stores are jammed and the budget is tight, but this really is the season of good will, isn't it? Shouldn't a boy get what he wants, if only he asks for it nicely? Pretty please, Mr. Claus, won't you take a look at my list?

Won't you reach deep down in your bag and grant me immunity from those silly old laws that keep a boy from running his car just as fast as he wants to, particularly if he happens to be running it on the byways of North Carolina? If the cops in that auto commercial can say to the fellow in the zippy little car, "The road is yours, so do with it as you please," or words to that effect, then why can't they say the same to me in my zippy new big car?

Maybe that's too much to ask for; shouldn't be greedy at Xmas time. So what about just a little gift, one that would have the pleasurable side effect of bringing joy not merely to me but to millions of others? It really doesn't seem too much, Mr. Claus, in fact if you'll grant me just this one gift I promise—cross my heart and hope to die—not to ask for anything else. I'll make my bed every morning and eat my liver and do my homework—hell, I'll even say my prayers—if only I can come downstairs Christmas morning and find an envelope with a one-way ticket in it.

Oh, no, Mr. Claus, it's not a ticket for me; I'm not *that*

greedy. No, it's a ticket for all those people who believe that the real purpose of education is political indoctrination. Don't they deserve a nice vacation—a nice *long* vacation—in some place where the climate is just to their choosing? No, not Cuba: Truth to tell (sssh!) we're really talking exile, not vacation, and at this time of year a holiday in Cuba might seem too much like, well, a holiday.

No, let's pack them all on a boat and send them off to . . . what say Albania, Mr. Claus? A bit of R&R in that socialist paradise should be just their cup of tea, shouldn't it? A bracing winter breeze zipping in off the Adriatic should do wonders for their sciatica, shouldn't it? You can send them to Kamenice (alt. 2352 feet): Surely the snow's on the slopes there, enough of it for skiing and other winter sports. Yes, I know the government isn't big on free speech and other such niceties, but then, neither are the folks we're sending there.

So get aboard your sleigh, Mr. Claus, and start the roundup. You might make your first stop in North Carolina—stick to I-85, because the scenic byways are crawling with state troopers —where in the pleasant old tobacco town of Durham you'll find a whole sleigh-load on the campus of Duke University. In the English Department alone you can round up enough suspects to fill an entire deck—make that the orlop deck, if it's all the same to you—of your ocean liner.

Make certain, for heavens sake, that while you're roping them in at Duke you corral Stanley Fish, chairman of the English Department and high potentate of whatever is flavor of the month in academic lit'ry criticism. It was Fish, you may recall, who denounced the National Association of Scholars as "widely known to be racist, sexist and homophobic" and who suggested that members of the organization, for the sin of being "illiberal," be denied appointment to committees at Duke responsible for tenure and related matters.

Once you've got Fish & Company securely padlocked away in their cabins—no portholes down there on the orlop, and no shuffleboard, and no captain's table—then you'd best point your sleigh west and head for Texas, where an effort is under way to transform the freshman writing course at the state university in Austin into what one resident cynic calls "Oppression English." If many in the—where else?—English Department have their way, a course intended to improve the basic writing skills of freshmen will be turned into a series of assigned readings in "difference," i.e., a consciousness-raising indoctrination in politically correct attitudes toward racism and sexism and any other ism that might happen along.

Fortunately the imposition of this curricular improvement has been postponed until the fall, so there's still time to whisk away the malfeasants before they can do further damage. If you're looking for names of the guilty, check in with a fellow named Alan Gribben, an English professor who's had the courage to lead the fight against this latest exercise in high-minded fascism. "If you really care about women and minorities making it in society," Gribben has said, "it doesn't make sense to divert their attention to oppression when they should be learning basic writing skills." Please, Mr. Claus, zip down that fellow's chimney and leave him a nice big sack of Swiss chocolate, Virginia ham and Australian wine.

Then, sir, westward ho! once more. Take that sleigh all the way to California, to the city of Santa Cruz. The weather may be lovely there this time of year, but this is no day at the beach for you, Mr. Claus. Your mission is to descend on the campus of the University of California at Santa Cruz and make away with the "five professors of good will"—the description belongs to Jerome Neu, of UC-Santa Cruz's philosophy department, writing last week in the *Wall Street Journal*—who have organized what they call a "World Culture" course. As Neu tells it:

> Signs of trouble emerged early. One professor, a biologist, began a lecture about Darwin with an apology for speaking about the work of a "dead white male." The same professor (himself a living white male, originally from Canada) choked with emotion at a session with other professors and graduate teaching assistants over the fact that he was not a member of any oppressed minority.

On Dasher! On Dancer! Pack 'em up and take 'em away! On Donder! On Blitzen! To the top of the porch! To the top of the wall! Now dash away! Dash away! Dash away all! Dash all the way to Massachusetts, where you've one final pickup to make. It's in the town of Amherst, on the campus of the University of Massachusetts, in the (!) English Department. There you'll find any number of right-minded people who, in the bottomless bliss of their rectitude, have managed to do what the folks in Texas only dream of doing. "The writing faculty here," the *Chronicle of Higher Education* reported last week, "has revamped the university's two freshman composition courses so all the readings raise issues of racial and social diversity."

The courses are called "Basic Writing" and "College Writing," but "Politically Correct Writing" is the real name for them. The woman who directed the formulation of the reading list, one Marcia S. Curtis—take down that name, Mr. Claus!—says, "I don't want the old canon that is all white, mostly male and European-centered," so she and her colleagues have come up with a multi-flavored list that may be a bit light on literary distinction but is heavy on what matters most in the groves of academe these days: "oppression" and "diversity."

Where are you going for Christmas, Marcia S. Curtis? You're going to Albania! The sleigh's leaving now, and in just a few hours it'll deposit you in the Port of Boston, there to join Stanley Fish and the other members of the holy flock aboard the U.S.S. *Dialectical Materialism.* It's a long trip across the Atlantic, but you can pass the time happily with group readings of Louise Erdrich and Bobbie Ann Mason and perhaps a mantra of the complete poetical works of Alice Walker. In no time at all you'll be making port at Durres, on Albania's gold coast, to be greeted by Premier Adil Carcani himself, toasting you with a flagon of Albanian champagne.

Bon voyage! And don't bother to write.

THOUGHT POLICE

ON PATROL

∽○∾

February 18, 1991

By any reasonable standard it was sophomoric behavior, though the student in question was a junior, and certainly it was a weird way to commemorate one's twenty-first birthday. According to a witness to the occasion, one Douglas Hann stood in a dormitory courtyard at Brown University last October and, well-oiled with celebratory alcohol, sang his hosannas into the skies. Among them were a shout of "nigger" and another of "faggot" and another of "Jew"—this last accompanied by an obscenity—and, to a black woman watching the display, the boast that "My parents own you people."

You'd think a fellow reaching his maturity would be capable of more mature behavior, but human beings generally, and college students most particularly, often possess a silliness far beneath their years. Inasmuch as this guy had been hauled up on earlier occasions both for alcoholic excess and for racial insults, he'd seem to be a particularly hard case. But Brown, which itself is a pretty weird institution, responded to this childish tantrum with an equally childish punishment. It gave him the Pete Rose treatment: banishment for life.

It did so under a rule enacted by the university shortly after the ascension to power of its president, Vartan Gregorian, in the spring of 1989. "I issue a solemn warning," Gregorian said then, "that it is the policy of my administration to take action against those who incite hatred. It is my intention to prosecute vigorously, and to expel immediately, such individual or individuals for any attempt to inject and promote racism and thus insult the dignity of our students as citizens of Brown."

Thus charged, the university wasted little time in enacting a disciplinary code forbidding "the subjection of another person, group or class of persons, to inappropriate, abusive, threatening or demeaning actions, based on race, religion, gender, handicap, ethnicity, national origin or sexual orientation"—a veritable shopping list of "minority" special interests. Violators of the code were made subject to expulsion, an important distinction from the dismissal penalty usually exacted by Brown for garden-variety academic violations: Dismissal can be reviewed and reversed after a period in purgatory, but expulsion is forever.

It was under this code that the case of Douglas Hann fell, and it was under the expulsion proviso that it was resolved. The Undergraduate Disciplinary Council, which is half student and half faculty/administration, heard the charges against Hann last fall and pronounced him guilty; its verdict of expulsion was upheld by Gregorian three weeks ago. Hann is now back at home in Pittsburgh, where he told the *New York Times* last week—while not denying that the episode occurred—that Gregorian "wanted someone" and complained, "I think it was just a political statement by the university."

The unfortunate truth—unfortunate, that is, because there is no pleasure to be taken in siding with Hann—is that he is almost certainly right, in essence if not in all particulars. To be sure the sense in which he is wrong is far from trivial: The revulsion against "hate speech" among university faculties and administrators is in most instances genuine and deep and must not be taken lightly. But viewed within the context of the wave of self-righteousness now sweeping through the campuses, the campaign against offensive speech must be viewed in other, less flattering, lights.

Yes, "politically correct" has quickly become a buzz phrase, and it's already time to grant it a merciful death. Those of us who are critical of college faculties and administrations have employed it just about to that point where "ad nauseam" are the only suitable words; we're in danger of becoming as guilty of oversimplification and obfuscation as are the very people whose policies so richly deserve our contempt. But the crusade against "hate speech" is an integral part of the overall process by which American higher education is attempting to enforce compliance to its own political orthodoxy, and it must be viewed as such.

In some measure it has nothing to do with politics and everything to do with damage control. The universities are scared of lawsuits and demonstrations initiated by minority groups, real or merely self-defined, and seem willing to go to elaborate lengths to ward them off. One effective strategy is to preempt each patch in the quilt of "diversity" by embracing its cause with a fervor to match its own. When a school proclaims itself at one with every minority group under the sun, including dozens previously unknown, how can any of them rise up against it?

But that's essentially lawyers' doing, a sly stratagem for contentious times. Far more disturbing is the astonishing assumption, which underlies all these attempts to quash offensive utterances and publications, that the university campus is no place for freedom of speech. The "hate speech" regulations not merely attempt to impose a uniformity of thought on the campuses; they also deny free expression to those who dissent from the consensus.

They do so under the guise of protecting persons and groups alleged to be vulnerable; they put a humanitarian gloss, that is, on a denial of basic liberties. Like it or not—and clearly the academic thought police do not—the freedom to speak one's mind no matter how disagreeable its thoughts is one of the foundations upon which this country exists; abandon it and we would abandon much of our essential corporate self. Americans really do believe, though from time to time that belief is severely tested, in the old chestnut attributed to Voltaire: "I disapprove of what you say, but I will defend to the death your right to say it."

But in Brown and other places similarly enlightened, this has been revised to read: "We disapprove of what you say, and therefore forbid you to say it." The result is that the college campus, heretofore celebrated as a forum for the free exchange of ideas, is rapidly becoming as restrictive as any institution in American society; by comparison the military and the boardroom seem absolute models of untrammeled expression. Speak your mind on campus and you run the risk of ostracism, or condemnation, or expulsion; in such an environment, everyone will soon be afraid of saying everything, so no one will say anything and the exchange of ideas so crucial to scholarly inquiry will dissolve in a nice warm bath of feel-good inoffensiveness.

Is that what the colleges really want to teach their students: That there's only one proper way to think, and all other thoughts are forbidden? That no matter what you think, keep your thoughts to yourself and speak only the approved words? Whatever the case, neither has anything to do with academic freedom—the cherished tradition to which defenders of tenure so ardently, and noisily, cling—and everything to do with suppression of dissent.

Of course it's offensive—repugnant, contemptible, loathsome, whatever you want to call it—for a college student or anyone else to go into a public place and shout words such as those used by Douglas Hann in his little scene last fall. But displays such as that are among the prices we pay for being not merely a free country but one of unexampled heterogeneity. One of the lamentable but inescapable truths about human beings—even American human beings! even college students!—is that not all of them love everybody else and that some of them are given to saying so in public. It's a truth about which the universities would do well to instruct their students, in the hope that they learn to observe standards of civility and tolerance; but telling them to keep their mouths shut is scarcely the way to teach them anything except blind obedience, and that's strictly a lesson for fascists.

RACISM FINDS A HAVEN

❧

August 12, 1991

The trouble with cultivating an image of journalistic raffishness, such as the one enjoyed by the *New York Post*, is credibility: It publishes a piece of serious reportage, and nobody takes it seriously. Such was the case last week, when the *Post* uncovered an astonishing exercise in bigotry and anti-Semitism masquerading as free academic expression; at first just about everyone kept at arm's length, and it wasn't until days later that responsible parties—if "responsible" is the word for them—began to deal, however gingerly, with the questions raised by the story.

It first appeared in last Monday's *Post:* a report of a speech delivered by Leonard Jeffries Jr., a professor at the City College of New York and chairman of its African-American Studies department. The speech was given on July 20 to the Empire State Black Arts and Cultural Festival in Albany; it was co-sponsored by the State University of New York's African-American institute and the governor's advisory committee on black affairs.

Apparently the speech was just about as long as an address by Fidel Castro—two hours!—and even loonier. Ostensibly speaking to the question of Afrocentric education, Jeffries launched into a tirade against whites generally and Jews specifically. He said that there has been "a conspiracy, planned and plotted and programmed out of Hollywood [by] people called Greenberg and Weisberg and Trigliani" and that "Russian Jewry had a particular control over the movies, and their financial partners, the Mafia, put together a financial system of destruction of black people."

That's not the half of it. Jeffries turned history upside down and informed his audience that "everyone knows rich Jews helped finance the slave trade." He also focused his attention on Diane Ravitch, formerly professor of teaching and education at Teachers College, Columbia, now assistant U.S. secretary of education. Ravitch, who is one of the most thoughtful, articulate and persuasive critics of multiculturalism, was dismissed by Jeffries as "a sophisticated, debonair racist" and "a Texas Jew."

None of this, and there was lots more, was a figment of the *Post*'s occasionally lurid imagination. It had originally been broadcast over NY-SCAN, a cable television station, and it had been videotaped. The *Post* merely transcribed Jeffries' remarks and reported them in a straightforward manner. But because the *Post* was the source the story seemed dubious in some eyes—mine, I am embarrassed to admit, among them—and it wasn't until two days later, when the *New York Times* lumbered in with its own report, that the authenticity of the original story was confirmed.

Still, the real or fancied opprobrium attached to the *Post*'s masthead enabled one of Jeffries' supporters, A.J. Williams-Myers, to tell the *Times* that "we need to look at the origin of the fervor in the first place," by which he meant not Jeffries but the *Post*—a clear case of ignoring the news and shooting the messenger. Williams-Myers, who is director of the aforementioned African-American Institute, said the *Post* was "race-baiting" and urged Jeffries' critics to "address the motives" of the newspaper.

But even should those motives be proved to be baser than base, yellow journalism run amok, it remains that neither Williams-Myers nor anyone else, much less Jeffries, has denied either the substance or the specifics of the speech. Not merely that, but another of his defenders—Donald H. Smith, chairman of the department of education at Bernard Baruch College—went so far as to call Jeffries "a very fine scholar" and to claim that, "if his remarks were, as the governor said, 'inaccurate,' then it is up to other scholars to do research to rebut it." But how, pray tell, does one "rebut" racism and anti-Semitism? These are matters not of scholarship, of proof and disproof, but of fantasy and hatred, neither of which is in the least susceptible to rational inquiry or argument. Jeffries is a "very fine scholar" who in all seriousness believes that blacks are intellectually superior to whites because they have more melanin in their skin, a form of racist claptrap similar in tone and spirit to the racial-superiority theories drummed up by the Ku Klux Klan and the White Citizens Council and other publicists for white supremacy. How can one expect a "scholar" in thrall to such hallucination to entertain disagreement, no matter how respectful or persuasive?

But if you doubt that Jeffries possesses a scholarly mind, tell that to the ranking officials of the City University of New York, of which City College is a part. Although Jeffries' race-baiting harangues have been a familiar part of CUNY life for years, this has not prevented him from gaining both tenure and the chairmanship of his department, not to mention a following at City College as, in the *Times*' description, "a popular, flamboyant lecturer."

More than that, what this has gained him in the current circumstances is the exceeding reluctance of all but a few at City College or CUNY to speak out forthrightly against the garbage he retailed in Albany last month. Thus the president of the college, Bernard W. Harleston, issued from the sanctuary of vacation a cautious statement lamenting any remarks by anyone that "undermine another racial or ethnic group," but also saying that "the college must . . . insure the right of its faculty and students to express their ideas without fear of institutional censorship."

There we go again: "academic freedom." It's the smokescreen behind which Jeffries hides and the justification given both by his defenders and by those too cowardly to oppose him. But talk such as Jeffries engaged in at Albany has nothing to do with "ideas"—it's bigotry pure and simple—and nothing to do with academic freedom. He's fully entitled to his absurd prejudices, and if he wants to shout them to the rooftops that's his business, but he scarcely deserves either the gloss of legitimacy that tenure provides or the endorsement implicit in state financing.

It is here that the Jeffries case differs from that of Douglas

Hann, who was expelled from Brown University for exercising his inalienable right to make an ass of himself in public. Hann's anti-black and anti-Semitic ravings were every bit as offensive as Jeffries' anti-white ones, but he was not speaking as an employee or representative of his institution. Jeffries does, not merely in his solo shot at Albany but in his continuing classroom appearances, so City College would therefore be entirely within its rights in disciplining or dismissing him. Unfortunately, though, those rights are compromised by official timidity and by the ironclad strictures of tenure, which severely limit an institution's ability to rid itself of unwanted or incompetent faculty members.

All of which probably means that once this little storm has blown over Jeffries will be back at the same old stand, vilifying whites and Jews and anyone else of whom he disapproves, under the aegis of his City College professorship. No doubt a slap on the wrist will be administered, but not much more than that. Jeffries has a constituency, after all, and college administrators can always disappear behind "academic freedom" if the alternative is giving offense to any element in the tense "multicultural" coalition that now rules on the campuses. If Jews don't fit into the coalition, well, that's just their tough luck.

The irony of this is both exquisite and painful. For nearly a century City College was a bright shining light for Jewish students in New York—"the haven of Jewish minds," as Irving Howe puts it in his book, *World of Our Fathers*. Jewish students "loved the place, loved it utterly, hopelessly, blindly," Howe writes, and quotes a member of an early class: "We knew it as gospel truth that this plain College was for each of us a passport to a higher and ennobled life." But that was 1906; this is 1991, and the passport has been rescinded.

BLACK VS. WHITE

◆◇◆

September 27, 1993

Having watched from the inside for more than a dozen years as the *Washington Post* struggles to make itself more responsive to and representative of the community in which it publishes, I find it preposterous that anyone could imagine it to be "racist" or "white chauvinist." Call it cumbersome or bureaucratic—call it, if you will, insensitive or arrogant—but "racist" or "white chauvinist"? No way.

Yet that is exactly what this newspaper was called last week, as were, by implication and extension, those of us who have published pieces in the *Post* taking exception to the Afrocentric program now undergoing a laborious birth in the public schools of the District of Columbia. At an extraordinary news conference, organizers of the program and parents whose children are enrolled in it let the *Post* have it with all barrels. Its coverage of Afrocentrism was called "a racist attack" by "white supremacists" and "an avalanche of blatant distortion and outright lies"; parents were warned to "guard against white supremacy and white chauvinism . . . so that they can see the white chauvinist orientation of the *Washington Post*."

However preposterous this may be, it is of a piece with other attacks this newspaper has weathered over the years; it will weather this one as well. As for me, I learned years ago that being called nasty names is part of the price one must pay for the privilege of being given a public forum for the expression of opinion. Being called those names isn't a day at the beach, especially when the names are as mean as the ones that were bandied about in the auditorium of the Ruth K. Webb Elementary School last Thursday, but it comes with the territory.

The more important question is: Precisely what good did the attack on the press do for the children of Webb School who are the Afrocentric program's alleged beneficiaries? It's easy enough to see what good the attack did for those who launched it: Apart from the pure pleasure of venting some pent-up spleen, the attack provided a convenient smokescreen for diverting attention from the program's manifest shortcomings. But what did it teach the children?

Perhaps it taught them that blaming the media is always a useful defense of last resort. No doubt this will serve them well in a culture in which media-bashing has become a widely popular psychological safety valve. Perhaps it taught them that another popular form of American self-deception—claiming victimization—is equally convenient when matters aren't going exactly the way one wishes they were.

Most likely, though, it taught them that the most direct path to racial unity is racial polarization. The attack on the media was not, as advertised, an attack on racism; it was an appeal to racism, an attempt to divide the District of Columbia into black and white and, thus, black vs. white. It is somewhat difficult to determine precisely what good this lesson will do for the schoolchildren, who ostensibly are being educated to enter an adult world that for a quarter-century has been trying, however imperfectly, to diminish both racism and its numberless manifestations in human affairs.

That such a lesson was administered in the auditorium of a public school is something to which taxpayers in the District of Columbia might wish to give prayerful consideration, but let's be charitable and chalk it up to the heat of the moment. As School Superintendent Franklin L. Smith said in the wake of the news conference, "People tend to get a little emotional . . . I guess they sort of felt like it was their one opportunity to lash out at the people that they felt were attacking them."

What is more disturbing is the prospect that the racism on

parade at the news conference may crop up, away from public scrutiny, in the Afrocentric program itself. That, in the eyes of many who sympathize with some of the program's goals, is what is most troublesome about it: It may simply substitute one form of racism for another. Leaving aside all the talk about "self-esteem," all the rhetoric about "the princes and princesses of African kings and queens," one is left with the central reality that Afrocentrism is—or has the clear potential to be—a program of racial indoctrination.

Programs such as that used to be familiar stuff in American education, though theirs was indoctrination of a different sort. Whether the cause was pure racism or just plain ignorance, American children in many parts of the country used to be taught that slavery was a benign institution and that Africa was of interest only to goldminers and students of tribalism. Then the civil-rights movement swung into full gear; one of its many salubrious side effects was that old assumptions upon which curricula had been based were challenged, and over the years those curricula were altered in order to take into account our new understanding of society and history.

It is worth noting, as a matter of historical accuracy, that although these changes were inspired by the predominantly black civil-rights movement, they were put into effect by a predominantly white hierarchy. In the 1960s and 70s, in the schools as in almost everything else, white control was general if not absolute. For curricula to be rewritten—as, for that matter, for the schools to be desegregated—white support was not merely useful but mandatory. The fact is that such support was mobilized, and in the curricula as elsewhere the great process of change got under way.

To say this isn't to assert "white supremacy" or "white chauvinism" but to make the point that society and history are considerably more complex than can be understood by those whose views are colored by racism or any other form of particularism. Whether Afrocentrism is inherently incapable of conveying the full breadth of this complexity is at least open to question, and the early returns are not promising. Doubtless there are many people involved in the Afrocentric movement whose motives are admirable, but there are others who seem considerably less interested in learning and teaching the truth than in indoctrinating African-American schoolchildren in a mindset the only appropriate word for which is racist.

The one bright spot is that Afrocentrism is almost sure to be yet another passing fancy. In the schools as in popular culture, fads come and go, often in response to deep if indistinguishable shifts in popular sentiment. As my colleague William Raspberry wrote a couple of days after the fiasco at Webb School, Afrocentrism doesn't look like a movement with much staying power, at least as an academic discipline.

But Afrocentrism is going to be around for at least a few years, so an unknown number of youngsters are going to be exposed to it. Some no doubt will get it in its most benign form: a course of study in which black history is accorded its proper place in world history and black accomplishments are duly celebrated. Others will be less fortunate. They will be fed a diet of half-baked history, half-baked science, half-baked literature in which the chief ingredient will be the self-deluding notion that black invariably is superior to white, "self-esteem" in the most dangerous sense of the term.

Maybe the students will be able to shrug it all off and go on to a more balanced understanding of the world in which they live. But the odds against their doing so are great. What we learn in our first years at school is the foundation upon which everything else is constructed; for the children at Webb, the great danger is that the foundation will be too shaky. To be sure there won't be many of those children, but to waste even one mind is a terrible thing.

BOMBS AWAY

‰

October 10, 1994

The National Air and Space Museum has done the right thing, but for the wrong reason. Its decision to tone down or expunge much of the anti-American commentary that had been written for next year's display of the Enola Gay, the plane that dropped the atomic bomb on Hiroshima, is self-evidently welcome. It is most unfortunate, though, that the museum reached it in response not to the facts but to pressure from special-interest groups.

The most outspoken and influential of these is the American Legion. It has lost much of the political clout that it enjoyed before Vietnam, when its leverage was roughly comparable to that now wielded by the National Rifle Association, but it is still the most prominent veterans' organization and it still commands attention in Washington. Attention is precisely what the Air and Space Museum granted it, during two remarkable closed-door meetings—one lasting twelve hours, the second ten—in which the Enola Gay exhibition's text and displays were discussed in exceedingly fine detail.

As a result of these discussions the exhibition will be considerably less inflammatory than had been planned by those curators who conceived and shaped it. Their stated intention had been not simply to present as much of the bomber as can be fit into the museum but to "address the significance, necessity and morality of the atomic bombings of Hiroshima and Nagasaki . . . [because] the question of whether it was necessary and right to drop the bombs . . . continues to perplex us." Among other things, they intended to tell visitors to the exhibition—many of them young Americans whose ignorance of history is infinite—that "for most Americans, this . . . was a war of vengeance. For most Japanese it was a war to defend their unique culture against Western imperialism."

In other words, the Air and Space Museum meant to turn an exhibition of a weapon of war into a philippic not merely against war but against the United States. Lining itself up with the zealots of academe who prowl the liberal-arts departments muttering against "American imperialism," the Air and Space Museum was prepared to use an exhibition of the technology of warfare as a springboard to leap into generalizations of the most sweeping and insupportable nature.

There are, obviously, a great many things to be said about all of this, many of which already have been said. There is no need for another homily on the transparent evils of political correctness, so one will not be delivered in this space. Still, there are other matters worth raising. The first is that the Air and Space Museum seems to have lost its way. Since when did it become not merely a museum of technology but also a forum for the enlightenment and conversion of the politically and morally obtuse? The Air and Space Museum is an independent agency of the United States government. Under precisely what authority is it seeking to engage in what can fairly be called anti-American propaganda?

A second point, as suggested earlier, is that the museum has decided to revamp its exhibition not because it has seen the error of its ways but because it is engaged in damage control. There is not the slightest evidence that any of those who put together the original design of the exhibition have been persuaded that the Pacific war was something other than American aggression against a Japan determined to protect its cultural heritage. To see the war in those terms falls somewhere between self-delusion and insanity, but that is not merely how certain people at the Air and Space Museum see it but also how they meant to persuade the rest of us to see it, especially—in the words of Martin Harwit, director of the museum—"those generations of Americans too young to remember how the war ended." There can be no doubt that, if only they had their druthers, the museum's curators would prefer to offer the exhibition in these terms, even after their twenty-two hours of face-to-face negotiation with veterans of the war and their representatives.

Which leads to the third and most important point. A common if unspoken assumption at this late hour of the twentieth century is that we are so fully in command of information that it is no longer possible for us to get the facts wrong. The insertion of time capsules in the cornerstones of new buildings, not so long ago a cherished custom, is no longer widely practiced because it is assumed that they are no longer necessary. Just as we have preserved all the information accumulated during World War II, so too we are preserving for future generations all the information about our own time. Capsules containing today's newspaper and copies of Top 40 recordings are no longer necessary because everything is saved, whether in its original form or on CD-ROM or some other form.

But the business at the Air and Space Museum reminds us that even in the age of information overload, historical truth is as mysterious and evasive as it ever was. You can preserve everything imaginable about the war in the Pacific, down to the most detailed and conservative projections of American casualties in an invasion of Japan, but that will not prevent someone so inclined from interpreting the mission of the Enola Gay as (a) a racist attack on the Japanese, (b) a way of proving the cost-effectiveness of the Manhattan Project and/or (c) a placating gesture to Harry Truman's political opposition.

You can assemble all the facts on earth, but you can't make people interpret them for what they are. Especially now, when the rank odor of deconstruction hangs over the scholarly community, it is easy for people to fabricate intellectual arguments for the triviality of facts and then to find whatever "meaning" they choose in such facts, or non-facts, as they are willing to "deconstruct" for their ideological convenience.

History changes because people change. Sometimes it changes for the better. Four decades ago it was commonly accepted among educators in the South and elsewhere that slavery, though "peculiar," was paternalistic and benign; we know better now, and have revised history accordingly. By the same token it is entirely possible that eventually historians will reach an understanding of the Enola Gay's mission that is more subtle than the one commonly held by those of us old enough to remember the day its ghastly load was dropped. But such a judgment must be the fruit of careful, dispassionate research and debate, not of ideology and moral smugness. The latter produce only bad history, which is precisely what the Air and Space Museum wanted to feed us.

PLAY 'FEELINGS' AGAIN

February 13, 1995

For years people have squabbled about the National Anthem. Some say it should be "The Star Spangled Banner," the notes of which no one can sing and the words of which no one can remember, while others say it should be "America the Beautiful," the music and words of which are at once elegant and accessible. But isn't the debate rather beside the point when it's entirely obvious that the real National Anthem is "There's No Business Like Show Business"?

You don't think so? You don't think so after eight years with a second-rate movie actor in the White House? You don't think so after an endless succession of political campaigns scripted by ad men and image specialists? You don't think so after a Super Bowl during which two newly deposed Democratic governors appeared in a commercial hawking Doritos? You don't think so after Mayor Clint Eastwood and Congressman Sonny Bono?

Well, surely you think so now. The events in Massachusetts of ten days ago leave no doubt that the bubbleheads are running the asylum. Appropriately enough, these events were staged at Harvard University, which takes a Hasty Pudding view of show business, part condescension and part adulation. All the more appropriate, they were staged at Harvard's Kennedy School of Government, named in honor of the president who certified style and glamour as the essential ingredients of late-twentieth-century American politics.

For reasons known only to the swamis who run the Kennedy

School, it presented a lecture entitled "The Artist As Citizen," written, copyrighted and delivered by the noted political theoretician Barbra Streisand. Not merely that, but the augustness of the occasion was certified by none other than the *New York Times*, which favored it with the presence of a reporter, a columnist and a photographer, all of whom combined to produce a grand total of seventy inches of column space devoted to La Streisand's up close and personal State of the Artist Address.

In speaking to this illustrious audience in this illustrious place, according to the *Times*, Streisand rebutted "those who criticized the stars circling President Clinton as 'bubbleheads' who should not meddle in serious matters of state." Those were the words of the *Times's* reporter, Maureen Dowd, who is soon to be elevated to the empyrean eminence of op-ed-page columnist. One who already basks in such glory is Frank Rich, who several days after the speech weighed in with words sure to make Funny Girl's heart flutter: "It's not enough for Ms. Streisand just to make her movies better—there's a whole country out there."

So precisely what was it that sent the *Times* into such ecstasies? It was a speech in which Streisand rambled on in this direction and that, proceeding (more or less) from this: "What can I say: I have opinions. No one has to agree. I just like being involved. After many years of self-scrutiny, I've realized that the most satisfying feelings come from things outside myself."

From there Streisand tottered off in defense of George McGovern and in opposition to Newt Gingrich, but no one seems to have paused to take note of this truly extraordinary disclosure: That Barbra Streisand, about whom Scott Fitzgerald unfortunately did not write a short story called "An Ego As Big As the Glitz," declared an end to "self-scrutiny" and a dedication to "things outside myself." This, which packed the approximate seismic punch of Elizabeth Taylor declaring herself a novitiate, went virtually unremarked; so much for the news nose of the New York press corps.

As anyone well knows who has followed her career from Miss Marmelstein to Colonel Cammermeyer, Streisand without ego is no Streisand at all. It used to be a regular stop on the Hollywood bus tours: "There's the Brown Derby, and there's Marlon Brando's house, and there's Barbra Streisand's ego." Now that it is no more, what will the tour guides do, and what bottomless resource will Streisand draw upon when she's "gotta go for it!" as she so memorably summarized her artistic sensibility in the course of a "forthright phone interview" with her fugleman Frank Rich?

Perhaps she intends to indulge herself in the luxury of deep thought, but if she does she's going to discover what many others already know: that as was once said of another La-La Lander, deep down she's shallow. Like a great many other people who have done very well in show business, Streisand has fallen into the trap of mistaking emotion for ideas, of assuming that because she *feels* something she must *think* it as well.

One need only listen to Streisand's recordings to realize that she leads with her gut rather than her head. Although early in her career she tried her hand at a few songs of subtlety and wit, in what passes for her maturity she has been content with flag-wavers and show-stoppers. She may have been Broadway for a while but she's all Vegas now, tugging at the heart-strings with a voice that over the years has come to resemble an orchestrion, if not a calliope.

She may think she's singing "Happy Days Are Here Again," but it's only "Feelings." Fine. As Streisand herself doubtless would put it, she's entitled. She's entitled not because she's rich and famous and self-indulgent to the max but because she's just another citizen of a country that for some reason accords to every more or less sentient adult the right not merely to think as he or she pleases but, alas, to vote accordingly. She's equally entitled— all things being possible on this Big Rock Candy Mountain—to hypocrisy as big as her ego, emitting dithyrambs about the down-trodden on the one hand while soaking her fans with concert ticket prices that border on the predatory.

She can feel any old thing she wants to feel and she can even pretend that her feelings are thoughts, but none of this entitles her to be taken seriously as anything except an entertainer, and not very seriously as that. Were her self-regard just a tiny bit smaller than it is, she would realize that her performance at Harvard was just that: a star turn. Were her ego really under control, she'd understand that Harvard was using her every bit as much as she was using Harvard, that each, in permitting its gaudy light to be shed upon the other, was merely engaging in an act of reflective self-regard. This being her stock in trade, it must have seemed like just another day at the office.

THE FIRST

THANKSGIVING

∽o∾

November 27, 1995

(A few notes made on Thanksgiving Day, 1995, after reading the front page of that day's New York Times, *which reported that "in schools in New York City and across the country, Thanksgiving is getting a makeover, as teachers recast the Pilgrim-and-Indian story to reflect the political and cultural sensibilities of the 1990s.")*

Once upon a time a foul band of blue-eyed devils set sail from England bloody England on a ship they named "Mayflower," in honor of the moving company that stole the Colts from Baltimore. Many days later, after thoroughly polluting the waters of the Atlantic Ocean, they made landfall at a pristine shoreline, which they dubbed "Plymouth" in honor of a planned obsolescent automobile and which they immediately turned into a medical-waste dump. They set up camp and began to build a city, which they called "Boston," in honor of an "Old Mr. Boston," whose spirituous liquors drove them to frenzy, pillage and rapine each day when the sun passed over the yardarm, and they settled down for what they called, with typical British euphemism, the "cocktail hour."

Soon enough the work of these brigands was witnessed from afar by indigenous persons of color, peace-loving souls who were at one with Mother Nature and, by way of proving this, were shod in Birkenstocks. They ordered their clothes from J. Peterman and ate only organic food grown on communal farms. They greeted the newcomers warmly and informed them that this place on Earth was called "Massachusetts," which they translated—they spoke perfect English as well as Latvian, Croat and Austro-Hungarian—as "Land of Pristine Natural Beauty Inhabited by Persons of Diverse Multicultural Perfection."

The English bloody English heard as much of this as they could stomach—about twenty-three seconds worth—before they did what English bloody English always do. They had a merrie massacre. They hauled out their bazookas and Uzis and put on what they liked to call "a turkey shoot," except that in this case the turkeys were the indigenous persons, whom the English in a characteristic outburst of imperialistic scorn had decided to call "Indians," since the English were incapable of distinguishing one oppressed indigenous person from another.

There was blood all over the ground, which was the cause of bottomless joy to the English bloody English, to whom no pleasure has ever been greater than the senseless shedding of the blood of innocents such as foxes, and if foxes aren't available they'll settle for innocent indigenous persons whatever their race, gender, class or sexual preference. By way of celebration they decided to set up a form of government that they called "democracy," the definition of which is: "a form of domination and oppression under which the moneyed classes control the ballot box through corruption, bribery and nepotism, in the process grinding the noses of innocent indigenous persons and all others making less than $75,000 a year into the dust."

The establishment of this satanic government took place in the middle of the summer, so the English checked their imperialist digital wristwatches and decided to call it "The Fourth of July." They constructed a huge edifice, which they called "Pentagon," and from inside it they brought out all manner of weapons of destruction, which they fired into the air spontaneously, creating a scene of carnage so pleasing to their tastes that they called it "a fireworks display" and vowed to have one on every subsequent "Fourth of July," as indeed they have, each time slaughtering hundreds of thousands of innocent indigenous persons not to mention bluebirds, muskrats, polecats and other children of Mother Nature.

The calendar rolled on. The weather began to cool. The English bloody English looked out into the fields and observed with cruel satisfaction the laborers toiling in the fields, hauling in the crops for sub-subsistence wages in a non-union shop. They cackled with glee as one unfortunate after another tumbled to the ground in exhaustion, pleading for the mercy that they scornfully denied. "Hah!" snarled their leader, Sir Newton of Gingrich-on-Pye, "Let's give them a holiday! A special treat: gruel with lumps of lard! We'll call it—*HAH!*—'Labor Day'!"

So it was done, and the laborers were permitted to leave the fields so they could go to "Wal-Mart," which the English bloody English had built overnight and thus forced out of business all the shoppes in which quaint indigenous persons had made their marginal but morally impeccable livelihoods. The laborers went to "Wal-Mart," where they were issued plastic squares that permitted them to buy as many La-Z-Boy armchairs, Harley-Davidson motorcycles and Jet-Ski personal watercraft as their hearts desired. Little did they know that they would be paying the interest on these capitalist baubles until the last drop of labor had been wrung from their innocent indigenous brows.

That got the English bloody English into autumn, but despite all this merrie pillage, brigandage and general rapine, their thirst for blood and pagan ritual was far from slaked. At night as the sun passed below the horizon and darkness descended, as they gargled "Old Mr. Boston" and glugged "Jack Daniels," the English bloody English howled at the moon and called out, "Fie, foh, fum, we be bloodthirsty Englishmen!" They roamed the land with their muskets, shooting down robins and other innocent indigenous birds before they could fly south to warm climes and certain enslavement.

It was a bloody autumn. The fur and the feathers flew. The innocent indigenous persons stayed away in their tents, eating their organic tofu and practicing sexual acts of a unique and highly indigenous nature. One of them, a brave called Thanks, had a bit too much of what the English snidely called "kickapoo juice"—it was actually an indigenous pinot noir, soft in the nose with a hint of balsam and a nip of cranberry—and decided to test the mettle of the invaders. He snuck out of his tented multi-family dwelling place and began to do tribal dances, while singing haunting melodies such as "Native American Love Call" and "I'm a Native American Too."

This infuriated the English bloody English. They hauled out their arsenals and shot the brave deader than dead. Sir Newton of Gingrich-on-Pye chortled and cackled, and then shouted, "By George, I've got it! We'll have a celebratory feast and we'll call it 'Thanks-killing.'" Even the English found this a bit too much, so over the years they toned things down. They replaced the slaughtered brave with a slaughtered turkey, and they called the day "Thanksgiving."

Will you have white meat or meat of color?

FOUR

∽o∾

POLITICALLY

INCORRECT

∽o∾

CHECKING OUT

⚭

February 10, 1992

What this campaign needs isn't the sex check it's getting from hypocritical and self-righteous members of the press, but a reality check—more specifically, a checkout check. If all the other bozos running for the presidency are as ignorant about American life as George Algernon Fortesque Leffingwell Bush proved himself to be last week, then this much is certain: the country really is going to hell, not in a handbasket but in a shopping cart.

In case you missed it, His Supreme Preppiness put in an appearance at a convention of the National Grocers Association, where he was shown a mockup of a state-of-the-art checkout lane. There, according to Andrew Rosenthal of the *New York Times,* he "grabbed a quart of milk, a light bulb and a bag of candy and ran them over an electronic scanner." Just as anyone could have told him, the price of each item promptly showed up on the cash register's digital display. But you could have knocked the Commander-in-Chief of the Army and Navy of the United States over with a feather duster. "This is for *checking out?*" he asked in wonder and awe, and later he told the assembled grocers: "I just took a tour through the exhibits here. Amazed by some of the technology."

It makes me think of a daydream I used to have when I was a boy. I was minding my own business when suddenly who should appear before me but the Father of His Country. "Why, General Washington!" I said. "Let me show you all the amazing things that have happened in your country." First I took him to the kitchen and showed off the stove and refrigerator. "My good-ness!" he said. Then I played a record on the Victrola. "A mira-cle!" he said. "An orchestra in a box!" Then we went for a ride in the car. "I can't believe it!" he shouted. "A horseless carriage!" Then I pointed to the firmament, across which a DC-3 was speed-ing. "No!" he exclaimed. "Man has the wings of a bird!" Then I woke up, happy as a clam, delighting in my role as tour guide for the Man Who Would Not Be King.

You could substitute George II for George I in my day-dream and nothing else in the plot would change. The man who runs the United States of America confessed last week, however indirectly and inadvertently, that he's so out of touch with the daily lives of his constituents, he doesn't even know how they go about buying the food they put on their tables. "Amazed by some of the technology," indeed!

No, presidents and would-be presidents of the United States should not be required to know which aisle the Hamburger Helper is in, but it would be nice if they had a clue to, say, the difference between a bar code and a price tag. By coincidence the Associated Press came out last week with its quadrennial the-candidates-are-richer-than-the-rest-of-us piece, its indignation clearly visible just below the veneer of reportorial objectivity, but that isn't the point. It may be a lousy reality, but it's reality all the same: To run for the presidency you have to have more money than most. Even Tom Harkin, the tinhorn "populist," owns three residences with a sum value of $547,106; a degree of financial independence is not merely necessary if one is to take the risk of running for office, it may be desirable as well.

But independence is one thing, ignorance is another. Though his press secretary nobly tried to cover for Bush—why, he'd seen him in a grocery store, oh, a year or so ago, right there in that quintessential American town, Kennebunkport—the plain truth is incontrovertible: The guy may be smack dab in the mid-dle of the Washington "loop," but so far as America itself is con-cerned, he's a creature from outer space. He masquerades as just one of the American guys, with his fake macho bonhomie and his affected appetite for pork rinds, but he comes from and is utterly a part of a world wherein real men clip coupons and the super-market is where the servants go.

Money does weird things to you if your family has had it for a few generations. You take it for granted; you're not grateful for its quiet, loyal, obsequious presence or surprised by the things it can do for you. If anything, people like Bush, with a net worth in the low millions, are more apt to think of themselves as toward the bottom of the economic totem pole because they hang around with people worth tens or hundreds of millions; some of these low-end high-enders have even been known to plead poverty, as they tool away from East Hampton in their understated Mercedes wagons, en route to golfing holidays amidst the gorse and grouse of Scotland.

There's nothing especially wrong with this so long as these people don't inflict the burden of their ignorance and innocence on anyone save themselves. But when they not merely persuade themselves that they are Representative Man but then presume to run the daily affairs of the rest of us, we're the ones likely to get taken for a ride. A person whose major beef in life is that his neighbor has a better view of Long Island Sound should not be relied upon to have an especially acute sense of what life is like for someone squirreling away $50 a month under the illusion that this will pay for his child's college education or his family's pro-tection against catastrophic illness.

Not merely that, but more: The person so isolated from daily American reality that he doesn't know how to shop for gro-ceries is denying himself one of the great pleasures and astonish-ments of our national culture. Take a foreign visitor on a tour, and the place that's likely to raise the greatest shouts of delight and envy isn't the computer salesroom or the baseball park, but the supermarket, not because the visitor is "amazed by some of the technology," but because the display of cornucopian plenty is almost too much for the alien eye to comprehend.

Me, I'm in the supermarket or the neighborhood grocery four or five times a week. This has nothing to do with being a man of the people—no doubt I've many conceits about myself, but that's not one of them—and everything to do with the sheer magic of the place. From time to time I talk about this with a friend who has become quite famous in a certain segment of American society but has managed to maintain as much privacy as our celebrity-haunted culture permits. What we invariably agree upon is this: It is difficult to imagine a fate worse than having a face so recognizable that you couldn't go to the supermarket without being molested by autograph-seekers and other pests.

Nor is the supermarket just a place for amusing oneself: poking around in the produce counters, eyeing the rye and the pumpernickel at the bakery, ferreting out the perfect fat-free "frozen dessert" in the freezer. It's also a place where those of us who tend to drift away into one ivory tower or another get a strong dose of how other people live. Has George Bush ever seen someone paying for ground beef and Wonderbread with food stamps? Has he ever gotten stuck in the detergent aisle behind a woman so halt that she can nudge along only in increments of inches, so alone that she has no one to help carry her load? Has he ever found himself behind a three-hundred-pound creature whose cart is filled with potato chips, cold cuts, cookies, processed cheese, ice cream—and Diet Coke?

Sure he has; and Placido Domingo sings country-western, too. The mere mental image of George Taliaferro Belmont Cabot Bush in the checkout line is enough to cause gales of laughter. Except that when he's president of the United States it really isn't all that funny.

THE TALK-SHOW AGENDA

⌇∾∾⌇

October 12, 1992

The campaign now gasping into the homestretch has been, by any civilized measure, a singularly uncivilized event. Perhaps it has not been the most degraded campaign of the century—that honor doubtless belongs to the campaign of 1988—but in one respect it has outdone all others: It is the first presidential election in which the candidates have been reduced to the level customarily occupied by authors hustling their books, faded movie stars grasping for one last jolt of celebrity and transvestites peddling their pathetic wares.

Years from now, when some perspective has been gained on this ludicrous show, the 1992 election surely will be known to historians as the Talk Show Campaign. Don't let the brief spasm of formal debates mislead you into thinking that they are the most important public forums that the candidates occupy this fall. The debates last a total of only four evenings. The TV show appearances, by contrast, have been at the center of the campaign for months and apparently will remain so right up to the end.

It is true that the debates are staged for television and thus can be described as TV programs, but that misses the point. The debates may well prove to be as shallow and frivolous as everything else this campaign has unearthed, but their basic purpose is serious; whatever else they may be, the debates are not intended as entertainment, as *show*. But the vast majority of the other television and radio programs to which the candidates are scurrying with such unseemly eagerness are just that: trivial amusements that reduce the candidates to the lowest common Hollywood denominator.

Where were last week's heaviest campaign barrages fired? On two talk shows. On Tuesday, Bill Clinton went onto the *Donahue* show, where he found himself in a spitting match with its blow-dried host over the tiresome subject of his antiwar activities of two decades ago; before it was over Clinton had called Phil Donahue's questions "a load of bull," apt words for just about any Donahue utterance. Then, two days later, who should surface on *Larry King Live* but George Bush; "maybe I'm old-fashioned, Larry," he said in his most oleaginous manner, but he thought Clinton's antiwar activities were "wrong."

What a spectacle it is: a candidate for the presidency of the United States engaged in a debate with an entertainer who specializes in slick pop psychology, and the president himself fawning over another entertainer, this one specializing in movie stars and other pop celebrities. Is this how the presidency is to be won in 1992? In confessional pleas to the priests of pop, uttered amidst commercials for deodorants, depilatories and sanitary napkins?

How did the talk shows come to acquire this central place in American political life? It's not that countless millions of Americans huddle around their television sets every time one of them comes on the air; Larry King's audience on CNN, as David Zurawik of the *Baltimore Sun* recently pointed out, is a couple of million at most. Phil Donahue's syndicated show may rake in a few more, but his numbers aren't going to cause many sleepless moments for the producers of *Roseanne* or *60 Minutes*.

Not merely are the numbers relatively small but the audience is, shall we say, a tad off-center. Some years ago Russell Baker wrote—he put the words in the mouth of a British acquaintance but they have the ring of pure Baker—that writing a letter to the newspaper is prima facie evidence of insanity. Can't much the same be said of calling a talk show? Listen for a while to the voices of the people who phone in their questions and protests and you get a pretty convincing portrait of Americans on the margin: people with exaggerated grievances, people who have an excessive liking for the sound of their own voices, people with too much time on their hands.

Are these really the people—not to mention the "hosts" who orchestrate these hours of confession and outrage—who should be setting the agenda for a presidential election? Do we really want the debates framed in terms shaped by people whose usual entertainment fare consists of women talking about their adulteries and television stars promoting their new shows? Is it possible for American public discourse to become more trivial or degraded than this?

The answer, no doubt, is in the affirmative, for each new day brings another step into the depths. But this particular step, it should be noted, is being made by the candidates with their eyes wide open. They go on the talk shows for the simple reason that, Clinton's dustup with Donahue to the contrary notwithstanding, they can be assured of friendly if not downright sycophantic receptions. On the talk shows—as on the early-morning entertainments that fob themselves off as "news" broadcasts—the atmosphere is cozy, intimate, pseudo-confidential; the candidate can talk directly to the voters, his message unfiltered by the skeptical questioning of the press.

Indeed it has been wondrous to behold how the candidates have shrunk from the ladies and gentlemen of the press corps this year. Reporters on the Clinton plane are captives, rarely allowed to see the candidate for questioning; those on the Bush plane are similarly isolated and controlled. The candidates want the voters to believe that by looking into the camera they are going over the press and speaking "directly to the people," but that is mere dissembling; they are simply chickening out of direct confrontations with the press.

This isn't to say that the press corps is the ideal medium through which candidates should be forced to give the public an honest reckoning. Reflectiveness is not exactly the salient characteristic of the press; it tends to be more interested in what will play on page one than in substantive issues of public policy, and its questioning tends to reflect this. By the same token, the press has more than its share of inflated egos and ladder-climbing careerists; too often these people are far more interested in getting themselves on camera than in asking hard, challenging questions.

The irony is that if anything, a case can be made that in switching from the news media to the talk shows, the candidates are merely exchanging one compliant medium for another. People in politics may grouse loudly and indignantly about the "hostile" or "negative" press, but the truth is that the Clinton plane is filled with people praying for White House assignments and the Bush plane with people praying to keep the ones they have now. Most of them are more interested in schmoozing with the eminent than with pressing them to come out from behind the plate-glass shield of campaign rhetoric; they're far more likely to throw gopher balls than spitters.

Still, for all its many faults the press—broadcast and print alike—does try to cover the news and does have some competence in doing so. Larry King by contrast may be likeable, hard-working and gregarious, but his territory is entertainment; Phil Donahue is hard-working, and he clearly delights in thinking of himself as an intellectual force, but his domain is confession and self-help. To put it as bluntly as possible: These aren't the people who ought to be asking the questions.

But that is just what they are doing, and the candidates love it. No one loves it more than Ross Perot, who not merely leaped into immediate political legitimacy on the strength of a single talk show appearance but is confining his campaign to advertisements and more television shows. Move over, Walter Lippmann, make room for Barbara Walters. Let's go on with the show.

THE SAME OLD SLEAZE

〜〜

January 17, 1993

Not to rush to judgment or anything like that but: Aren't things getting out of hand just a wee bit ahead of schedule? An administration-in-waiting that makes much self-satisfied noise about its purity can be expected to founder soon enough on the shoals of ineptitude and cupidity, but coming aground before it's spent a single day in office is a novelty even in a place so routinely sordid as the nation's capital.

Consider the president-elect. Bill Clinton has been heaving aside his campaign commitments with the gay abandon of a stripper tossing her knickers into the cheap seats. He's rewritten Robert Frost's famous lines so that they now read: "But I have promises to break,/ And miles to go before I wake." Not merely that, but since the campaign we've learned what somehow had been covered up: Clinton is congenitally, perhaps pathologically, tardy. He thinks nothing of keeping other people waiting an hour or more while he does whatever it is that he apparently imagines to be more important. Congress no doubt will love him for that.

Consider too those who have been swept into his embrace. His Commerce secretary-designate not merely considers himself somehow too grand for ordinary conflict-of-interest stipulations but went into a pout when he was told to cancel a few pre-inaugural parties that were to be thrown in his honor by precisely the sort of people who create conflict-of-interest problems. His attorney general-designate turns out to have been the employer of illegal aliens. His wife's brothers hired a lawyer to solicit financial support for the inauguration from the sort of big corporations that invariably find themselves scrambling to get on the good side of the federal government. Et cetera.

If it all has a slightly familiar ring, that should come as no surprise. One obvious reason is that it's taking place in the official Washington of the 1990s, a place and time where venality has been elevated to a fine art. Beyond that, Clinton has openly admitted his desire to emulate the transition and early administration of Ronald Reagan, who not merely presided over the sleaziest White House since that of Warren Gamaliel Harding but who made politics and lowest-common-denominator show business indistinguishable from each other.

If anything, the inauguration festivities that will keep Washington transfixed for most of the week give every promise of being more Reaganite than Reagan himself could imagine. The inauguration of 1993 is shaping up as a far cry from what the country's founders intended it to be—a high and solemn ritual of the civil religion—and is being turned into a celebration of greed and vulgarity along the lines of those two great spectacles of the Reagan years, the Los Angeles Olympics of 1984 and the Statue of Liberty centennial of 1986.

No expense is being spared to make this the tackiest inauguration ever, and no effort is being spared to dump the tab for its excesses upon precisely the people whom Clinton had led us to believe would no longer be invited to sup at Washington's most exalted tables. The Clintonites call their inauguration "An American Reunion: New Beginnings, Renewed Hope," but all the evidence indicates that it's nothing more than the same old sleaze; the only change from the Reagan years is that the same people are dumping the same money into different pockets.

Most of the $25-million bill for the inauguration, as the *Washington Post* reported last week, has been picked up by "192 corporations, wealthy individuals and labor unions that made interest-free loans to the inaugural committee." These include the likes of AT&T, Boeing, General Electric, the National Association of Letter Carriers, Salomon Brothers and the Tobacco Institute, none of which has ever been suspected of harboring even a teeny-weeny interest in such nonsense as federal contracts and/or regulations.

The name for it is influence peddling, though Rahm Emanuel, co-chairman of the inaugural committee, claims that "this is not about money." What else, precisely, it might be about remains a mystery, though a well-aimed stab in the dark might suggest it's also about advertising and promotion. Not all the corporations rushing to fling their dollars into Clinton's inaugural pot are in it to stir up conflicts of interest; some just see it as, in the immortal words of an unnamed spokesman for General Motors, "a real marketing opportunity."

The Clintonites are doing nothing to discourage them from that conviction. The Clinton inaugural makes the Super Bowl look like a model of commercial restraint. Though in the past we have been led to believe that the inauguration of a president is the people's business, bits and pieces of this one have been sold off to four broadcast operations for their exclusive, or semi-exclusive, use. We're not talking about the swearing-in itself —not much sex appeal there, alas, though Linda Bloodworth-Thomason probably could tart it up—but about various entertainment galas and the big bell-ringing celebration.

The producer of the inaugural gala, Harry Thomason, was asked last week by David Zurawik of the *Baltimore Sun* about "how ownership of TV rights to such a public event could be determined." He received a disingenuous and revealing reply. Thomason said:

> [Home Box Office] is giving the political parts—the walk across the bridge, the bells, the arrival and everything—to any network and news organization that wants to carry it. Now from the entertainment section—and this is all on an honor system—others will be able to carry a couple of minutes of whatever they want. But we're strictly going on an honor system, because this is a public event on public land.

If that seems like dissembling to you, that's how it seems to me, too. In so many words, what Thomason said is: We've sold rights to a public event, some parts of which are more public than others, but anyone is free to steal HBO's satellite transmissions, except we hope they'll be good little campers and decline to do so. "Honor system"? In American *television*? Surely the man jests.

But when it comes to the making of money there's no joking at all. The Clinton inauguration is merely the latest step in an entirely logical progression that eventually will reduce everything in American public life, and much in American private life, to mere opportunity for commercial gain. The inauguration of a president is no longer a ritual of transition and renewal, it is an occasion to cash in, one in which a vast company of the terminally greedy participate: firms and individuals elbowing each other for "marketing opportunities" and political influence, entertainment luminaries scrambling to put themselves at center stage, and by no means least the very "public servants" who have been entrusted with the American people's business.

For a week or two back in November there was a glimmer of hope that Bill Clinton's administration might be an exception to this sordid pattern. But that glimmer was snuffed as soon as Hollywood and TV and big-time advertising were given carte blanche to run this inauguration in their accustomed style. The clear message is that sleazeball Washington can take heart: Under the Clintonites as under the Reaganites and the Bushies, it's going to be business as usual.

For those of you out there who'd let yourselves believe otherwise, speedy disenchantment no doubt is painful. Getting the honeymoon out of the way before the wedding march has been played is a weird way of doing a marriage. But try to look at it on the bright side: The quicker you disabuse yourself of your illusions, the sooner you can get back to good old cold, nasty reality.

THE KENNEDY 'STYLE'

⊷

November 22, 1993

Like everyone else, I can't forget it. I'd just finished my customary lunch-hour tour of the book and music shops of Times Square. I walked through the lobby of the *New York Times*, where I was then employed. As I waited for an elevator, I heard a woman talking frantically: ". . . Dallas . . . the president . . . shot . . . may be dead." As soon as I reached my floor I raced to the wire-service ticker, there to stand horrified vigil through the afternoon and into the night.

I was twenty-four years old. More than half my life has been lived since that awful day. In some ways I put it behind me ages ago; in others I will never be rid of it. In this I am very much like millions of others of my generation, the one that was most deeply and irrevocably shaped by the assassination of John Fitzgerald Kennedy.

This will naturally be disputed by those of Kennedy's own generation, men and women now in their seventies who saw Kennedy's rise to the White House as their own assertion of national leadership. But by the time this came to pass they were mature adults with considerable experience of life, including that of warfare. My generation by contrast had entered adulthood on the wings of Kennedy's presidential candidacy; for better or worse he was the embodiment of our future, and his violent death called everything into question.

People who are too young to remember the 22nd of November, 1963, cannot begin to imagine how ghastly a day it was.

Other events left their variously indelible marks on the memory of twentieth-century America—the Titanic and the Lusitania, the stock-market crash of 1929, Pearl Harbor, the death of Franklin Delano Roosevelt, the Hiroshima bomb, Sputnik—but none was as traumatic as this. The nation had become accustomed, thanks to Roosevelt and Eisenhower, to durable, impregnable presidencies; the bullets that killed Kennedy seemed to shatter the institution itself, leaving the ground beneath us no longer rock-solid but shaky and uncertain.

To be sure we do well to remember a couple of things. One is that in November of 1963 the country was not exactly the paradigm of placidity that we now like to recall; not merely had it been through a great deal of upheaval in the late 1950s, but the first two and a half years of the Kennedy presidency had not been exactly triumphant. The other is that the assassination did not paralyze the country; to the contrary, Lyndon Johnson seized national leadership with unexpected sensitivity to psychological nuance and got us back on course with impressive speed.

The Kennedy presidency wasn't Camelot, and Oswald's bullets didn't plunge us from a golden age into a dark one, mythology to the contrary notwithstanding. But for a long time that's how it seemed. Even those of us who had been dissatisfied with the actual if not symbolic progress of the Kennedy administration were unable to resist the great wave of sentimentality and hagiography that swept across the nation. It was as though the rivulet of emotion that had been stirred by the death of James Dean eight years earlier suddenly had become a mighty ocean, engulfing the entire nation in grief and hero-worship.

The comparison with James Dean is by no means idle. Both the movie actor who died in an auto crash and the president who was killed by an assassin became, immediately after their deaths, figures of irresistible mythic potency. The realities of their lives were utterly irrelevant to the symbolic weight that their images assumed. To say that they were worshipped by millions of Americans is no exaggeration; if Kennedy's cult was vastly more populous than Dean's, their essential nature was the same.

Kennedy-worship lasted a long time. God knows I was for

much of that time one of the loudest crooners in the choir. I bought all the funereal newspapers and magazines that poured forth after the assassination. I devoured the gospel chapter and verse as pronounced by such major prophets as William Manchester, Theodore Sorensen and Arthur Schlesinger, and such minor ones as Evelyn Lincoln, Red Fay and Ken O'Donnell. I gobbled up each lugubrious television broadcast that celebrated each Kennedy anniversary, however minor; had videotape machines existed in those days, I would have filled my entire cathedral with Super Hi Grade Kennedyiana.

By now the Great Awakening has subsided. That a few pockets of religiosity remain was attested to last week by the broadcast of various lamentations—the one I half-watched, "Jack," on CBS, was an especially lurid mixture of prurience and piety—but time has healed most of the old wounds and stories about Kennedy's all-too-human shortcomings have closed the others. Thirty years after the fact we may at last have managed to put the assassination behind us.

But not entirely. The impregnable presidency is forever a thing of the past. The vulnerability of the White House is now taken for granted in a country that has become accustomed, if not entirely inured, to assault by firearms as a means of expressing personal grievance. One unexpected but direct consequence of this is that the presidency is so isolated from the body politic by the extreme protective measures now favored by the Secret Service that it exists in an impenetrable cocoon; given the violent directions in which our culture is evolving, it is impossible to imagine this cocoon becoming anything except even less accessible.

Yet however distant the presidency may have become, it assumed in the wake of the assassination a place in the popular imagination that is paradoxically intimate. Whether John Kennedy had what we like to call "style" is perhaps a matter of taste, but he left us with a bottomless yearning for presidents who can fulfill our fantasies about the image of leadership. This has more to do with Kennedy's death than his life. Certainly he was a man of great wit and presence; having been privileged to attend a couple of his press conferences, I can give personal testimony to both. But his much-celebrated interest in literature and the arts was largely a public-relations sham, and if one assumes that "style" has something to do with being a gentleman, then in no sense can he be said to have qualified.

But it was his "style" that lived on after his death, that was made holy by the circumstances of that death; it is his "style" against which that of every subsequent president has been measured. Kennedy was no martyr, yet he became one not merely in the popular imagination but, more important, in the calculations of those who manipulate that imagination. Style was everything for Kennedy, so it is certainly appropriate that style is all he left us, but it is a poor tool for the governance of a nation. As legacies go it leaves a lot to be desired.

SHOOTING THE RAPIDS

✺

March 14, 1994

Here we go, hurtling down the rapids of Whitewater into a furious eddy of political opportunism and journalistic exhibitionism. The government of the United States will grind to a halt for a year or more, thank God, and the high-octane newsfolk of the Nation's Capital will bore us all to tears with interminable recitations of imaginary outrages, but who cares? It's going to be one hell of a ride.

One hell of a ride, that is, for those who care to climb aboard. In a nation of some 250 million souls, perhaps 3,260 will sail on the Good Ship Clinton as it tests the mighty Whitewater. This is the approximate total population of the United States Congress, the Republican and Democratic National Committees, the Executive Office Building, Nader's Raiders, the *New York Times*, *Wall Street Journal* and *Washington Post* editorial departments, the Amalgamated Op-Ed Columnists of the United States, the National Gossip Columnists Union and the ink-pot brigade at the *American Spectator*.

For all these people Whitewater is going to be the most fun a wonk could possibly imagine, a vast cesspool loaded to overflowing with recrimination and mendacity and implication and hallucination. Political careers will be lost and made therein, and so too will Pulitzer Prizes. Television anchor personages will bliss out as each new bucket of slime leaves yet another prominent politico in midair, headed for a most unbecoming pratfall, while the mightiest men and women of the White House and the Hill will shout unto the mountaintop their bottomless contempt for base journalistic merchants of "innuendo and rumormongering and gossip and sensationalism."

Thus it was put last week by one Margaret Williams, who works high on the staff of the First Lady, or First Person, and who had just finished giving testimony at a legal hearing where, she said, she was "really encouraged to be part of something where findings of fact are actually important." In thus speaking Williams betrayed herself as new to Washington, where findings of fact are utterly trivial by comparison with the trade in hearsay and the public display of self-righteousness.

Usually the former is assumed to be the business of journalists and the latter of politicians, but newsfolk are getting big for their britches these days and have started to encroach on the territory of others. Journalists have taken to preening their moral superiority much as ducks take to brackish water. The journalists in question are not those who report the news, most of whom more or less manage to keep their opinions in check, but my fellow members of the columnists' associations, upon whom no checks at all are imposed save those of bad taste, which are universally ignored.

The most garish and glorious show in town is not the one in the White House or the one on the Hill but the one at Columnists, Inc. It is only just beginning; by the time we reach the third act it should make *The Phantom of the Opera* look like *The Old Curiosity Shop*, but even the early moments of the performance have been delightful.

None more so than last week's brilliant swordplay between Frank Rich, he of the *New York Times*, and Liz Smith, she now of *New York Newsday*. The former, in case you missed it, is the former Butcher of Broadway who last year was elevated from his post as theater critic to the heavenly precincts of the op-ed page, perhaps to become its token white male of the future. Though new at columnizing and still using his baby teeth, Rich has given evidence of prodigious skill at tut-tutting, which is the columnist's chief business, as when he tut-tutted Hillary Clinton for "ducking the press" re Whitewater but granting an audience to four New

York gossip columnists "who could be counted on not to ask about Whitewater."

"Oh, really?" asked Liz Smith last week by way of ladylike rejoinder. "As I say," she continued, "opinion-writing is not reporting. It's thinking, regurgitating and *guessing*." Slap! "As a matter of fact, when Linda Stasi, Cindy Adams, Jeannie Williams and I had tea with Mrs. Clinton March 2, we *did* ask her about Whitewater." Slap! Slap! "Our questions were substantive without going for the jugular." Slap! Slap! Slap! "If [Rich] bothered to *read* the columnists he was so sure about, he'd have seen Mrs. Clinton's answer to the Whitewater question. It may not have been a good answer, but so far as I know, it's the only answer she has yet given and it appeared exclusively in this column." Slap! Slap! Slap! *SLAP!*

Liz Smith is a nice lady who just happens to have a case of gossipitis, an exotic disease that leaves the afflicted convinced that the most important people on earth are Elizabeth Taylor, Frank Sinatra and Ivana Trump. The ailment produces delusions, such as that gossip columnists "ain't all that different from any other breed of reporter," as Smith put it in her slashing riposte to Rich. "We operate in diversity," she said, neatly aligning herself with the armies of correctness, "and we're as good and as bad as most of the rest of what passes these days for journalism."

You can say that again, lady, and no doubt you will as the curtain rises on Act I, Scene 2 of the Whitewater melodrama. It's a populous play, starring not merely Frank and Liz but also Parson Will and Mother Goodman and Doktor Krauthammer and Saint Quindlen and Detective Safire and Bullyboy Buchanan. It's better than *Oh, Calcutta!* Not since the previous H_2O scandal of two decades ago has there been such a glorious orgy of journalistic Taking Sides. Don't you want a seat right down in the Front Row?

Hmm. You say you don't? Turn up the lights, stage manager, let's have a look at the house. Good Lord, it's empty! It's the best show in town and no one's watching! The *Wall Street Journal* took a poll last week and found that 34 per cent of Americans think Whitewater is "just political" while 41 per cent "don't know enough to say," which means that 75 per cent of Americans *just don't care*. Small wonder that a Washington eminence identified as a "Democratic analyst" complained to the *Journal*: "How can the public not be paying attention when every news outlet is going crazy with this?"

What that bad little public needs is a good spanking. No doubt Parson Will and Saint Quindlen would be happy to do the honors.

NATIONAL DAY OF

WHAT?

~∞~

May 2, 1994

From the Washington office of the American Civil Liberties Union went forth last week a fax wherein it was declared that, "in respectful observance of the National Day of Mourning," the office would be closed "for eighteen and one-half minutes," such being the duration of the notorious gap in the White House tapes that Watergate buffs so fondly remember. The observance seemed entirely appropriate to the occasion, but soon enough word went forth from the ACLU that the fax was merely a "joke."

Joke? The biggest joke last week was the National Day of Mourning. The very thought that the government of the United States in all its bureaucratic majesty could be brought to a halt in "mourning" for Richard Milhous Nixon—psychological basket case, moral pygmy and unconvicted criminal—bids fair to take the breath away. What next? A postal holiday for John Dillinger's birthday? A national moment of silence for the soul of Lizzie Borden? A granite monument on the Mall for John Wilkes Booth?

The Day of Mourning, we were variously advised, was for "reconciliation" or "forgiveness" or "unity" or "conciliation." It seems to have occurred to no one that although it is well and good to bury the hatchet with those with whom one has honorably disagreed or done battle, that wasn't what the sponsors of last Wednesday's bipartisan orgy of bathos were up to. For reasons ranging from self-interest to empty-headedness, they wanted us to believe that the various offenses committed by Nixon against the people and the Constitution of the United States had somehow vanished into the ether, that all we need know about him now is that he had been a man of great resilience and that he had given his life to "public service."

It won't wash, at least not in *this* Maytag. To call Richard Milhous Nixon a public servant is to make a mockery of the words and of the ideals they represent. Richard Milhous Nixon was a servant to nothing except his own ambition, his bottomless need for approval and applause. Though his resilience was not without its admirable aspects, he was in all other important respects a man bereft of redeeming qualities, one who should be remembered not for his last two decades of desperate self-resuscitation but for being the only president of the United States who found it necessary to declare, in denial of the truth, that "I am not a crook."

Nixon's misdeeds were, in number and consequences, truly breathtaking. He rode to prominence on the tide of McCarthyism and was never thereafter reluctant to wave the Red flag if it would advance his interests. His Checkers speech is by any honest reckoning the most cynical—and the most embarrassing—single performance in the history of national politics. His ardent embrace of Spiro Agnew's divisive rhetoric helped open the fault lines that divided the nation in the 1960s and 1970s. As for Watergate, it was anything except the joke so many now make of it; it was a constitutional crisis of the gravest magnitude, one that came into being solely to advance the political ambitions of Richard Milhous Nixon.

So much attention was focused on Watergate in the 1970s that we have forgotten the other crucial instrument of Nixon's 1972 presidential campaign. In his determination to win, Nixon made one thing perfectly clear: He would win dishonestly. Not merely did he dispatch his little band of Inspector Clouseaus to spy on the Democrats and steal their paltry secrets, but he undertook a calculated, concerted effort to win the electoral votes of the South with divisive racial strategies.

Judging by such as I have read of the millions of words that

Nixon's death has unleashed, each of us remembers him in different ways and for different reasons. What I remember is the "Southern strategy" that Nixon conjured up in collaboration with John Mitchell, who made as much a mockery of the words "Justice Department" as Nixon did of "public service." This strategy was designed for the 1972 campaign and was firmly in place more than a year earlier, when Nixon issued a statement on a school busing case in Texas, deliberately giving aid and comfort to those who were resisting efforts at calm, orderly compliance with the Supreme Court's ruling in the Charlotte-Mecklenburg County case.

Many people in the South disliked busing and not exclusively because they were racists; many worried about making children the instruments of social change and, more specifically, about how their own children would fare. But throughout the region there was a widespread sense that compliance was preferable to violence and that the time of resistance and evasion was over. As president of all Americans, Nixon might reasonably have been expected to give official encouragement to these people. Instead he aligned himself not with what was best in the South but with what was worst, forfeiting such moral capital as he may have possessed in his determination to woo the followers of George Corley Wallace.

He won the election, but he lost any claim to the approval of history that he so fervently desired. If I may be pardoned the unpardonable offense of self-quotation, in August of 1971 I wrote: "The South has come, however slowly, to understand that the law must not be tampered with for political expediency, and it has committed itself to obeying it dutifully. For the president of the United States to imply that it can be evaded is unconscionable, and a disservice to every Southerner who is working earnestly for racial peace."

It was easy for Nixon to speak and act as he did because he was a lawyer who neither understood nor believed in the law. Sworn to uphold it, he twisted it to his convenience and violated it outright if that too served his interests. In the most literal sense of the word, he was a scofflaw: He scoffed at the law, ridiculed it, dismissed it as irrelevant to the higher purpose of his own ambition.

That he was twice elected to the presidency of the United States is testimony to the skill with which he did all of this as well as to his good fortune in drawing hapless opponents. The American people have been willing to overlook what they regard as minor faults of character in their public officials, and Nixon was a beneficiary of this tolerance. But that we have known for decades of his contempt for the law—and thus by extension for the nation that tries to live by the law—and still insist on genuflecting before him is evidence of nothing except innocence, ignorance and self-deception. Day of Mourning indeed! Good riddance is more like it.

THE INNER CLINTON

✎

January 9, 1995

A cat may look on a king, 'tis true, but time marches on and kings depart. A proverb that suited the 16th century seems a trifle dated when no self-respecting cat would be seen in the company of such as now pass for royalty. Instead we must rewrite our proverbs to suit the temper of the times, which is why that old saw now reads: A personal development guru may look on a president.

That is what happened last week when William Jefferson Clinton—president of these United States, commander-in-chief of its armed forces, leader of the free world and, all in all, the very model of a modern major domo—permitted himself to be looked upon by not one but two eminent personal development gurus and actually allowed them to address the presidential presence.

Precisely what words these gurus uttered in that space so suffused with the Clintonian aura has not, as of this writing, been made available for public delectation, but no doubt it had something to do with getting in touch with the inner presidential child. Inasmuch as we live in a New Age in which the inner child speaks to us with a force once reserved for the voice of Jehovah Himself, it seems safe to assume that the president was invited to hear the words of his subterranean pipsqueak and that he did so with the utmost solemnity.

What a wonderfully, quintessentially American scene that must have been! To imagine it in its full glory requires a gift of creativity vastly greater than the one bestowed upon the poor scrivener into whose word processor these sentences slouch to be born, but one need not be a Thomas Pynchon or even a Tom Clancy to picture the president in bucolic retreat at Camp David, a fire crackling in the presidential fireplace, a jug of lo-cal apple cider gurgling in the warming pan, the great man himself flinging wide the sturdy log door to welcome—with a jolly "Ho! Ho! Ho!"—his distinguished visitors.

Their names, the nation was informed last week, are Stephen R. Covey and Anthony Robbins. Covey may well have been recommended to the president by none other than Newt Gingrich, who has found Covey's services useful in the formulation of a lecture called "Personal Strength in American Culture." Robbins, who practiced the fine art of janitorial engineering before finding his true calling, is known and loved by television viewers from coast to coast, indeed was described in this newspaper last week as "probably the nation's most famous personal success guru."

Small wonder these champions of fulfillment were invited not merely to look on but also to speak unto the president last week. Sad though it is to say, "personal success" has not been high on the Clintonian agenda of late, devoutly though the president may have wished it otherwise. But did His Slickness pout? Did he sulk? Did he whimper? Not on your life! He called for his pipe and he called for his bowl and he called for his gurus two.

In so doing he demonstrated nothing so much as that he is all-American to the core. For generations it has been the national custom to summon, in moments of fragile self-esteem, the counsel of a personal development guru. Over the years the purveyors of such counsel have gone by various names, "guru" being merely the latest in a long line, but call them whatever you will, they have offered the same product: the quick fix, the painless cure-all, the keys to the kingdom, the acne-free complexion.

American innocence is often evoked when portraits of the national character are painted. What possibly could be more innocent, and thus more American, than this pervasive conviction that self-fulfillment, personal growth, managerial competence and riches beyond imagining can all be found within the pages of a book written with the energy, not to mention literary style, of a Texas high-school cheerleader? Historians may talk about the frontier as the defining experience in American culture, but isn't the quick fix every bit as important?

Certainly that would seem to be so, especially now that the quick fix has been given the presidential imprimatur. In the past that imprimatur tended to be fixed upon the likes of Billy Graham and Norman Vincent Peale, television preachers who were more or less equally accomplished at inspiration and at golf. The encounters between the presidents and these divines were always conducted with great publicity, calculated as they were to show the presidents as men of God as well as state.

But this latest encounter between a president and his swamis-in-waiting was a clandestine business about which neither the chief executive nor the swamis has been willing to speak. This will immediately suggest, to those familiar with presidential conduct as disclosed over the generations, that matters of great import took place, since it is in the nature of the presidency to transact frivolous business in full public view and serious business behind closed doors: in smoke-filled rooms in the days of Roosevelt, incense-filled rooms in those of Clinton.

Precisely what this business is we can only guess, but given the nature of the guru racket as now operated, we are likely to see a "new" Bill Clinton. The first hint of what has yet to be revealed may have been contained in the front-page photograph that showed the president and the speaker of the House flashing grins of Grand Canyon dimensions, grins so eerily alike that it was quite impossible to tell the Clintster from the Newtster.

Perhaps mastery of that grin is the first of *The Seven Habits of Highly Effective People*, which happens to be the title of the most famous epistle of the aforementioned guru, Stephen R. Covey. By the time the remaining six have been accomplished we may well find, while surfing through Cableland, Clinton himself, right there on Channel 73, lecturing us about "How to Let Your Inner Child Light Your Way Along the Passage to Self-Fulfillment, Instant Karma and a Trump Tower Penthouse."

From there it won't take long—say, about two months after the 1996 election—for Clinton to launch a whole new career as the nation's Guru in Residence. He can do PBS specials with Bill Moyers. He can do best-selling books and audiotapes and video cassettes. He'll show us how to win friends and influence people, how to survive the coming Depression, how to shed cellulite, how to make love to a person of our preference, how to make certain that every day in every way we get better and better. In time Slick Willie will metamorphose into Uncle Bill, and he will at last attain what has so far been unattainable. He will become a Highly Effective Person.

LONG MAY IT WAVE

⋙∾⋘

July 3, 1995

What a relief it is to know that our elected representatives are manning the barricades, defending us from threats to the Republic so ghastly as to chill the blood. Never mind that these threats haven't been raised since Jerry Rubin and Abbie Hoffman last walked the land. What matters isn't the threats but the illusion of bold action against them, and when it comes to illusion, or delusion, nobody but nobody can top the United States Congress.

Thus it was that last week, while Sarajevo tumbled and Japanese-American relations crumbled and the hills of south-central Virginia turned to clay, what did Congress do? The House of Representatives approved by a vote of 312 to 120 a proposed amendment to the United States Constitution that reads, in all its glory: "The Congress and the States shall have the power to prohibit the physical desecration of the flag of the United States."

Talk about fighting yesterday's battles! Flag-desecration went off the radar at about the same time as Sonny and Cher and the Nehru jacket, but you'd never know it from the guardians of the national honor up there on the Hill. Mustering all the courage of little boys making rude gestures after the bandidos have moved on to the next town, the House spanked the miscreants of the 1960s and 1970s with the biggest board it could lay its hands on. The loud noise you heard a few minutes later came from the beyond: The ghosts of bygone days yelling, "Ouch!"

When it comes to the problems facing these United States, flag desecration must rank somewhere up there with leprosy and bubonic plague. Tacking an amendment onto the Constitution in order to fight it is a bit like installing a popgun at the bow of a battleship. Not merely it is irrelevant, it is also subject to the kind of question in which lawyers delight, i.e., what, exactly, is "desecration"?

According to Webster, to "desecrate" is "to violate the sanctity of by diverting from sacred purpose, by contaminating, or by defiling." Let's agree, for the sake of argument, that the American flag is "desecrated" when someone burns it or tears it apart or otherwise violates it in order to make some political, ideological or cultural point. But does desecration stop there, or does it somehow manage to find its way into that venue most beloved by your basic generic congressman, the American marketplace?

A two-hour stroll through a major shopping mall last week suggested that the honorables may have opened a bigger can of worms than they, in their wisdom, had bargained for. The first sighting was in Speedo Authentic Fitness, which proudly displayed jackets, bathing suits, T-shirts and tank tops, all adorned with the American flag. A few doors away, at Herman's Sporting Goods, more Speedo suits were on display, racing briefs for men and tight suits for women, all of them wrapping the most intimate (and at times malodorous) parts of the human anatomy in the Stars and Stripes.

Out of sporting goods and into general apparel. The Limited was having its "Great American Sale," featuring a "USA" pullover with a flag on the sleeve and a "USA" T-shirt similarly designed. Britches Great Outdoors had a rugby shirt with a flag motif, as well as bathing suits and T-shirts featuring the flag. At the General Nutrition Center, of all places, workout clothing with the flag splashed from the bottom of the trousers to the top of the shirt was on sale. Accessory Lady had socks with two different flag designs, flag button covers and flag picture frames. Lerner had prominently on display a heavy-duty shirt sporting the flag, the Gap had a flag shirt for children, and Peace Frogs had flag-motif boxer shorts. Victoria's Secret, alas, had no flag unmentionables.

In the home-decoration department, Hecht's offered a broad line of "Americana" goodies, among them a "Patriot Check Tablecloth," napkins and napkin rings featuring the Stars and Stripes, "decorative runners" featuring the same, and flag place-mats and tablecloths by Bardwill. A few steps away, it had a Ralph Lauren "Polo Bear" beach towel on which a bear was depicted wearing a flag sweater, and a "Polo University" beach towel with a "USA" flag design.

Housewares of a more evanescent sort were for sale at Rite-Aid, Hallmark and the Card Shop: picnic supplies for the great patriotic holiday now under way, among them paper plates and napkins, "Proud to be . . ." paper tablecloths, not to mention "Celebrate America!" sun visors. All of these were decorated with representations of the flag, none exactly reverent.

That was what a fairly quick tour of the mall produced—a mall that retailers would call "upscale," mind you, not an Ocean City T-shirt shop or a roadside Harley-Davidson souvenir stand. No doubt either of these would have produced a far grander if rather less tasteful selection of patriotic gewgaws, including the usual run of love-it-or-leave-it whimsy.

Yes, one man's desecration is another man's marketing op-portunity, but what was for sale at that mall looked every bit as much like desecration—"diverting from sacred purpose"—of the American flag as whatever was done to it by some long-haired weirdo at some college campus some two and a half decades ago. If there is a legal or moral distinction between burning the flag on the one hand and using it to cover one's private parts on the other, the niceties of that distinction are beyond my grasp.

The difference in the minds of the honorables apparently is that the latter is done to make a buck and the former to make a point, a point that members of the current House of Representa-tives didn't like twenty-five years ago and still don't like today. They're entitled. But a constitutional amendment? If that isn't *ex post facto* overkill, what is it? Sure, burning or defacing the flag is a silly and distasteful way to express one's opinions; it suggests that those opinions are about as mature as the means of expressing them; but it is—up to now, anyhow—a protected form of expression that has twice been affirmed by a Supreme Court of which a majority of the justices were appointed by conservative presidents.

Well, nothing's new under the sun, least of all hypocrisy, and there should be plenty of fun ahead once the lawyers get their hands on the 28th Amendment. Is "desecration" in the eye of the beholder? Sooner or later the courts will tell us, to the lawyers' everlasting profit.

CHECKING OUT: II

～∾～

August 19, 1996

No matter what you read or where you looked, the word in the media last week was that when Bob Dole went to the podium in San Diego he was under great pressure to deliver "the speech of his life." The phrase was flavor of the week, so frequently and monotonously was it repeated. But a few hours before the actual event it took on an unexpected twist, when a reporter for NBC News announced that "the speech of his life" would be made before a television audience of "ten to fifteen million people."

This was meant to impress, but it did quite the opposite. It was the most depressing evidence yet of the degree to which the American electorate has dropped out of politics. In a nation of 260 million, 10 million is less than 4 per cent, 15 million is less than 6 per cent. If one reckons a voting-age population of 190 million, the figures are still depressing: 10 million is barely over 5 per cent, while 15 million is just under 8 per cent.

Another way to put it is that substantially more than 90 per cent of Americans eligible to vote apparently declined to watch Dole's speech accepting the Republican presidential nomination. Still another way to put it is that no one in the United States watched the speech except the cadre of fourteen-year-old children in charge of political affairs at the Clinton White House. The speech, like everything else at the convention, seems to have been made into a vacuum.

If a vacuum is what it was, count me as part of it. The statement is scarcely made as a boast, but it remains that for the first time in my life I allowed a national convention of one of the major parties to run its entire course without watching a single moment of it. This was not solely the result of indifference or vacation-induced laziness. I knew that the convention would have no drama, and a couple of hours worth of NBC's coverage of the Olympics had given me as much touchy-feely, up-close-and-personal "news" as I was capable of stomaching; advance word had it that the Republicans had whole tureens of the stuff on the menu.

It may be as well that I was encouraged in this inattention by a number of news stories and reminiscences about conventions past that were published as the Republican festivities were about to begin. The brunt of all these was that television had backed away from "gavel-to-gavel" coverage for any number of reasons, chief among them that the primaries had taken the suspense out of the conventions and that the American people have become disenchanted with politics to the point of utter ennui.

Both arguments are valid. The primary system, which assumed its present all-encompassing dimensions in the early 1970s, was intended to democratize the nomination process, taking it out of the hands of the "bosses" in their "smoke-filled rooms" and handing it over to "the people" in all "their wisdom." This has not proved to be the case. The primaries have turned out to be captives of an activist minority, to be highly susceptible to special-interest voting blocs, and to be manipulable by big money. So much for vox pop.

By the same token, public indifference to politics is real and easily documented. In large measure due to the rhetoric of Ronald Reagan, the ancient patron saint whom the Republicans canonized at every opportunity last week, Americans are deeply suspicious of and hostile to government and, by extension, all those who participate in it. Ours may be meant to be a democracy run at the consent of the governed, but any such consent now granted is by default; certainly it is not willingly given.

All of which is true and all of which is lamentable, but there is yet another reason to lament the vacuum in which the public rituals of American politics are now conducted. In a nation so vast as ours geographically and so heterogeneous in population, occasions for the affirmation of national unity are absolutely necessary. The political conventions used to serve such a purpose. No matter how much conflict they aroused, they were followed by all of us attentively and seriously. We understood that the shape of our lives was to some degree affected by what took place, and we saw it as our civic responsibility to pay heed.

This is not to sentimentalize the conventions of the past. As one who prefers the selection of candidates by political professionals to the beauty-contest process of the primaries, I nonetheless readily concede that bad candidates were chosen by the old rules and that shady deals were struck. But the close attention given the conventions by the general public was a tacit reassertion of the central importance of politics, in the best sense of the word, to our national life.

No such declaration is made any more. The event that draws the attention of more Americans than any other is the Super Bowl, in competition with the Academy Awards and the Miss America contest. What binds us is not government or country but our obsession with entertainment and glitz. What we affirm, to the extent that we affirm anything, is the trivial.

The blame for this, when blame is cast, usually is ascribed to the various malign forces that "run" the country: politicians, the media, the entertainment industry. Obviously all are to some degree at fault, but the central truth is that we get what we deserve. If we are dismayed by tawdry, exploitive movies, television and popular music, we neglect to acknowledge that in the marketplace over which we have ultimate control, this is what we choose. By the same token, if we are disenchanted with government that is at once bloated and ineffective, this is because we demand on the one hand that it serve our every whim yet refuse on the other hand to support it either with our tax dollars or our active participation.

When you come right down to it, the probability that "the speech of his life" by a man who may well become the next president of the United States was seen by less than 10 per cent of those eligible to vote for him is nothing short of appalling. Not merely does our indifference to this event deprive us of a shared experience in the rituals of public life, but it makes a mockery of all our gripes and protests about government and those who operate it. We live, after all, in what is ostensibly a representative government, not a dictatorship or an oligarchy. If we decline even to observe its processes, much less participate in them, what claim do we have to criticize its operations?

SPINMEISTER

∽o∾

September 16, 1996

Certainly it is true that the matter of Dick Morris and his tattle-tale whore has produced more than its share of bathetic journalistic nattering. Those of us who have been granted the license to air our opinions in public too often do so with little regard for anything except our own self-righteousness, and the Morris business is precisely the sort of story—an arrogant, unprincipled inhabitant of the corridors of power caught, quite literally, with his pants down—that provides an irresistible temptation to make pious fools of ourselves.

Still, two wrongs don't make a right. Just because various journalistic homilists cast errant thunderbolts from their pulpits doesn't mean that Morris's behavior is somehow excusable or even admirable, yet that seems to be what David J. Garrow wants us to believe. Writing last week on the op-ed page of the *Washington Post*, Garrow chastized several writers for innocence and naivete, then praised Morris for his "understanding of the public dynamics of personal reputation," arguing that his "refusal to go through a public ritual of shame and apology has been tactically brilliant and already is speeding his resuscitation." Morris and his wife, Eileen McGann, according to Garrow, "have handled Morris's sex scandal with considerable class and splendid skill."

These are the words of a man who was awarded a Pulitzer Prize for a biographical study of Martin Luther King Jr. and has also written a book called *Liberty and Sexuality: The Right to Privacy and the Making of Roe v. Wade*, but they sound for all the world like standard-issue Washington damage control, not to mention situational ethics. To Garrow the tawdry side of Morris's private life is "of no moment whatsoever" and "of no public relevance"; what matters to Garrow is that Morris and McGann "have handled Morris's sex scandal with considerable class and splendid skill," while the moral implications of his behavior—not to mention his betrayal of the trust of the president of the United States—are nonexistent because, so Garrow would have us believe, everyone knew Morris was a sleazeball from the outset and should not have expected any better of him.

Or that at least is what Garrow appears to be saying; his line of reasoning is so shaky and his prose so muddy that he could well be saying precisely the opposite. There can be little doubt, though, that in essence he offers nothing more than another variation upon the orthodox faith of Washington's power crowd, the essential tenet of which is that so long as you stay out of jail, you are morally impeccable. It is hard to distinguish between Garrow's tortured logic and that of such earlier apostles of the Washington Creed as Richard ("I am not a crook") Nixon and John ("Watch what we do, not what we say") Mitchell.

Cynical *realpolitik* such as this sounds natural coming from the likes of Nixon and Mitchell—or Lee Atwater or James Carville or anyone else who turns politics into profit—but coming from a member of the professoriat who has set himself up as an authority upon, if not indeed an exemplar of, the higher morality, it is not pretty. Perhaps Garrow has wearied of *la vie académique* and is trying on the battle garb of hard-ball political consulting. Whatever the case, his supine homage to Morris's "maturity and intelligence," his "audacious tenacity," is as ludicrous as it is distasteful.

It is also very much in tune with a culture that no longer believes private morality has any bearing on the performance or trustworthiness of public figures. In the not so distant past this conviction was honored silently, as the press declined to publicize the personal shortcomings of political leaders and the public pretended—or may actually have believed—that they did not exist. Then we went through the Gary Hart Period, during which we indulged ourselves in the fancy that if a person couldn't behave decently in private, he probably couldn't do so in public. Now we have reached the end of the road: We will gobble up a whole plateful of gossip—Gennifer Flowers, Sherry Rowlands, you name it—and then pronounce it "of no moment whatsoever," "of no public relevance."

Not merely is it irrelevant, it is the raw material of private gain. Thus we have the spectacle of Morris and McGann at luncheon with Harry Evans and Tina Brown—oh, to have been a fly in *that* soup!—apparently to negotiate for-profit schemes to benefit not merely the unrepentant whoremonger but also Random House and the *New Yorker*. This was followed by the even more spectacular appearance of Morris at another Manhattan luncheon, this one held by the *New Yorker* to flatter would-be advertisers. With the magazine's reportorial and editorial staff in the role of Greek chorus, Morris lectured these eminences "about his ethics and insights," according to the *New York Times*. It must have been a very short luncheon.

According to one who was in attendance, Morris denied that he had betrayed Bill Clinton and minimized the importance of his dalliance with Sherry Rowlands: "He spoke in sweeping terms about how the American public no longer cares about these things. I think he said, 'You journalists are the prudes in this country.'" Perhaps he is right, but if so it is a sad commentary on the state of public—and private—American morals. If ever there has been a fox–henhouse relationship, it is the one between the press and the higher morality. The press has the morals of a cat burglar, or a pusher, or a madam, and is about as reliable a guardian of the public morals as Al Capone; but in the country of the blind, the one-eyed man is philosopher-king.

It would be easy to claim that the rise of amorality is largely limited to the power circles of Washington and New York and Los Angeles, where profit and publicity are the essence, but that, in the words of the great moralist Richard Nixon, "would be wrong." As a survey last week in the *Washington Post* made clear, the public itself no longer cares about the private lives of the people whom it chooses as its leaders. Though sentiment runs overwhelmingly against Bill Clinton's personal life and his standing as moral exemplar, it runs overwhelmingly in favor of him as presidential candidate. Presumably David Garrow would say that Clinton is a keen manipulator of "the public dynamics of personal reputation" and would applaud him for that; but to this prude in the pressbox he—just like his erstwhile Svengali—is merely the personification, as well as the chief beneficiary, of our moral bankruptcy.

A Joyful Noise

unto the Lord

❧

February 10, 1997

Among the institutions upon which Washington prides itself, surely special honor must be accorded the National Prayer Breakfast. Held but once a year—evidently on the implicit understanding that once a year is quite sufficient—this august occasion assembles under one roof the most extraordinary collection of duplicity, of human hypocrisy, that has ever been gathered together in Washington, with the possible exception of when Richard Nixon prayed alone.

It was held once again last week, with the usual results. There we had the newfound bosom buddies, Newt Gingrich and Jesse Jackson, raising their voices in unison unto the Lord, along with those of some four thousand other worshippers at the altar of high-profile piety. The breakfast, which is sponsored by various congressional prayer groups—how's *that* for an oxymoron?—has as its theme what Nelson Rockefeller liked to call "the brotherhood of man and the fatherhood of God," or "Bomfog," as reporters covering him abbreviated it. Its real theme is the brotherhood—these days, the personhood—of spin.

It's of more than passing note that this event is held at breakfast rather than at lunch or dinner. In the culture of official Washington, each of the day's three meals has its own highly ritualized significance. Lunch, the most important of the three, is when the players play and the deals get done. Dinner, depending on whether it is eaten in a public or a private place, is when (a) the ingestion of seas of overpriced liquor and French wine is followed by Packwoodesque passes and Tidal Basin follies, or (b) dainty sips of postprandial coffee are accompanied by the smug homilies of journalistic bigfoots and their tongue-tied acolytes.

Breakfast, by contrast, is when nothing of consequence happens. Except for the poor slugs who ride Metro or the Beltway to ordinary jobs at ordinary wages, "this town"—as the smuggest of the smug so delight in calling it—is not an early-rising kind of place. Nothing of importance gets done until everyone is awake, which is hardly the case at the National Prayer Breakfast, which is exactly why it is held at breakfast. Think "National Prayer Lunch," and you have thought the unthinkable.

Usually the star of the National Prayer Breakfast is the likes of Billy Graham, one of those prayer-and-power preachers such as littered the landscape back in yon days when Ike was president and all was right with the world. But Billy Graham is an old man now, and those who have followed in his train don't quite measure up. Think Jerry Falwell or Jimmy Swaggert or Jim Bakker, and you have once again thought the unthinkable, at least National Prayer Breakfast-wise.

So they had to fetch up someone else this year, and they fetched up Bill Clinton. As the *New York Times*'s man on the scene put it, the once and future president's "speeches often echo a preacher's cadences," and indeed he wasted no time getting into the Elmer Gantry mode. He ascended unto the pulpit, and within moments had launched himself into orbit. When he finally came down, he got the kind of ovation that only official Washington can deliver: an explosion of universal humbug. Too bad he wasn't in a smalltown Southern church, because he could have stood at the door to hear the parishioners' heartfelt praise. "Them was fine words, preacher, fine words."

Trouble was, it was all sound and fineness, signifying nothing. "This town," quoth he, "is gripped with people who are self-righteous, sanctimonious and hypocritical. All of us are that way sometimes. I plead guilty from time to time. . . . Cynicism and all this negative stuff is just sort of a cheap excuse for not doing your best with your life, and it's not a very pleasant way to live, frankly—not even any fun."

Now, before you go running off to the amen corner for a bit of ecstatic shoutin' and stompin', put yourself into rewind and think about it for a moment. *Of course* he meant it. He *always* means it. No matter what he says, no matter how wildly and extravagantly it contradicts what he said only six minutes ago, Bill Clinton always means what he says. He is a man of his word, and if you just stand in place long enough, sooner or later he'll come sailing past with the words you want to hear.

Not merely that, but this time around the words really *were* fine. Not exactly eloquent, but to the point. Washington isn't merely "gripped" by all the slime mentioned above, it is a cesspool. The two main reasons why the people's business rarely gets done here are that special-interest groups lobby it to death and that official Washington, when it isn't kowtowing to the lobbies, is engaged in an endless food fight, the purpose of which is to grind the other guy's nose in the swill while keeping one's own above the fray.

Official Washington is a petty, cynical, childish place, as Brother Clinton so unctuously made plain. Why, he got to "this town" and before he knew it, "our friends in the Congress and the Republican Party . . . were real mean to me over something." When he was told that he was the scapegoat for congressional Democrats who had treated his Republican predecessors similarly, he said with a plaintive air, "I didn't even live here then."

No, he lived in Little Rock, which when it comes to the ways of official Washington isn't exactly the Land of Oz. By comparison with Washington's, the stakes in Little Rock politics are small, but the politics is every bit as vicious. Little Rock is one of the last stops in Washington's farm system, and those who master the game there are pronounced ready to play in politics' equivalent of what baseball players call The Show.

All of which is to say, when Brother Clinton gets into his preacher-man mode, watch your wallet. A roomful of Washingtonians being lectured on ethics by Bill Clinton is the equivalent of a houseful of banty roosters being harangued on home security by Br'er Fox. Either lecture should be listened to with a couple of caveats firmly in mind: (a) he knows the subject, all right, and (b) just to what use he'll put that knowledge depends on what's in it for him.

But then it is also useful to bear in mind that this latest Clintonian homily was delivered at the National Prayer Breakfast. So far as official Washington is concerned, the National Prayer Breakfast is strictly window-dressing. Once a year you get up a few minutes ahead of schedule, slip into the suit, and trudge off to a hotel dining hall to break a little bread and whisper a little mumbojumbo. Then it's back to business as usual—slash and burn, hit and run, take no prisoners—in a little world where the only prayer that counts is: Lord, don't let me get caught.

TEE HEE

〜o〜

February 2, 1998

It is tempting beyond measure to let the scene now before us play out as burlesque, opera-bouffe and penny-arcade porn show. That, judging by the tone of most public discussion—not to mention the wickedly dirty jokes flashing through the Internet—is what the vast majority of Americans apparently have chosen to do, with what the press chooses to represent as a collective shrug of their shoulders.

The prevailing interpretation of this popular indifference to the charges against the president, as expressed by those few talking heads and scribbling hands that have extracted themselves from media hysteria long enough to attempt serious analysis, is that this is a good thing. For too long, we are told, Americans have been too priggish about concupiscence in high places. We should emulate the Italians, these Solomons tell us, or better yet the French, and their weary, Old World view that what public people do in private is their own business and nobody else's.

If this were in fact how the American people had reacted there might be reason to take comfort in it, but there is little hard evidence that this is the case. To the contrary, we have greeted all these sordid rumors and accusations not with a blase yawn but with a childish snicker. We have reached a terribly unhappy hour in our nation's history, the import of which can now scarcely be imagined, yet the most we can muster for it is a giggle, a tee hee, as if the grand dame across the table had just sat down on a poo-poo cushion.

Watergate was the "long national nightmare." Is this scandal, by whatever clever coinage one chooses to call it, to be the long national joke? It is beginning to look that way, yet there is nothing funny about it. One of the few people to attempt a sober, pun-free inquiry into it, the British journalist and historian Paul Johnson, pointed out in the *Wall Street Journal* last week that what is at stake is our respect for and belief in the presidency. Johnson, a great admirer of this country and its government, wrote that the presidency "is the central institution in the land, and the one whose externals—solemnity, dignity and credibility of utterance—are most essential to its successful functioning." He said, accurately, that "over the past two centuries, few of the key offices in the world have been so consistently occupied by such good men," and added:

> As a result, Americans still believe in the presidency, just as the British, at least until recently, believed in their royal family. Both gave the peoples they served a sense of security and reassurance. Citizens could go about their business confident that their country was structurally sound and presented a dignified face to the world. In the past few years, however, we in Britain have seen our monarchy humiliated and ridiculed, exposed and belittled—partly through the fault of the younger royals but mainly through the destructive assaults of intrusive journalists and writers. The institution has lost much of its magic and allure—and, perhaps even more important, its exemplary role as a standard-bearer in manners and morals. As a result we are all the poorer. The monarchy has shrunk, and we have shrunk too. We feel shame and a sense of loss.

Shame and loss are what we Americans should feel, yet we merely titter with Leno and Letterman. Leaving aside for the moment the performance of the press, consider what "exemplary role" the White House now plays: The president, according to reliable reports, has admitted in sworn testimony to what he denied in 1992—a long extramarital affair in Arkansas with Gennifer Flowers—a lie that may well have greased his way to the presidency; despite incessant public comment—not all of it lurid or prurient—about his sexual appetites, the president is likely to stand accused of indulging those appetites, within the White House itself, with one or more women to whom he is not married; faced with accusation upon accusation, innuendo upon innuendo, this same president retreats into his bunker from which he resolutely, steadfastly, angrily refuses to do the decent thing and tell the truth to the American people; from that same bunker, this most astonishing of all, the First Lady—the *First Lady*—goes on national television and charges, with a straight face, that the investigation of her husband's manifold affairs is the work of a "vast right-wing conspiracy."

This is *funny*? Even if the president is innocent of every charge against him—Paul Johnson is right to believe the country's best interests will be met if he is able to "serve out his term, if not exactly with honor, then at least with some degree of capability"—his stonewalling and his retreat into lawyerly evasions are acts of moral and legal cowardice that scorn not merely the office he occupies but the people who put him there. As for the "right-wing conspiracy," this is despicable demagoguery, bearing absolutely no resemblance to widely known facts, suggesting that the White House has simply come unhinged.

That we in the press have been merrily dancing around, heaving fuel onto all these fires, is a given. Never mind that many of those piling it on most heavily could not qualify for work in any self-respecting newspaper, magazine or broadcast operation. The public sees us as indistinguishable, and to the degree that those of us in the mainstream press find little alternative to chasing desperately after the supermarket tabloids and Internet gossip pages, the public is right. As one who came into this business nearly four decades ago with a deep belief in its probity and responsibility, I am embarrassed to the quick by its behavior in the present crisis.

But I am no less embarrassed by, or for, my country. It's not just Bill Clinton and his entourage who are dragging the presidency into the mud, it's all of us. The American public, feigning a Gallic sophistication it could never in a million generations achieve, is too complacent and self-involved to confront—or care about—what is being done to the highest office in its power to bestow. Richard Nixon disgraced the presidency, which at the time and for many years thereafter seemed the worst that could be done to it. But Bill Clinton has done worse. He has made not merely himself but the office itself the object of mockery and ridicule. Yes, at moments it is hard not to laugh, but this is no joke.

PART TWO

✂⊶

FIVE

THIS
SPORTING LIFE

✂⊶

POETS ANONYMOUS

≈

April 1, 1991

Yes, Your Honor, I confess: I wrote it. But there were extenuating circumstances. I was young, and I was under the influence—no, not of controlled substances, but of uncontrolled prose. I couldn't help myself. The typewriter—that's how long ago it was, I used a *typewriter*—went onto automatic pilot. From the bottom of my heart, I apologize.

What, Your Honor? You say an apology isn't enough? But, ma'am, what more can I do? No. Surely you don't mean it. I'd rather wash out my mouth with an entire cake of Lava soap, or copy every word in *Remembrance of Things Past*, or run backwards around the Central Park lake at midnight. I'd rather do anything on earth than *that*.

You insist. Did I hear you correctly, Your Honor? You said, "I insist." No appeal to a higher court? I have to stand right here and take my punishment like a man. I have to quote my own words. In public. In front of all these people. Just like this:

> As any true baseball fan will tell you, it is called the World Series precisely because it is the most important thing in the world. It is not merely the coronation of a champion, but a ritual of affirmation, an occasion when those fortunate few and we envious millions before our television sets join in celebration of the joys of baseball and the richness of memory.

Yes, Your Honor, I know. God knows, I know. It's terrible. It's baseball prose at its absolute dreamy romantic worst. "The richness of memory." Lord have mercy. Mea culpa. But I was thirty years old and didn't know any better. Please don't make me quote any more of it. But you insist. Oh, all right. You're the judge:

> Because baseball is a game at once so stark and so intricate, it is the perfect spectator sport; it gives to each person who watches it the material of memory: a treasure chest to be opened, in the privacy of the mind, whenever the impulse strikes.

Your Honor, if it makes you feel any better, just reading the words aloud gives me a sore throat. "The material of memory." Lord have mercy. Mea culpa. Look, I was thirty years old and like a lot of other hack journalists of that day and time I'd been reading too much Roger Angell. None of us realized that he'd cornered the market; all of us thought that if he could get away with elegantly elegiac baseball prose, so could we. It was like influenza; we all caught a case. Everybody was doing it.

If it will improve my chances, Your Honor, I'll now admit in public what I did a couple of years ago in private. Yes, Your Honor, I am a member of PA. You don't know what that is? It's called Poets Anonymous. It's an organization of journalists and academics who are united in their common determination to end their addiction to writing poetic prose about baseball.

Against the soft green background of their field of dreams, the players take their balletic steps toward the infinity of fate. . . . I'm sorry, Your Honor, I just did it again. I took the pledge in 1989, after reading one baseball novel too many, and I swore that I would renew it each spring with the approach of Opening Day, that hallowed moment in the calendar of American memory when the child in each of us begs to be born anew. . . . Ouch! I thought corporal punishment had been outlawed, Your Honor!

Well, anyway, ma'am, what happened was that all of us started reading Roger Angell, and before you knew it the pages of every American newspaper and magazine and literary quarterly were filled with the excrescences of tinhorn Angells who figured that if he could write, "Baseball's time is seamless and invisible, a bubble within which players move at exactly the same pace and rhythms as all their predecessors," then so could they. We, actually. Mea culpa.

We didn't do it anywhere nearly so well as Angell, but we tried. Lord knows we tried. Remember what that great old newspaper hack Gene Fowler once said? "Writing is easy," he said. "All you do is stare at a blank sheet of paper until drops of blood form on your forehead." We sat and we stared and we sat some more and we stared some more, and eventually we came up with poetry. Or at least that's what we thought it was. Newspaper poetry, actually, which is to poetry as . . . well, you know the rest of it.

But we didn't know. I swear, Your Honor, we thought we were writing up there in the big leagues, writing with the likes of Edgar A. Guest and James Whitcomb Riley and Rod McKuen and even Carl Sandburg, except we were writing about the poetry of baseball instead of the poetry of cows and cornfields and dear old friends and fog creeping in on little cat feet. We thought we were doing what all newspaper retainers and assistant professors of English dream of doing, which is to say we thought we were writing literature, and so what we did was, we wrote a whole lot more of it.

You thought the excesses of the 1970s were sex and drugs and rock 'n' roll, but I'm here to tell you, ma'am, that the worst of them were perpetrated by we owlish little guys who sat in front of our typewriters and produced endless dithyrambs about the evanescent yet eternal beauty of the centerfielder as he swoops through a ring of fire toward the gossamer streak of white that the batter has launched into the heartbreakingly green expanse that rolls across the . . . I'm sorry! I'm sorry! I'm sorry!

The mists of memory. Or is it history? Didn't I write that somewhere along the way? "The mists of history"? That's where I've put all this stuff, Your Honor. A couple of years ago I went cold turkey. It wasn't easy, and as you can see from time to time the old addiction just sneaks up and takes control before all the strictures of Poets Anonymous have had a chance to take effect.

I'm like the former smoker who craves a coffin nail with that first sip of coffee; sometimes the urge is overwhelming.

But I'm fighting it, Your Honor, and Poets Anonymous has been a great help. Not merely does it require us to read the collected baseball prose and poetry of W.P. Kinsella, Donald Hall and Barry Gifford, which is enough to drive any poet manqué to swear off simile, trope and blank verse. Not merely that, but it forces us to stand up in front of the membership and read our own prose, just the way I read those ghastly sentences of mine right here in court only a few minutes ago. Every night we PA members sit around and confess our sins—baseball as a metaphor for American life, the manager as authority figure, Pete Rose as tragic hero—and the more we do so, the more determined we are never again to repeat them.

But it's hard, Your Honor. The spirit is willing but the brain is weak. You can be right there at the word processor, minding your own business and trying to squeeze out another few hundred words for the next day's edition, when suddenly the moon floats over the iridescent bowl of light wherein players walk along the basepaths to the immortality that is Cooperstown while in the stands around them the hushed throng prays for their enshrinement and . . . Stop me before I gurgle again!

Oh. That's just what you had in mind. Poets Anonymous isn't enough for you, Your Honor? You're putting the full force and majesty of the law to work? If I ever again write baseball poetry you'll *what?* No! You'd never do that. Sentenced to watch *Field of Dreams* every night for the rest of my life? Oh no, Your Honor, if it comes to that please show mercy. Please just send me right off to the chair, with a one-way ticket to the Great Ballpark in the Sky.

THE BEST YEAR

OF MY LIFE

❦

October 7, 1991

When we sit around in the dark evenings of the winter all too soon to come, reminiscing wistfully about the glory days of Memorial Stadium and beerily mourning their irrecoverable loss, there will be talk aplenty about the most glorious days of all: the incredible World Series of 1966, the day Frank hit one clear out of the park, the twi-night doubleheader in October of 1982 when the Orioles barged back into the pennant race, the night one year later en route to a world championship when Tippy—can you believe it?—picked off the side.

Glory days indeed. I was lucky enough to be there for the last two, and I'll remember them for as long as I'm blessed with memory. Yet now that the final Orioles game has been played in Memorial Stadium and we turn our attention to the new place improbably called Oriole Park at Camden Yards—why not, Brady Anderson asked last week, just go ahead and call it "Babe Ruth Oriole Park at Camden Yards Where Cal Ripken Plays"?—what sticks in my mind is none of the above but a game played in the old ballpark on the night of September 26, 1979.

Nineteen seventy-nine: It was—absolutely, conclusively, inarguably—the best of times. Late in the fall of the previous year my wife and I had moved to Baltimore from Miami, bearing the going-away present friends had given us: tickets for all the Orioles' 1979 home games against the Red Sox. We were Boston fans, and we looked forward to seeing Yaz & Company in person. What we didn't know was that by March we'd swap those tickets for an Orioles' season-ticket mini-plan and that by late April we'd be Baltimore fans of the most insufferably insistent and loquacious variety.

The Orioles weren't expected to be much that year. After the great teams of the late 1960s and early '70s, they'd slipped from three straight second-place finishes to a most improbable fourth. Attendance in 1978 had been barely over a million—the average "crowd" was 14,407—and nobody thought the club record of 1.2 million, set in 1966, was in any danger of being broken. You could walk up to the box office any old day or night, ask for the best tickets in the house—and get them.

If, that is, you really wanted to see a team that most people thought was headed back to fourth, or worse. It was a respectable club, to be sure—in those days the American League East was so strong that a team could finish at 90 and 71, as the Orioles had, and get no higher than fourth—but the Yankees and Red Sox and Brewers positively bristled with power, while the Orioles were Jim Palmer plus a batch of competent unknowns. It looked to be another summer of quiet games played out for small stakes before sparse crowds.

That's the way it started. After an Opening Day victory on a gelid April afternoon, the team settled into a sub-.500 rut in which it seemed all too comfortable. After eleven games the Orioles were 3 and 8, and empty seats were everywhere. But then they went to New York, of all places, and started to win, of all things. At one point they ran off a nine-game winning streak, and on May 18 they settled into first place. As it turned out they stayed there every day save one for the rest of the year, but we had no idea of that at the time. All we knew was that we were right in the middle of the pennant race no one had predicted and that it was more fun than any of us could have imagined.

What was even more amazing than the action on the field was the action in the stands. Late in June we were joined by friends from New York—the same ones who were with us yesterday for the final-game obsequies—and were unanimously astonished to be part of a crowd of more than 45,000 for a Saturday-evening doubleheader. Why, in nine *playoff* games between 1969 and 1974, the Orioles had only once drawn more than 45,000, yet here it was June and the place was fairly close to packed. What was going on here?

The answer had to do with something more than baseball and explains why the end of baseball at Memorial Stadium leaves me in a condition embarrassingly close to grief. What was being reborn in the summer of 1979 wasn't just a baseball team but a city. Throughout its history Baltimore had been an odd place, intensely proud of itself, even arrogant, yet possessed by a civic inferiority complex: Washington, too close by for comfort, was too powerful; Philadelphia and New York, up to the north, were too big and too rich. Throw in Boston for bad measure, and the most you could say for Baltimore was that on the East Coast, it was the Fifth City.

But things were happening. A proposal to rejuvenate the grungy old Inner Harbor had been narrowly, reluctantly approved by the city's voters; construction was under way, as it was as well at any number of center-city projects. The city's complacent echt-WASP establishment had been jolted out of its inertia by the mayor, William Donald Schaefer, and by private interests led by an extraordinary man named Walter Sondheim.

Baltimore was stirring to life, and for whatever reason the baseball team it had for so long taken for granted became the most visible and potent symbol of its regeneration. Crowds at the stadium just got bigger and bigger, until by season's end attendance had broken the old record by 400,000; to think that yesterday's crowd broke *that* total by fully one million! Not merely were the crowds big, they were noisy and good-natured. A bearded, long-haired cab driver named Wild Bill Hagy led cheers upstairs in Section 34: "The Roar from 34," we called it. Soon enough the whole stadium began to join in, and it became the refrain for an entire summer: "O-R-I-O-L-E-S!"

It was a summer of unceasing apprehension as the Orioles somehow held onto their lead against the challenges of all those teams who looked so much tougher on paper. Through June and July and August their lead fluctuated with excruciating uncertainty between one game and eight, but just before Labor Day they pulled away and on September 22 they clinched the championship.

Four nights later they played their last home game. They beat the Tigers 13-2 for their 101st victory of the year. All of which was nice but none of which meant a thing. What mattered was that late in the game the "O-R-I-O-L-E-S!" cheer was booming all around the ballpark, yet up in 34 Wild Bill Hagy was in his seat: The cheer was being led from the Orioles' dugout by the manager, Earl Weaver, and the catcher, Rick Dempsey.

That was only the beginning. Just about everyone in the crowd of 17,205 hung around to the end, and when it was all over something certifiably miraculous happened: The entire team ran out on the field and led the crowd in the cheer. The place was bedlam; never has the noise of happiness sounded so loud in my ears. A few months later, trying to put into words what happened that night, I wrote: "I was laughing. I was crying. I was so hoarse I could barely talk. I was seized with joy, with gratitude, with an inexpressible sense of community, of belonging."

Yes, those words seem pretty corny now, read in the cold light of a dozen years' distance. The only thing is, they were and still are true. What happened in Memorial Stadium that season, what came to its dreamlike climax that evening, had just a little to do with baseball and everything to do with a city discovering, and celebrating, itself. If there was a tear in my eye yesterday when they closed the old place down, that's why.

HAIL, CHIEF WAHOO

❧

August 2, 1993

What a joy it is to flee the cares and woes of the workaday world and escape into the Elysium of sport. What a relief it is to leave behind the machinations of sordid publishers and cynical authors—or should it be cynical publishers and sordid authors?—and collapse into the universe of play. As we say here in Tough City, when the going gets tough, the tough get going: to the ballpark.

Which is exactly what I did last week. I didn't drive the five miles to Camden Yards; the Orioles were on the road, getting their annual dose of cold reality at the Skydome in Toronto. Me, I put a round-trip total of 744 miles on the car, that being what it takes to travel from Northwest Baltimore to the southern shore of Lake Erie, where dwell Chief Wahoo and his Tribe.

All of which no doubt sounds peculiar in the extreme to all save those fortunate few who for one reason or another have, at some point in their lives, fallen under the peculiar spell of the Cleveland Indians. Peculiar, that is, for the obvious reason that spells cast in Cleveland tend to be hexes rather than charms. The city that in recent years has been famous for setting its lake on fire and electing as mayor the singular Dennis Kucinich is also known, in baseball circles, for adding whole new universes of meaning to the phrase "cellar-dwelling."

Thus it is that if one chances to say, as I did upon several occasions in advance of departure, "I'm going to Cleveland for the weekend," the automatic response is, *Why?* None among

American cities, with the possible exception of those twin New Jerseyan monuments to urban decay, Newark and Camden, labors under so heavy a burden of opprobrium as Cleveland; surely none does so less deservingly than that city.

The fact of the matter, as I discovered last week, is that those of us who puff out our chests when we tell the world that we live in Washington or Baltimore have ample reason to look north toward Cleveland in envy. Take both of our symphony orchestras, roll them into one and put them under the baton of, oh, Herbert von Karajan redux, and you wouldn't come within a country mile of the Cleveland Orchestra, which went to the mat with Tchaikovsky and pinned him flat, all this under the stars at a summer amphitheater called Blossom toward which even Wolf Trap must bow in admiration. While you're at it, take a bow in the direction of Cleveland's cultural center, just beyond the downtown district; it makes Baltimore's little cluster of museums look strictly bush league and holds its own against those marble monuments to official culture in Washington.

But culture hadn't a thing to do with my presence in Cleveland last weekend. I was there to make a gesture to my long-lost youth, to see the Indians play ball in their final season on the shore of the lake in what is now called Cleveland Stadium but was known in its glory days—and thus forever will be known by me—as Municipal Stadium. Treasured friends had moved from Baltimore to Cleveland early this year, had acquired season tickets to the Indians (merrily abandoning their loyalty to the Orioles in the process), and had invited us to come to the ballpark; it was an invitation not to be refused.

That's because in all fifty-three of my years I had never managed to find my way into Municipal Stadium. The list of ballparks in which I'd seen the national pastime wasn't half bad, considering that I'm neither a sportswriter nor a nostalgia nut—Griffith Stadium, Forbes Field, the Polo Grounds, Fenway Park, Yankee Stadium, Atlanta-Fulton County Stadium, Comiskey Park, Shea Stadium and, of course, dear old Memorial Stadium—but somehow I'd never made it to Cleveland. Suddenly it became clear that, with the Indians gearing up to move next season into their own Camden Yards clone, it was now or never.

Why Cleveland? Because the spell, or the hex, hit me about forty-five years ago and never quite went away. It must have been sometime during 1949 that my parents went on a business trip to New York. They returned to Virginia bearing gifts for me and my siblings, mine being a book called *Player-Manager*, ghostwritten on behalf of the estimable Cleveland shortstop, Lou Boudreau, who the previous season had done just that: played *and* managed the Indians to their first world championship since 1920.

To say that I fell in love with the Indians is an understatement. From then until 1959 the Tribe was my team; that year, on a day that will live in infamy, they traded Rocky Colavito to the Detroit Tigers, breaking my heart and sending themselves down the long descent into terminal mediocrity. But that betrayal was yet to come. During the 1950s I huddled by my radio, by day and by night, listening to games played by the great teams managed by Al Lopez and featuring stars so bright as to glow into eternity: Al Rosen, Bobby Avila, Larry Doby, Al Smith, Vic Wertz and Luke Easter, not to mention a starting five of—can you believe this?—Early Wynn, Mike Garcia, Bob Lemon, Art Houtteman and Bob Feller, as well as the best brace of stoppers ever paired, Don Mossi and Ray Narleski.

Those *were* the days. To be young and a Cleveland fan was sheer heaven—until, that is, the first game of the 1954 World Series, when Willie Mays raced to the deepest reaches of center-field in the Polo Grounds and robbed Vic Wertz of a stupendous extra-base hit. In the process he also robbed the Indians of the world championship they clearly deserved—they may well have been, for that one season, the best ballclub ever—because they never got untracked after that.

But all this is ancient history, cherished only by me and a handful of others who still recall the glory days. For me they were glorious even though I had never set foot in Cleveland and hadn't the foggiest idea of what the ballpark, much less the city, looked like. To be sure I got a quick look at both four years ago when, passing through on business during the off-season, I persuaded a guard to let me have a look at the ballpark, but that mainly reinforced me in the conventional view that it is far too cavernous for baseball—a place that swallows the "crowds" of 15,000 usually drawn by the Indians these days.

A week ago, though, the place was jumping. A crowd of nearly 55,000 had been drawn by the lively young Indians ballclub and by the prospect of free, 1948-vintage Indians caps. We got there an hour early and were still too late for caps—the supply of 25,000 had already been exhausted—but that wasn't the point. Baseball was the point, and there was plenty of it: a slugfest (no other cliche will do) won by the Indians 11-9 and featuring two monstrous homers by Albert "Ding Dong" Belle.

The baseball was fine but the people were even better. Before the game got underway, sitting in our friends' wonderful third-base-side seats, my wife and I realized we were seeing something that's become almost as much ancient history in Baltimore as Memorial Stadium itself. Baseball fans.

In the stands at Municipal Stadium, not a single necktie was to be seen, not a single beeper, not a single business suit. The yuppies and the lobbyists who've taken over Camden Yards—the crowd at the All-Star game was the worst yet—wouldn't be seen dead at Cleveland Stadium. It was full of kids and young people. The mood was noisy and exuberant. Indians' rallies were greeted by thunderous crashing and banging of the old wooden seats, and the vendors were up to their elbows in soda pop and beer. In my section an attendance pool was quickly organized, attendance being something of a novelty in Cleveland; I put my $1 on 57,800, and lost by 3,400 empty seats.

It was a hell of an afternoon: old-fashioned baseball played before an old-fashioned crowd in an old-fashioned place. It took me more than four decades to get there, but I made it just in time. Thank God, or Chief Wahoo, for that.

HOMEBOY

∽◦∾

August 9, 1993

One of the cardinal precepts of the conventional wisdom in this part of the world is that two of the Mid-Atlantic's principal cities, Baltimore and Washington, are steadily growing into one. Almost all the evidence supports it, from the bedroom communities that now connect them to their designation by the federal government as a "combined metropolitan statistical area," but every once in a while someone rises to say: "Whoa! What's going on here? What's the big hurry?"

That's what happened last week. The person who delivered this latest point of order is an unlikely instrument of romantic rebellion or, depending upon one's point of view, unseemly impertinence. He is short, his countenance is most charitably described as unprepossessing, and though he speaks softly, he does so in the less than dulcet tones of ethnic Baltimore, his home town. But when he spoke last week, it was to a very large and almost entirely startled audience.

His name, as all of us now know, is Peter G. Angelos. Within the month he will become the majority owner, managing general partner and chairman of the board of the Baltimore Orioles, the baseball team that he and a number of others arranged to purchase last week for the numbing price of $173 million. But it isn't the price that concerns us here, newsworthy though it most certainly is. Rather, it is the manner in which Angelos seized command.

He took the prize, Angelos said, for Baltimore. Not for Baltimore-Washington or Washington-Baltimore, but for good old Balmer all by itself. Bidding against an art dealer from New York named Jeffrey H. Loris, Angelos went in with one thought foremost in mind: "I was not going to let . . . people say that a New Yorker got the best of a Marylander." Once the prize was won, Angelos had this to say: "I want to make it very clear that the control of the ballclub is in Baltimorean hands."

To readers outside Baltimore and its immediate suburbs those words may seem mere local pride or provincial bluster, but such a view fails to take into account the Baltimorean cast of mind. As one who has lived in that city for a decade and a half I would not presume to intimate understanding of its psychology—just as it takes six hundred years of rolling to make a fine English lawn, so it takes several generations of residence to produce a true Baltimorean—but I have been there long enough to acquire a sense of it; this tells me that Angelos spoke not merely from his own heart but from that of the entire city.

What he was saying was that the Orioles belong to Baltimore, not to some amorphous megalopolitan construct and not, God knows, to New York. By implication he was also saying that Baltimore has its own identity, one not to be submerged in the waves of outsiders—in Baltimore these days, "outsiders" is a euphemism for "Washingtonians"—who are threatening to turn the city into something of a Rust Belt theme park, complete with Ye Olde Harbour and quaint Little Italy trattorias. Baltimore, he was saying, is quite capable of standing on its own, thank you, and can even buy back its own baseball club.

Probably you have to live there to understand just how much resonance Angelos's words, and the assumptions behind them, carry in Baltimore. For much of the twentieth century Baltimore has labored under a civic inferiority complex, as New York and Philadelphia to the north and Washington to the south have become the urban giants in a part of the world to which Baltimore once thought it could lay claim. With an odd (and oddly touching) mixture of resentment and resignation, Baltimore has stood by as its port has been eclipsed by Newport News, Philadelphia and others along the Atlantic; as its steel mills have shrunk in the face of competition from Asia and elsewhere in the United States; as its middle-class population has fled to the suburbs and its city neighborhoods have rotted; as its beloved teams, the Orioles and Colts, have either fallen under alien ownership or decamped altogether.

Baltimore is a poignant and beguiling mixture of conflicting longings. On the one hand it wants to be what the lobbyists in the field boxes at Camden Yards would call a "player," holding its own at the table against the high rollers who have so often made sport of it; it takes a certain pride in knowing that high rollers now come to Baltimore to play. But on the other hand it wants every bit as much to be itself, an agglomeration of small towns masquerading as a big city, a place where the waitresses still call you "Hon," where an impenetrable local patois is still spoken, where a little guy from the neighborhood can still become owner of "them Oreos."

In Washington and elsewhere the assumption in recent years has been that Baltimore is grateful for outside attention, even if that attention is patronizing, and indeed this is not without truth. Baltimore yearns almost plaintively for recognition by the national press and basks excessively in such as it receives. It still looks more in envy than indifference upon Washington and New York, and it still is prone to self-disparagement.

But the past decade has been good for Baltimore's self-confidence. Not merely has its new baseball park received fawning praise from experts foreign and domestic; not merely is its decrepit old Inner Harbor now a tourist haven for hundreds of thousands of visitors each year; not merely are there now people who commute from Washington to Baltimore, as opposed to the one-way reverse flow of the past. On top of all this, compounding it all, is an elusive yet palpable sense that the old inferiority complex is a thing of the past. So many people have told Baltimore how terrific it is that Baltimore is actually starting to believe them.

It is this, I think, that is as important as anything else to an understanding of what Angelos did and what he said. Fourteen years ago, when Jerold Hoffberger put the Orioles up for sale, no local buyers could be found; ditto for five years ago, when the team went back on the market after the death of Edward Bennett Williams. On both occasions there was plenty of locally generated hot air about keeping the ownership in the city, but no one put his mouth where his money was.

Angelos's bid for the team, by contrast, was a gesture of individual and communal defiance. Jeffrey Loria "could have gone to $200 million," Angelos said after the auction, "but I would have told [my lawyer] to go to $201 million." Buoyed by the city's new confidence, Angelos decided to become the embodiment of it. In so doing he sent, however unwittingly, a message to Washington: Baltimore and Washington may be headed for the altar, but if it's all the same with you, we'd like a marital contract.

As it happens I was in Camden Yards last Tuesday night when Angelos and his fellow purchasers made their quasi-triumphal appearance in the owner's box. It was a pleasure to see him there and later brush past him in the Eutaw Street esplanade. To be sure the happy smile he sported probably will fade under the limelight. For one thing, the press is bound to take a look at his financial affairs. Though no one seems to question his probity, people do tend to find it miraculous that a lawyer in the seemingly eleemosynary practice of representing asbestos victims could end up wealthy enough to purchase 51 per cent of a $173 million baseball club.

Those questions will come along in time, as will complaints from fans when one free agent or another isn't signed by the new management. But right now no one in Baltimore seems to be worried about such matters. The city is proud that local people will soon own the ballclub again, proud that it plays in the prettiest ballpark in America and prouder still that poor old Baltimore now is home ground to the most expensive sports franchise in the universe. Put *that* in your pipe and smoke it, high roller.

BASEBALL A LA BURNS

❧

July 8, 1994

Thanks in substantial measure to the machinations of Tony LaRussa, manager of the Oakland Athletics and widely regarded as a genius among what passes for baseball's intelligentsia, the Athletics and the Baltimore Orioles frittered away an astonishing three hours and forty-three minutes last Thursday night in the course of playing a nine-inning baseball game. If you think that's conclusive evidence that Western civilization is boring itself into extinction, think about something even more persuasive. Think about Ken Burns. Think about *Baseball.*

Baseball is Burns' nine-part, eighteen-hour public television documentary about the National Pastime. The program has been in the works for half a decade, enough to make it "long-awaited," as we masters of journalistic prose like to say. But if you are one of the millions who long await, you got a clue last week that *Baseball* may be far more protracted than the most interminable Baltimore–Oakland snoozer, and vastly more insufferable.

This clue came in the form of "The Making of *Baseball,*" a thirty-minute preview of the documentary. Presumably it was offered by public television as a tantalizing peek at riches soon to come, but from where I sat it was about as enticing as a strip tease by the circus fat lady. It was not so much a preview as an act of institutional self-abnegation wherein PBS flung itself in adoration at the feet of Burns, who on the evidence supplied in these thirty minutes scarcely needs additional ego-reinforcement.

Obviously PBS is counting on Burns to do for it in September 1994 what he did a few years ago with *The Civil War*, i.e., get universally adoring reviews and attract hordes of the chattering classes to PBS programming. Perhaps that will happen; strange things happen every day. But what seems more likely is that even the most malleable will find eighteen hours of Burns' *Baseball* about, oh, twelve hours more than they really want, and that boredom will lead to disenchantment.

This is because "The Making of *Baseball*" suggested nothing so much as that Burns has allowed self-infatuation to cloud his judgment and that no one working for or with him has the courage to question his decisions, even the most egregious. Thus we have for example this matter of length. "I haven't even begun to worry about it getting too long," Burns said during last week's hagiography, a comment that went without challenge even though *Baseball* at eighteen hours will make *Roots* seem like a sitcom. The explanation is simple: Burns works in "an open atmosphere," the reverent narrator told us, "though every final decision is Ken's."

Open, schmopen. Consider "the connection between the Negro Leagues, segregation in the United States and the rise of fascism in Europe," all of this being "part of the story of baseball." In the immortal words of Dave Barry, I did not make that up. The "connection" exists in the mind of Ken Burns, and when he put it to his assembled staff no one raised more than a timid objection. How indeed could anyone, when none other than Burns declared that "it is absolutely true." He saw an exhibition at the Holocaust Museum that established this "connection," Burns told his awe-struck colleagues, and he spent a whole month doing research to assure himself of its validity. Then he railroaded it into *Baseball* and thus eventually, in all likelihood, into the minds of the series' watchers.

Well, let's raise one hand in objection. The notion that the segregation in the United States that forced black ballplayers to set up their own professional league somehow aided and abetted the rise of fascism in Europe that in time led to the Holocaust . . . wow. It's approximately as loony as the notion, popular among certain brain-dead Americans, that the Holocaust didn't happen at all. If anything it can be said to be the left-wing mirror image of that right-wing fantasy—a reduction of complex and painful human experience to conspiracy theories and hallucinations. Burns wants, he said, to "bind these parallel lines together," but that's not binding, it's warping.

This exercise in oversimplification in the service of self-righteousness is presented to us by one who makes a great display of presenting himself as a "historian." In the sense that Burns deals in the raw material of history this is true, but his real business is the manipulation of images and emotions, which is to say the business of television. Make no mistake about it, he is good at this business. *The Civil War* was in many if not all respects a fine piece of work, and doubtless there will be some of the same in *Baseball*. But like other masters of the television medium, Burns in the final analysis is more interested in entertaining and moving us than in instructing and enlightening us.

Thus we had Burns exclaiming at one point in last week's broadcast, "I just love that image!" and later telling his pet pianist, "That was perfect in my book," after a threnodic rendering of "Take Me Out to the Ball Game." Thus too we had a member of his staff talking about "laying sound effects onto silents," which is to say tarting up old film and photographs with manufactured sound. This isn't history but historical fiction, an entirely legitimate genre—viz., the "Histories" of Shakespeare—but one not to be confused with history itself.

The danger is that those who practice this genre and those who consume it will permit themselves to be thus confused; it's especially dangerous at a time when television has turned image and reality into a hopeless muddle. But if this causes Ken Burns any self-doubt or qualms, there was no sign of it in "The Making of *Baseball*." What we were given instead was a man serenely confident in the absolute rectitude of his vision and fawningly reinforced in this illusion by the T-shirted staff—looking for all the world like the inner circle at Ben & Jerry's—assembled at his quaint New Hampshire fastness.

Thanks a lot but no thanks. No doubt there will be a great deal of fine old film in *Baseball*, but the price of seeing it looks to be too high: emotive music, ponderous narration and ideological indoctrination. It all begins the night of September 18, which happens to be when the Yankees play the Orioles at Camden Yards. When it comes to life's little choices, this is the easiest imaginable.

Ho, Hum

✈

September 19, 1994

So we are in for a moratorium on baseball. So what? You'll get no cries and lamentations from this quarter, no middle-aged white-male bleats about a body blow to the American psyche or the loss of American innocence or the death throes of the National Pastime. Baseball is a game, and notwithstanding the superior performances of a handful of players, recently it hasn't been much of one. A timeout is in order.

This isn't to say that the timeout has been called for the right reason. To be sure, the players were entirely correct in walking out. The job market rights they seek to protect are the same ones enjoyed by all other American workers, except that baseball players enjoy fewer of them. Their salaries may seem excessive to those of us who work at least as hard for far less, but their careers are brief and the amount of money they make for their employers is immense. That they are so widely criticized for wanting to make as much as they can is a tribute to the public-relations expertise of the owners' flacks as well as to the surpassing ignorance of Joe Six-Pack.

Speaking of ignorance, not to mention stupidity, the World Championship in that department goes to the owners, whose inability to practice even the most primitive forms of self-government is why we are in this mess. They have done a fine job of convincing people that the players are the villains in this melodrama, but the real problem is that they are incapable of managing their own affairs with enough efficiency and fairness to assure that the playing field is more or less level for all twenty-eight major-league clubs. Rather than tidy up their own house, they are insisting that the players do the dirty work for them. Anyone who finds their case sensible and legitimate should be packed away to the funny farm.

But the particulars of the controversy that led to the walkout are only part of baseball's problem. Baseball has become paralyzed by bureaucracy, not in the front offices—though no doubt there's plenty there—but on the playing field and in the dugouts. A game that not long ago was distinguished by daring and imagination is now the prisoner of convention and caution. Baseball has always been played "by the book," but the book has become so bloated and cluttered with footnotes that it's no longer readable or workable.

Thus we have the evolution of "the percentages" into the dullest chapter of the book. Managers and pitching coaches now waste hours of their time, and ours, pondering the percentages during conferences on the pitching mound during which play is stopped, and then changing pitchers as many as five times in a single inning to squeeze every last drop out of the percentages. The result is not merely games that routinely run more than three hours—in the minor leagues as in the majors, as I discovered during a recent inspection of the Rochester Red Wings—but games that are as dull as they are long. Baseball has always depended on a delicate balance between its passive and active elements; now it is all passivity and inertia and delay, thanks to decisions made by managers who are terrified that independent thinking might lead them into risk and error.

A few games into the 1994 season, my little delegation to Camden Yards in Baltimore became sufficiently exercised about the three-plus-hour ballgame to go on a strike of our own. We established, for ourselves and our guests, the Two-and-a-Half-Hour Rule: After two and a half hours of play, we're out of there. Someone could be pitching a no-hitter or someone else could be hitting homer after homer, but if they can't finish the job within two and a half hours, they can finish it without us. No doubt this had minimal impact on the Orioles, apart from a few beers or lemonades that went unsold, but it made us feel good.

Another thing wrong with baseball is an excess of metaphor. Having in the fairly distant past made my own inept contributions to this unhappy trend, I herewith apologize and slip into my hair shirt, pausing to note only that in the years since, matters have gotten a whole lot worse. Baseball as metaphor has become an industry, employing broadcasters, journalists and other ne'er-do-wells in a concerted campaign to smother the game under blankets of Meaning that are only marginally connected to reality. Like the structuralists and radical feminists and Marxists who are twisting the interpretation of literature and history into a vehicle for their own ideological fantasies, the baseball-as-metaphor crowd is turning the game into a singularly repellent junk heap of tired imagery and bloated sentimentality.

Speaking of which: Did you see the front page of the *New York Times* last Thursday? Right there, under the headline "In Memoriam" in Gothic type, All the News That's Fit to Print featured a diatribe by one Robert Lipsyte, who, after complaining that baseball "had become an increasingly sour male soap opera," launched into the following:

> The game was encouraged, after the Civil War, as a big, nonviolent spectator sport to contain and pacify the European immigrants . . . ; to escape women's marching toward the vote, and to whip the white boys into shape for foreign wars and the Industrial Revolution.

Wow. What on earth are the editors of the *New York Times* smoking? Has the *New York Times* been taken over by the Duke University English Department or, saints preserve us, by Catharine MacKinnon and Andrea Dworkin? Is it really now possible to postulate, on the front page of the newspaper of record, a conspiracy theory the essence of which is that baseball was a creature of "the merchants and their politicians" whose intent was to provide an opiate for the masses, to oppress women and to train cannon fodder? No other word will do: Wow.

In the Department of Nutty Fruitcake, that takes all the

prizes they're giving out: Baseball not merely as metaphor but as malign instrument of white male empowerment, domination and privilege. It was bad enough when they started talking and writing it that way in the English departments, worse when it crept into the history departments, downright crazy when—I swear this is true—the geography departments caught the disease. But the *New York Times*? On the *front page*?

Sic transit gloria mundi.

SAY GOODNIGHT,

BASEBALL

∽๑๏๛

April 24, 1995

On the sports front of the *Philadelphia Inquirer* there appeared last week a striking color photograph of the Phillies' second baseman, Mickey Morandini, making an off-balance throw to first. Above it was a headline that read: "Hopelessly Hooked on a Spring Rite." Sipping my coffee, I thought: Yes, damn it, that's right. Baseball really is back, the spring rite really is irresistible, and I'm hooked again.

Then I read the smaller line immediately below: "The opening of the Pa. trout season brought out scores of anglers. This time, the strikes were welcome." So much for that little burst of sentiment. After the strike of 1994–95, and facing the very real possibility of a strike and/or lockout of 1995–96–97–9?, everybody feels ambiguous and uncertain about baseball. When a lifelong fan glances at the sports page and in all innocence manages to confuse baseball and trout fishing, there's reason to believe that nothing will ever be the same again.

Between the lines, as they say in the game, it will always be the same. As the players finally take the field this week for the belated opening of the 1995 season, it will still be pitcher and catcher, fielder and runner, bunt and double play. But off the field, not merely in relations between players and owners but also in how the rest of us feel about the game, things really have changed. The question is whether any of these bozos to whom the health of the sport has been entrusted have even the remotest idea of what is going on or what to do about it.

There's precious little reason to believe they do. The players have made a big deal throughout their truncated spring training of signing autographs free of charge, and before yesterday's exhibition game at Camden Yards the Orioles came out en masse for a half-hour signing session, but as the season wears on this will change. Too many people clamoring for signatures aren't innocent little towheads but cynical jerks who'll turn around and sell the autographs they collect. The players know this and understandably resent it; combine that with their natural truculence, and it's safe to predict that it will be "Shove off, kid," as usual by, say, June.

As for the owners, the oceans will part and the skies will rain liquid gold before those creeps wake up. A few teams have run exculpatory advertisements and a few have made token price concessions to lure back fans, but generally the assumption is that the customers will come back on their knees, begging for more $3.50 cold wieners and $4.50 warm beers. If the Baltimore Orioles have made a single friendly gesture to the thousands of season ticket owners whose money they sat on throughout the strike, no word of it has reached this quarter. Apparently they assume that the Rockies may crumble, Gibraltar may tumble, but a sold-out Camden Yards is here to stay.

Dream on. From the 1960s to the 1980s, Dodger Stadium was filled to the rafters as Los Angelenos applauded the long parade of Dodger greats from Sandy Koufax to Orel Hershiser. But Koufax is long in retirement, Hershiser is a Cleveland Indian, and the Dodgers are begging for customers. Nothing lasts forever. It's the most fundamental of all truths of human existence and the one that none of us ever manages to understand until it's too late. If you and I can't get our hands on it, try to imagine how little is understood by the major league baseball owners, who collectively and multiplied by seventy-five still make you and me look like Albert Einstein's older brother.

These guys don't understand anything. They don't understand that whatever claim baseball may once have had to being the national pastime is now forfeited, almost certainly for good. They don't understand that far more Americans care about football and basketball than care about baseball, and that both of these sports have been far more attentive than baseball to the best interests of their fans.

That's why in the spring training now nearly ended, the spring training that was to see baseball turn over a new leaf, game after game ran far past three hours, and it wasn't just from letting all those minor-leaguers get a taste of big-league action. It was because nobody anywhere has done a thing to reverse the steady lengthening of the average game, a phenomenon that in and of itself explains why this semi-ex-fan will be at Camden Yards at least twenty fewer times this season than any previous.

Baseball is all public relations—mostly lousy PR, at that—and no action. It tells us it loves us, but acts like a two-timing spouse. It raids our pocketbooks with price increases for everything from tickets to programs to soft drinks, then it turns around and offers us—take it or leave it, buster—a game that offers fewer and fewer spectator pleasures every year. But does baseball worry? Does baseball care? Of course not. Baseball is forever, remember?

So why are we going back to the ballpark? Everybody has their reasons, though probably they're mostly old folks' reasons, since younger fans play hoops and once my generation buys the farm, say goodnight, baseball. Well, my reasons have mostly to do with friends and family, less and less to do with players and games. Once Cal Ripken sets his unsettable record—and I do hope to be there the night he takes the field for consecutive game 2,131—my statistical interest in the game will be dead. I'll go because there are a few people I see only once a year, during ballpark weekends, and I'd badly miss them; to see them is worth the cost of the tickets, and then some.

At the risk of indulging in *béisbol* sentimentality, it's true as well that baseball connects me, as it does so many others, to my past. Not just my childhood, which in fact was big-league-deprived, but all those years from 1958 to the present when I made up for lost boyhood ballgames in parks from the Polo Grounds to

Fenway to, most loved of all, Memorial Stadium in Baltimore. It is indeed true, as the sentimentalists insist on reminding us, that baseball is a continuum; once you get on board it is harder than you might think to hop off.

So a week from today, when the Orioles open at home, I'll be there. Whether I'll have it in me to join the standing ovation with which Baltimore's ever-forgiving fans will salute their team, I won't know until the time comes; but if I do, it will be in this spirit:

Welcome back, damn it.

2,131

⤔

September 4, 1995

D*eo volente.* Those words—Latin for "God willing"—appeared with such frequency in the correspondence of genteel, God-fearing Victorians that they were often boiled down to *D.V.* The will of God was evoked for everything from the historic ("The Union will survive, *D.V.*") to the most routinely quotidian ("I will see you on Sunday, *D.V.*").

The will of God is a matter about which relatively few Americans now trouble themselves, but it might not hurt to give it a thought from time to time. That has come to mind with increasing frequency as the ladies and gentlemen of the sporting press have fallen over themselves in celebration—or in a handful of infantile instances, derogation—of what all assume to be an absolute certainty, i.e., that two nights hence Cal Ripken Jr. of the Baltimore Orioles will break one of the few remaining sports records once thought to be "unbreakable."

To none of these folk—or to anyone else, for that matter—does it seem to have occurred that the most appropriate way to depict the coming events is not as "when Ripken breaks Lou Gehrig's record" but as "when Ripken breaks Lou Gehrig's record, *D.V.*" In this most resolutely secular and self-satisfied of ages, we seem to have lost the understanding that nothing in life is certain, that everything proceeds at the will of God or whatever higher power in whom or which one places one's belief or disbelief.

This is a pity not merely because it underscores the absence of both faith and humility in our lives but also because it diminishes our appreciation of what Ripken has done. In part this is hardly our fault. An accomplishment that requires nearly a decade and a half for completion tends to be taken for granted because of the sheer monotonous longevity of it all; no doubt medieval Europeans grew similarly blasé about the great cathedrals that rose in their midst, stone by stone, decade by decade. We cannot be expected to remain in a state of constant astonishment and thus to some extent must be forgiven the complacency with which we watch Ripken's consecutive games march steadily toward that historic number, 2,131.

But in playing every single game for more than thirteen seasons, Ripken has built himself—and us—a cathedral so monumental and amazing that what we should do in this hour of its completion is stand back and soak in the wonder of it all. What he has done defies not merely everything we know about the capacity of the human body and mind to withstand stress but everything implied in those words, "God willing." Any student of human experience knows that what is customarily willed by God, or fate, or whomever, is not surpassing strength and endurance but ordinary human weakness and fallibility.

Whether Cal Ripken is a religious person I do not know—given how much has been written about him, this itself is remarkable—but if he is, he must be tending sedulously to his prayers; if he is not, he must be thanking his lucky stars. During this season of Ripken's ascent to the pantheon of baseball's own deities, two of the game's other bright stars, Matt Williams of the San Francisco Giants and Ken Griffey Jr. of the Seattle Mariners, have seen their seasons ruined by precisely the sort of injuries that Ripken, over and over again, has been spared.

It's difficult to watch Ripken at play and not believe that the higher powers have given him special dispensation. Last Tuesday night at Camden Yards he took a full cut at a pitch and fouled it off his foot: fouled it off *hard*. Stoicism being the ballplayer's assigned lot, he showed little more than a flickering grimace, but when his time at bat was over he headed right for the clubhouse, a trainer close on his heels. The apprehension that rushed through the stands was palpable.

Yet at inning's end there was Ripken, buoyant and boyish as ever, dashing from the dugout, racing his teammates onto the field. Not a trace of a limp could be detected in his stride. If he felt pain—say it's so, Cal: Say that even *you* can feel pain—he didn't show it. Instead he played the game through to its conclusion and was back at the same old stand the following night, shaking off a blow that would have sent most ballplayers, not to mention most ordinary mortals, to the podiatrist and then to the disabled list.

Absolutely amazing: There are no other words for it. When it comes my time to look back over a happy lifetime and count its blessings, among the richest outside the immediate precincts of home and work will be the privilege of having been in attendance at the unfolding of Ripken's entire career. I was there for his first at bat, his first chance in the field, his first home run, and I will be there (*D.V.*) two nights hence to join in celebration of The Streak.

The pleasure that Ripken has afforded me takes two forms. One is Ripken the shortstop. If we have been guilty of taking his durability for granted, so too have we taken for granted his skills, which are at once brilliant and workmanlike. His streakiness as a hitter is a nice bit of fallibility that reminds us that he is, after all, human, but inconsistency at the plate has never led to inconsistency in the field. He covers everything, but with such consummate ease and lack of melodrama that we tend to forget just how good he really is. The other night when he got a ground hit through short, my first thought was, "That would never have gotten past *our* shortstop." I was right.

Then there is Ripken the man. The vogue phrase "role model" is hardly dignified enough to convey what Ripken is. The old-fashioned "exemplar" is more to the point. An exemplary person, the *Oxford English Dictionary* reminds us, is "of a kind liable to become an example: remarkable, signal, extraordinary." Cal Ripken Jr. is all of those things. He is modest, funny, generous, public-spirited, loyal, intelligent and fearless. If there is anything wrong with him, apart from an unfortunate tendency to hit into double plays, I do not know what it is. At a time when there is too little for which to cheer, he evokes for me the days when I loved baseball without qualification and rooted for my favorite players with innocent enthusiasm. Whether the coming great event will be the last time I find it in me to cheer without restraint or reserve I do not know, but cheer I most certainly will. *Deo volente.*

BOONDOGGLE

❦

February 5, 1996

It should be obvious by now, to all save the venally self-interested or terminally self-deluded, that the case for highjacking the Cleveland Browns and spiriting them away to a publicly financed stadium in Baltimore has completely collapsed. It is clear that this undertaking enjoys little public support in Maryland generally and Baltimore specifically and that reports of its alleged economic benefits have been wildly exaggerated; we know as well, as many have known all along, that it is plainly and simply wrong. Yet it continues to enjoy the ardent backing of people and institutions in Maryland whose influence is wholly disproportionate to their numbers.

The immediate and most obvious beneficiaries of stealing the Browns from Cleveland are the team's owner, Arthur Modell, and the Maryland Stadium Authority and others connected thereto, the construction industry notable among them. Others prominently and noisily in favor of this state-sponsored theft are the governor of Maryland, Parris Glendenning; the Greater Baltimore Committee; and the *Baltimore Sun*'s editorial-page editors. In varying degrees, all of these have money, power and influence; what they do not have is popular support, so it will be interesting to see whether they will be able to bully the Maryland General Assembly into doing their bidding.

There is reason to hope that they will not. Last week seventeen of Maryland's forty-seven state senators—six short of a majority—introduced legislation that would undo the structure now in place for financing the $200 million cost of the Baltimore football stadium. On the day that they did so, a poll disclosed that this stadium is opposed by 62 per cent of Marylanders and 59 per cent of Baltimoreans; the poll also showed that Glendenning's scheme to spend $78 million of state funds to serve a privately financed Washington Redskins' stadium in Prince George's County is opposed by nearly 70 per cent of both Marylanders and Prince Georges residents.

That was last Tuesday. The next day another major load hit the fan: A study by Maryland's Department of Fiscal Services, which provides economic analyses to the legislature, reported that the lavish economic benefits of the Baltimore stadium as touted by Glendenning and others are largely fiction. It projected 430 to 689 new jobs, as opposed to Glendenning's 1,394; state and local taxes generated of $4–$7.5 million, as opposed to $9.2 million; an annual economic impact on the state of $27–$58 million; a cost for each job created of $98,858–$225,321, as opposed to $31,731.

The response of the stadium's supporters to this damning news was to circle the wagons and start sniping. The Greater Baltimore Committee, which previously had kept its own counsel, decided that "we should get into the fray," according to its director, Donald Hutchinson; the governor's communications director, John Frese, a former reporter for the *Sun*, said that "we need to do a better job of getting the message out"; and the *Sun* itself weighed in with a thunderous lead editorial.

This last is an extraordinary document, a piece of lunacy that surely startled even readers long accustomed to the *Sun*'s penchant for editorial-page self-righteousness. Under the headline "Third-rate or first-rate?" it begins with a wild exaggeration—"There is no better way to turn Maryland into a third-rate state than for the General Assembly to kill plans for a football stadium in Baltimore"—and then winds its way through one insupportable claim after another. Among them:

> Baltimore's downtown needs an NFL team because it brings in cash for restaurants, bars, hotels and shops. . . . If Maryland turns its back on the National Football League,

the rebuff will long be remembered nationally. . . . NFL teams are treasured because they stamp a city as first-class. . . . It would be a severe loss, felt for many years to come, if Maryland drops this touchdown pass.

Savor that final bit of editorial-page slumming in sports-page argot for a moment, then think about it: There isn't a shred of demonstrable truth in any of these assertions. Study after study in city upon city has shown that throwing public money into arenas for privately owned professional sports teams produces marginal benefits at best and entails immense costs, as well as diverting funds from public services of greater importance and broader effect. This is especially true of football teams, which play only eight regular-season home games each year and which bring in few visitors who spend significantly on hotel accommodations and restaurant meals.

The notion that Maryland's reputation in the business community will rise or fall on whether the state subsidizes a millionaire's football playpen is so outlandish as to defy rational rebuttal. It is the equivalent of saying that the University of Chicago enjoys no standing among serious educators because it abandoned big-time football, or that Baltimore's own Johns Hopkins University is a third-rate institution because it competes in small-time Division I-AA football.

Certainly it is true that Maryland has had its problems with business, but this has to do with high taxes and low incentives rather than with major-league sports. If Maryland wants to prostrate itself before business, why not do so directly? If the goal is to bring in new industry and investment, how on earth is that going to be accomplished by handing Arthur Modell the keys to the state treasury?

The plain fact of the matter is that apart from the greed and influence of special interests whose actual numbers are exceedingly small, there is no constituency in Maryland for this boondoggle. Nothing could possibly be more telling than the strong opposition to it within Baltimore. That city's heart was broken when its beloved Colts were stolen a decade ago, but its ordinary people know that what the movers and shakers want to do to Cleveland is exactly what was done to them—and they want no part of it. Baltimore wants a team, all right, but it wants its own team, not one with a rich tradition in another city.

If anything there is a stronger case for spending $78 million to keep Jack Kent Cooke happy in Prince George's County. At least he would only be moving from the District of Columbia to one of its fastest-growing suburbs, and at least he would be spending his own money on the stadium itself. But when one considers the strained resources of Maryland's treasury and the genuine needs of so many residents of this traditionally compassionate state, the mere thought of using public funds to beef up the bankrolls of millionaires whining about their entitlements is outrageous. May those seventeen rebellious state senators go forth and multiply.

COMMON THEFT

❦

March 25, 1996

What happened in the Maryland General Assembly last Thursday was a foregone conclusion, had been a foregone conclusion since Day One in the fall of 1995, when it was revealed that Maryland had bribed the owner of Cleveland's Browns into forsaking that city and setting up shop in Baltimore. It was clear from the outset that if more bribes had to be paid in order to close the deal, paid they would be; pay them is what the governor and his legislative henchmen did last week.

Thus Baltimore now has a professional football team, though there is little evidence that this particular team—not to mention this particular owner—is the one that the football lovers of that city had wanted. As an added bonus, Prince George's County now has a team as well: the Washington Redskins, spirited across the District of Columbia line by Jack Kent Cooke, a man of large accomplishment whose vision seems to have shrunk in his late years to little more than luxury boxes, parking lots and off-ramps.

Much tumult and shouting was staged in opposition to these two preposterous projects, some of it in this space, but surely few making the noise really believed that it would come to anything. As a reporter for the *Baltimore Sun* wrote last week, "Leadership, with its financial power and its ability to confer favors, almost always wins." Although "leadership" is not a word often associated with the mush-mouthed Parris Glendenning it remains that he occupies the governorship and that its powers of bullying persuasion are considerable.

Bullying is exactly what went on last week. Legislators from Montgomery County, where the most vocal if not most dedicated opposition to the stadiums had been centered, were bought off with $36 million for school construction, money that would not be forthcoming unless they swallowed their "principles" and voted for the stadium scam. Next thing you know they will be swallowing their "principles" and voting for slot machines at the state's horse-race tracks and casinos at Ocean City or—why not?—Smith Island.

The entire episode should, though doubtless will not, be a useful lesson for those members of the punditocracy who of late have wondered why it is that Americans have grown so cynical about government. The causes most commonly advanced have to do with ethereal matters such as the ever-widening gap between the rich and everyone else, or the failure of government to deliver on its promises, or the suspicion that government favors certain groups in society to the exclusion of others. To one degree or another there is merit to all of these claims. But what about just plain bad, unrepresentative government?

It would be difficult to imagine a more brilliant example of same than the Cleveland Browns affair. The Redskins business, though not much more savory, is somewhat alleviated by the short distance the team will move, the small degree of inconvenience to be suffered by its customers, and the willingness of its owner to pay for his own playpen if not for the infrastructure attendant thereto. But the Browns business is another mess altogether; the Browns business is a blatant case of the positioned and privileged abusing the powers of government—not to mention flouting the will of the people—in order to feather their own nests.

As was previously noted here and elsewhere, polls taken over the winter showed a clear majority—generally 3-to-2—of Marylanders opposed to the stadium deals; even in Baltimore, where one might expect chauvinism to prevail over common sense, the same majority opposed the Browns deal. Newspaper

and broadcast stories repeatedly found widespread and often bitter opposition, not merely because people thought there were
better ways to spend the state's money but because there was surprisingly general agreement that stealing the Browns from Cleveland was an injustice in which Marylanders did not care to take
part.

The Browns deal had everything against it. Not merely
were the people of the state clearly opposed, but it soon became
self-evident that the governor and his gofers had cooked the
books in order to make the transaction seem more beneficial to
the state than it possibly could be. The argument that a football
team staked to a $200 million park in Baltimore would improve
the state's "business climate" was specious on its face. Beyond
that, the dependence of the deal upon funds raised through state
lotteries meant that the money to keep Arthur Modell on Easy
Street would be extracted from the pockets of low- and middle-
income Marylanders whose gambling habit the state has sedulously encouraged.

It was a stinker on all counts, but it's a done deal now. That
is because government functioned in its non-representative mode,
mocking both the will and the interests of the people in order to
fatten the pockets of the rich: not merely Modell but also the
contractors and the other businesspeople who will band together
to construct and operate the stadium. Thanks to the "personal
seat license" fees that will be charged to season-ticket holders few
ordinary Marylanders will be able to afford to see the team play,
and the jobs that the stadium will bring their way will be marginally remunerative ones in the concession stands and ticket booths,
but then ordinary people were never part of the equation.

It will be said in rebuttal that government works this way all
the time, that this is the way of the world, and indeed this is so;
that's why it was said up front that last week's vote was a foregone
conclusion. But one would have to look long and far to find a
more repellent instance of cynical, non-representative, special-interest government than this one. It smells as sweet as a three-
weeks-dead skunk in the middle of the road, and one can only

hope that the stink still lingers the next time Maryland goes to the voting booth.

In this corner, that's that; the say has been said and the subject is closed. What a pity it turned out this way. As a loyal resident of Baltimore, I had wished ever since the theft of the Colts in 1984 for a return of pro football to the city, not out of any personal interest but because the team had meant so much and its loss had been such a blow. A new team honestly wooed and won would have had my enthusiastic support. But the still-unnamed team the city is now getting—what about Baltimore Burglars?—gets no cheers from me at all, and I very much doubt that I am alone.

CHILDISH THINGS

March 1 1 , 1 9 9 6

The collegiate basketball competitions with which the nation is afflicted at this time of year are, so we were informed last week by the *New York Times*, not so much basketball games ad nauseam but "male-bonding rituals" during which "fans in the stands are boys again." Balding, paunchy alumni crawl out of the ruts their lives have become and are once again "immersed in bygone days, when there was no mortgage to pay, no employer to please, no burdens to bear."

Clearly what we have here is journalism venturing to test its toes in the rank waters of sociology and pop psychology, and the temptation to make fun of it as such borders on the irresistible. But what we also have here is something that looks very much like the truth. How else are we to explain the madness that sweeps through middle-class America each March when schoolboys in their underwear compete to see who can toss more balls through souped-up peach baskets?

That observation may sound sour, but it is not thus intended. If allegedly adult human beings want to retreat for a few days into the cocoon of youth, if what gives them comfort is a weekend's beer binge reminiscent of frat days lost, if it really matters to them whether Ole Sasquatch is able to beat the spread, much less beat Semiotics State . . . if that is how they get their jollies at this desperate time of year when spring seems a dream more impossible than that of the 1969 New York Mets, well, more power to them and may they dream happily ever after.

Once it was my dream too. Several millennia ago it was my incalculably good fortune to enter the University of North Carolina just as college basketball was beginning to compete seriously with college football for the attention of the country's sporting gentry. Sitting in the wooden stands of Woollen Gymnasium one late fall afternoon in 1957, watching the national championship Tar Heels as they dashed out of their dressing room and onto the court where the previous season they had performed so many improbable heroics, I was just about as thrilled as any eighteen-year-old kid has any right to be, and I stayed thrilled for many years to come.

Inasmuch as most of my early adulthood was spent in North Carolina, it would have been astonishing had I felt otherwise. North Carolina is a great state, perhaps even the greatest state in the universe, but its adult population loses all perspective, common sense and equanimity when college basketball season rolls around. Grown men—lawyers by day, or bankers, or even medical doctors—wrap themselves in the colors of their alma maters and scream themselves bananas at the Atlantic Coast Conference tournament, surely one of the most ludicrous displays of adult infantilism this side of a political convention. Their wives—lawyers by day, or bankers, or even medical doctors—wave pompoms and sing school songs and give women of opposing affiliations looks that can, and sometimes do, kill.

For years I was a happy participant in this lunacy. My idea of perfect heaven was driving from Greensboro to Chapel Hill, stopping en route for barbecue at Allen & Sons, howling like the proverbial banshee as the Tar Heels turned State or Wake or Duke into peanut butter, then rehashing the whole business during the jubilant drive home. At the time I was in my late twenties and early thirties and could be forgiven.

But many years have passed, and with them has come much change. Some for the better, some for the worse. The great stain on North Carolina basketball in my youth was that it was a white boys' game; one need not be Sherlock Holmes to deduce that this is true no longer. On the other hand, college basketball is now a very big business, one that is no less loath to exploit players than is college football, and one that—for me if for no one else—has lost much of its power to give delight as it has become ever more commercialized and ever more divorced from the real life of the campuses it ostensibly represents.

These are matters that have been chewed over in this space in days gone by, to no apparent consequence, and there can be no doubt that they have much to do with my disaffection from a game I once loved. But for me, as perhaps for a few of those reading this, a more telling explanation may be found in the words of one of those male bonders who spoke to the *Times* about the ineffable experience of the Big East tournament.

"Because I see these kids," he said, "I remember I was young once." True enough: Me too. But as the years have crept along one after another and as I have acquired something bearing a filial resemblance to maturity, I find that on the ever less frequent occasions when I see "these kids," I am reminded that I am a kid no longer, that the games of youth are more interesting to me as memories of yesterday than as momentous encounters of today. At the risk of sounding terminally stuffy, I am reminded that when I became a man, I put away childish things.

Lord knows it took long enough. Only a few weeks ago I half-watched on television as the Tar Heels made stirring comebacks against various opponents, though admittedly I snored through some of those comebacks. But a week ago, without even knowing it, I cut the cord completely. Last Sunday afternoon I took a walk, read a book, worked on a model ship, did the things people usually do on a cool, quiet Sunday. Not until quite late that evening did I realize, with a mild start, that it had not once crossed my mind to turn on the Duke-Carolina game and that—*mirabile dictu*!—I did not care who had won it.

This wasn't the Rubicon I crossed, just the last bridge into adulthood. Yes, readers familiar with what goes on in this corner will object that I retain a residual affection for the Baltimore Orioles even after baseball's recent, self-afflicted troubles, which is perfectly true; I will admit that it is good to see video clips out of spring training, to contemplate the Orioles in their putative glory, to believe that someday the temperature may actually climb to sixty degrees. Baseball does that to me. But big-league baseball is a game played by semi-grown-ups who are paid—to put it mildly—for their labors. College basketball, like college football, is boys paid under the table, or not at all, to perform for the pleasure and profit of adults. One consequence of growing up is that this no longer seems acceptable to me, and certainly is no longer anything to cheer about. Pardon me, boys, but I'll skip the bonding this time around.

THE FATCATS' GAME

⤙⤚

October 14, 1997

At the end of a long several months in which there have been more interesting and important matters to attend to than major-league baseball and its various self-inflicted crises, it is pleasant all the same to reach the middle of October and have a contest for the American League pennant between two engaging teams representing two engaging cities. As it happens, there is more to this postseason activity than baseball; there is also evidence of how baseball has changed and, for whatever it may be worth, an explanation for why my own interest in it has declined so precipitously in recent years.

The second of these matters is intimately connected to the first. Had baseball—Baltimore Oriole baseball, too—not changed so much since 1979, it seems safe to assume that my own interest in it would not have changed so much either. Through my youth and into my early middle age, baseball was a constant; relatively minor alterations in its character such as divisional playoffs and the designated hitter took place, but the game itself and the atmosphere in which it was played remained the same, and so did my allegiance.

Now all has changed. Free agency, welcome and long over-due, had the expected effect of driving players' wages to exorbitant heights and the unanticipated one of severing players' loyalties to teams and the cities they represent; loyalty was never very high in baseball's priorities, but now it is so uncommon as to be genuinely remarkable when it occurs, as in the celebrated example of Cal Ripken Jr. "The Oriole Way" and "Dodger Blue," sentimental phrases but accurate representations of old-fashioned, work-ethic constancy, have been replaced by here today, gone tomorrow, as practiced both by players forever on the run and front offices trying to keep costs under control.

Two other aspects of the game are vexing and offputting. One, which has been bemoaned here before, is the excruciatingly slow pace at which it is played. This is not a matter of baseball's allegedly relaxed, rustic character; in the days when baseball was far closer to its country roots, games routinely were played in under two hours. Now they commonly take more than three, sometimes much more, at a pace that is not agreeably measured but merely dull. This is explained in part by the long between-innings delays mandated by television commercials, but far more by the dilatory behavior of managers, coaches and players and by the steadfast refusal of umpires to enforce the game's time limits.

The umpires not merely officiate the game, which they are supposed to do, but they interpret its rules arbitrarily, capriciously and highhandedly, which they are not. There are as many strike zones as there are umpires to call them. If I persistently, willfully ignored and violated the rules of grammar, the ethics of journalism and the stylebook of the *Washington Post*, I would be fired, as I should be. But within the culture of baseball it is assumed that each umpire is a law unto himself—responsible, apparently, to no one save himself—and that this is as nature itself dictates. The result is a condition bordering on anarchy, in which one can only guess from one pitch to the next what the rules actually are.

These, I had thought for some years, were the reasons for my gradual withdrawal from the game I once loved. But in recent days it has dawned on me that deeper changes have taken place, that not merely the game but the cocoon in which it is played has changed, and not for the better. No doubt my perspective on this is strongly influenced by my own years in Baltimore and my abiding affection for that city, but no doubt as well there are many others in other cities—Cleveland, to take the most obvious and immediate example—whose testimony would be similar.

It is no exaggeration to say that when I began attending

Orioles games in 1979, baseball was still a people's game. Seats in Memorial Stadium were plentiful and reasonably priced, and most of those who sat in them were ordinary Baltimoreans. Their relationship with the team was complex; they loved it dearly and venerated its players, yet attendance was so low that the team's relocation was always a real possibility. But they knew their baseball, appreciated hard effort even if the results were not always commensurate with it, and were generous in their affection and admiration for all players.

In the third game of this year's first playoff round, by contrast, the Oriole relief pitcher Terry Mathews was greeted upon his arrival at the mound in Camden Yards with boos and catcalls so vicious as to defy comprehension. It is true, as Mathews himself readily admits, that he does not resemble a baseball Adonis and that he had a few bad outings late in the season, but this vituperative, hateful response was shameful, a civic embarrassment. In the days that follows, it turns out, Mathews "received numerous letters from people, most of them in the Maryland area, just letting me know" they were on his side.

Perhaps not too much should be made of "most of them in the Maryland area," yet Mathews's remarks appeared in the *Baltimore Sun* on the same day last week that the *Washington Post* ran a front-page story about the heavy attendance at Orioles games from the Washington area. It quoted a longtime Orioles fan as saying, "These are not the people I went to Orioles games with when I was a kid," and it paraphrased a ticket broker in Reston who "said Washingtonians account for closer to 40 per cent of Orioles attendance, especially when the team is winning."

Perhaps not too much should be made of "especially when the team is winning" either, yet one doesn't need a degree in sociology to figure out that there's a huge difference between Baltimore's old-shoe culture and Washington's frontrunner culture. Obviously many of those who drive from Washington to Camden Yards are just as ordinary and old-shoe as thee or me, but many have too much money, too little patience and absolutely no connection with what baseball once was and what Baltimore still is.

Waxing indignant or sentimental about this is pointless.

The big-bucks ambiance of Camden Yards is a direct outgrowth of the free market in baseball talent, and the price all of us have to pay to keep baseball alive. The post-1979 ownership of the Orioles, from Edward Bennett Williams to Eli Jacobs to Peter G. Angelos, would have been foolish and irresponsible had it failed to attend so sedulously to today's realities. But this doesn't mean all of us have to march in lockstep. Me, I'm watching the Orioles and Indians on television, confident that whichever proves the winner, it will be a good team from a good place. They're just not playing my game any more.

SAYONARA

❧

November 10, 1997

"I want to make it very clear that the control of the ball-club is in Baltimorean hands." With those words Peter G. Angelos presented himself four years ago as the new majority owner of the Baltimore Orioles, as a homegrown Lochinvar riding to the rescue, wresting his fair city's crown jewel from the grasping hands of a buyer with—horrors!—a New York City address. At the time the news looked great, and was treated as such in this space. But a lot can happen in four years, and a lot most certainly has.

A lot, too, has been said and written about the latest Angelos caper, his disdainful, contemptuous treatment of the ballclub's manager, Dave Johnson, and what we can now see as its inevitable result: Johnson's resignation under merciless pressure from what he clearly regarded as the best of all possible jobs. Nowhere, to the best of my knowledge, has this chain of events been applauded, and nowhere does Angelos now seem to be seen as he clearly sees himself, as the savior of all things Baltimorean.

He'll get no applause here. For four years I have watched with mounting astonishment as Angelos, who once seemed so bright an adornment to Baltimore's firmament, has staged a display of petulance, arrogance, touchiness, willfulness and capriciousness not seen locally since the departure of William Donald Schaefer from the mayor's office. A city that thought the glory days of "The Oriole Way" would return with local ownership has been sorely disappointed and, judging by news reports last week, no longer holds any affection for the endlessly self-regarding Angelos. What we have now is not "The Oriole Way" but "The Angelos Way," and it's a sorry substitute.

"The Oriole Way" was once as deeply ingrained in the character of the Orioles as a civic inferiority complex is ingrained in that of the city they represent. Cal Ripken Jr. makes indirect reference to it in the title of his fine autobiography, *The Only Way I Know*, defining it as "the knowledge learned over a long period of time of the best way to teach and play baseball—or, if not the best way, as good as any."

It was born of necessity. From their arrival in Baltimore in 1954 by way of St. Louis until the beginning of their present prosperity in 1979, the Orioles had to make do with small revenues from small attendance in a small market. Thanks to the likes of Paul Richards, Larry McPhail, Hank Bauer, Hank Peters and Earl Weaver, the Orioles became the American League's dominant team by bringing players up through their own system, steeping them in the game's innumerable fundamentals, requiring strong loyalty to the organization and returning it in kind.

The result, beginning with the team that won a most unlikely World Championship in 1966 and holding steady through the one that fell a single game short in 1979, was a succession of Oriole clubs that had a few star players and highly competent supporting casts. The 1979 club, which gave me the happiest baseball hours of my life, was typical: Mike Flanagan, Scott McGregor, Ken Singleton and Eddie Murray on the front lines, John Lowenstein, Don Stanhouse, Dave Skaggs, Rick Dempsey and Pat Kelly bringing up the rear. Good men all.

"The Oriole Way" was about many things, but mainly it was about character. The players worked hard, kept their egos in check—if there's ever been a more admirable, decent ballplayer than Ken Singleton or Mike Flanagan, I'd like to hear about him—and played as a *team*. The audiences before which they performed may have included too many empty seats, but those who showed up knew baseball and understood two important things: that the character of these teams was precious and that it reflected, in some degree, the character of the city itself.

I've written about that before, doubtless in a sentimental fashion, and won't do it again today. Suffice it to say that "The Oriole Way" began to fall apart during the successive ownerships of Edward Bennett Williams and Eli Jacobs. The former—sly, funny, irresistibly engaging, obsessed with power and influence—wanted to move the club to Washington but for various reasons found his hands tied; "The Oriole Way," implying as it does self-effacement and workaday anonymity, just wasn't his way. It wasn't Jacobs's, either; he was a cold fish whom the city must thank for much that it loves about Camden Yards but who knew absolutely nothing about baseball and provided no useful leadership.

Not all the changes that took place in the Orioles during the reigns of these men can be blamed on them or those who worked for them. Baseball was changing, and Williams and Jacobs were smart enough to go with its flow: expanding the team's market to include Washington and Northern Virginia, installing skyboxes and other revenue-producers to underwrite the immense salaries that even bench-warmers now command. To give the devil his due, much about the Orioles that many now assume to be the doing of Peter G. Angelos was in place, or well on the way to being there, long before he seized command.

But it's his team now, and he's obviously determined that its character will reflect his own. This requires us to reflect a moment upon the making of Angelos's fortune, which was earned by representing mostly blue-collar workers, in industrial Baltimore and elsewhere, whose employers had exposed them to asbestos, the debilitating effects of which for a long time were known to few. Climbing one's way to a skybox at Camden Yards on the backs of the proletariat is probably no uglier than ditto with leveraged buyouts or video rentals, but the qualities it suggests—combativeness, legalistic pettiness, greed—are not exactly those of "The Oriole Way."

The odd thing about Angelos is that he really seems to want to run the club right, but doing so runs against his grain. As the saying goes, he talks the talk but he doesn't walk the walk. He is, as the *Baltimore Sun* pointed out in a thoughtful editorial last week, "a walking, talking, flesh-and-blood contradiction," whose longing for "a legacy as rich and warm and grand as Baltimore" is "being dragged to earth by his own cold, petty distractions." Incapable, apparently, of self-criticism or self-doubt, he is equally incapable of responding judiciously to criticism or doubts expressed by others.

Thus it is quite impossible to believe that these words, or any others said or written since last week's melodrama, will sway Angelos from the course he is determined to pursue. That's his choice. Mine is to take a hike. "The Angelos Way" is not my way.

✺

SIX

AVE ATQUE VALE

✺

WALKER PERCY

⌇⌇

May 1 4 , 1 9 9 0

Walker Percy called his second novel *The Last Gentleman*, but that distinction belonged to Percy himself. As the obituaries have pointed out, he was a splendid writer—a deft and witty stylist, a thinker of depth and originality, a passionate believer in domestic love and other quiet virtues—but he was if anything an even more splendid human being; it is about this, upon the unhappy occasion of his death, that I wish to say a few affectionate words.

I make no claim to have known Percy well or to have been an even marginally consequential part of his universe. We had one of those brief friendships that are brought about by circumstances and wither away once those circumstances have altered. In looking back at the mementos of our friendship I am startled to realize that it occurred nearly two decades ago, and that in all those intervening years I saw Percy only one more time; yet my recollections of that distant time are as vivid and pleasant as any in my memory.

It is with no pride that I confess to having come late to Percy's work. In the fall of 1961 a friend pressed upon me a copy of his unknown first novel, *The Moviegoer*, some months before it became the quite unexpected winner of a National Book Award; but I was too callow to appreciate the book's subtleties, and remained so for many more years. Not until 1971, when I reviewed Percy's third novel, *Love in the Ruins*, did the full weight of his accomplishments dawn upon me; with the zealotry of the belated convert, I then joined his most ardent partisans.

A year later I received what seemed to me an astonishing document: an invitation to be a judge for the 1973 National Book Award in Fiction. To a thirty-three-year-old journalist working on a small newspaper in North Carolina, this seemed a summons from heaven, and I accepted with stunned alacrity. The greatest astonishment, though, was yet to come. A few weeks later a second missive arrived from New York, this containing the names and (!) home addresses of my fellow judges. I could scarcely believe my eyes: Evan S. Connell Jr., Leslie Fiedler, William H. Gass and, yes, Walker Percy.

If ever there was a pygmy among giants it was me. I hadn't a clue about how to behave among such eminences, but in the months to come, as books steadily poured in from New York and as the silence of my fellow judges grew ever louder, I realized that someone had to take the lead. I began to send out round-robin letters with lists of books I thought worthy of consideration for the award and I urged my fellow judges to do the same; this, miraculously, they did, so that by the time we came to New York in late February of 1973 to choose the finalists for the award, each of us had a fair idea of what the others had in mind.

We met for lunch at the offices of the National Book Committee at 1 Park Avenue. Fiedler and Gass were old friends, but the rest of us were strangers. Providentially—in all senses of the word—a bar was at hand, so we repaired to it and in short time established the amenities. We had lunch and set upon our deliberations, but before we began Percy said, "Since Mr. Yardley went to the trouble to get us in touch with each other, shouldn't we elect him chairman?" This time it was my ears I couldn't believe; but the others immediately assented, and suddenly I was in charge of the show.

A few months later Percy told me: "What was odd was (1) no group has ever gotten along better and (2) no group has ever been more divergent in its opinions." How right he was. From our first conversations in February until our final ones in April, we got along famously, and agreed about almost nothing. That we managed to settle upon a dozen finalists was a tribute more to our shared desire that each juror have his preferences represented than to our ability to find common literary ground. We were as odd a literary quintet as has ever been assembled, and what's odder is that we knew it and delighted in it.

Our second and final official meeting took place on the evening of April 9, at a round table—not *the* Round Table—in the Rose Room of the Algonquin. I have the bill before me: $145.55, a scandalous sum by the standards of the day, much of it going for four pricy bottles of French wine. (Later Percy offered to buy me some cheap red wine "in return for that $10 Pommard you laid on us—no wonder the NBC is broke.")

We got right down to business. Percy and I voted for Eudora Welty's *The Optimist's Daughter*, Connell for John Williams's *Augustus*, Fiedler and Gass for John Barth's *Chimera*. In very little time it became clear that no single book could get five votes; we decided, for better or worse, to divide the award. Percy and I, less determined in defense of our candidate than were the others, ended up the losers. The 1973 National Book Award for Fiction went to *Augustus* and *Chimera*.

When it fell to me as chairman to announce the award the next day, there was much hissing and booing. On April 11 the *New York Times* called the divided award "an unprecedented display of public disagreement" and said—heaven knows where this piece of misinformation came from—that "the meetings of the five fiction judges had been noisy and argumentative." This more amused than irritated my fellow judges, but what especially tickled Percy was that the *Times* described me as a "courtly young Southern critic"; he ribbed me about it for weeks.

After handing out the awards on April 12 we took our two winners out for drinks and decided we'd done all right; Percy and I agreed that we liked the men better than their books, and with characteristic courtesy Percy worried that the passing furor over the divided prize might somehow diminish the pleasure that Barth and Williams clearly took in it. Then the next morning we flew off to our distant residences, all of us relieved that a difficult job was over, but all of us I believe quite genuinely sorry that we had no further cause to meet.

In the ensuing years Percy and I stayed sporadically in touch. His letters were short, funny and kind. When I sent him a copy of my first book, not in hope of favors but as a gesture of friendship, he responded with a note so generous that it made me feel the entire enterprise had been worth all the trouble and uncertainty it entailed; for more than a dozen years that note has hung, framed, above the desk where these words are written, as prized a possession as any I own.

Downstairs, on a shelf in the living room, stands the other cherished memento of this brief friendship that has meant so much to me. It is a paperback copy of *Love in the Ruins* that came quite unexpectedly in the mail one day in the late spring of 1973. On its flyleaf Walker had written these words:

> To Jonathan—
> Here is, I swear, the first paperback off the press—
> To Jon, best of all judges (of wine anyhow) and books too—then how come, with the 2 best minds in the South, we didn't do better?
> Come to Louisiana—Walker

FREDERICK EXLEY

✑

June 29, 1992

In death as in life, Random House picked up the tab. For two decades the publishing firm had subsidized Frederick Exley out of the old-fashioned conviction that his novels were worth supporting even if they did not sell; the total outlay must have run into scores of thousands. Then, last week, Random House shelled out a few hundred more for a small, black-bordered announcement on the daily book page of the *New York Times*: Exley, aged sixty-three, was dead.

The news shouldn't have come as a shock, but it did. We had fallen out of touch. It had been three or four years since the phone had rung at some odd, inconvenient hour, bringing Exley's slurred voice and raucous complaints back into my life. He was writing mystery novels, he claimed in the last of these foggy conversations, or he was going off to Hawaii with some new bimbo, or some God-forsaken book reviewer had stabbed him in the back ... I don't remember; Exley's phone calls tended to dissolve into a blur.

He made them at all hours and to Lord knows how many people. From time to time I'd run into someone at a party or a meeting and somehow it would come out that both of us were hooked into Exley's network. Comparing notes, invariably we'd end up trying—and failing—to answer the essential question: Was he always drunk, or did he just sound that way?

That's what killed him, of course, and that's why the news of his death should have come as no shock. Fred Exley had been drinking himself to death for four decades, so the real surprise was that he had made it all the way to sixty-three. Yet there had seemed something inextinguishable about him, or perhaps it was something indistinguishable in us: The belief, or the hope, or the wish, that he could once more write a book as good as his first.

Its title is *A Fan's Notes*. A fictionalized memoir of "that long malaise, my life," it was published in the fall of 1968. I carried it off with me then on a year's academic sabbatical, but my colleagues beat me to it. They read it in great gulps of admiration, as soon enough I did too. We became the first of Exley's cults. We went back to our jobs in 1969 and started to write about him, in newspapers from Florida to New York to North Carolina to California; we were, Exley told me once, the "intellectually elite," though I think he had his tongue in his cheek.

That phrase occurs in the first of about a dozen letters I received from him; I sensed that he wrote when he was sober and phoned when he was drunk, which is why there were so many more calls than letters. Somehow he had learned that I was at work on a "reconsideration" of *A Fan's Notes* for a magazine, and he had called a few days before to inquire about it; now he was writing, in the clear hope that he could orchestrate the timing of the piece to his best advantage.

In this respect as in so many others, he was an odd and contradictory man. He detested the raw politics of the literati and kept himself mostly aloof from their maneuverings, yet he wasn't above putting in a good word for himself. He wasn't one of those writers who only calls or writes just as a new book is about to come out, but he believed passionately in his work, ached to the very center of his soul over the neglect under which he labored, and wanted so desperately to find readers that he had no compunction about smoothing his path in any way possible.

In the event it was all wasted motion, for there was a basic fact over which Exley had no control: Readers loved and hated his work with equal intensity, and it was strictly a roll of the dice as to where the review copies landed. His second book, *Pages from a Cold Island*, had the misfortune to find its way into the hands of Alfred Kazin, whose censorious review for the *New York Times*

Book Review cut Exley to the quick; the phone lines smoked and sputtered for weeks, but none of Exley's boozy profanity could undo what Kazin had done.

Did Exley yearn for a place on the best-seller lists and damn fate—or Kazin—for denying him one? Perhaps so; most American writers do. Yet he wanted readers more than money, admiration more than celebrity. Quite apart from the funds he required to keep the distilling industry operating at full capacity, his needs seemed to be relatively modest. If he wanted a trip to Hawaii or the Super Bowl he could usually find a magazine to underwrite it—though he rarely produced a piece in return—and friends were always happy to house and feed him.

His deeper need was for acceptance and friendship and praise, which is why he was on the phone all the time. His life, like his books, was a struggle against what he considered a meaner trick fate had played on him than mere neglect: "I understood, and could not bear to understand, that it was my destiny—unlike that of my father, whose fate it was to hear the roar of the crowd—to sit in the stands with most men and acclaim others. It was my fate, my destiny, my end, to be a fan."

Exley pursued that theme through all three of his books. In *A Fan's Notes*, he wrote about how the heroics of Frank Gifford, the football star, "had sustained for me the illusion that I could escape the bleak anonymity of life"; in *Pages from a Cold Island*, he evoked the "real literary life" as exemplified by Edmund Wilson, who lived a few miles away in upstate New York; in *Last Notes from Home*, he described his complicated relationship with his older brother, fallen honorably in military service.

His themes were large, but only in *A Fan's Notes* did he give them full expression. The almost certain truth is that he was that most frustrating of literary creatures, a one-book writer, but unlike many others thus afflicted he struggled to do more. It was a struggle that aroused deep sympathy among his readers and friends. I admit without chagrin that my reviews of his last two books were more favorable than my actual judgment, not as a favor to a friend—it would be presumptuous to claim friendship with a man I never met—but out of a desire to give him encouragement: to help push him over whatever great obstacle it was that kept him from ever again reaching the heights he had attained in *A Fan's Notes*.

That he failed to do so pained him deeply; the title of his last book should be read for what it is, a sad, weary declaration that he had said all he had to say, that he was spent. Yet to conclude from this that his life was sad, that he was a failure, seems to me utterly unwarranted. The obvious reason is that he wrote *A Fan's Notes*, a book unique and durable that will be read long after his brief obituary notices have faded. It is a piece of classic Americana: a minor classic, no doubt, but one with its own distinct place in our literature. Most writers, knowing they had left so substantial a monument, would die happy.

A second reason is that he had a hell of a good time. The boozing was a pity and a waste, but it was his choice and he lived with it, just as he died by it. He had a great many friends, some just telephone friends but many others real ones, and they cherished him as greatly as he cherished them. In his quirky, sloppy fashion he was loyal and generous, as many writers whose work he liked and publicly supported would be quick to attest.

But the most important thing about Fred Exley is that he lived what he believed. Writing was incalculably important to him. He accepted gladly the "apartness, confusion, loneliness, work, and *work, and work*" that serious writing demands, and he applied himself to the task with true devotion. That he fell short of his aspirations is self-evident, but so too are the honor and dignity of his labors.

LAURIE COLWIN

❦

November 2, 1992

The friends of Laurie Colwin gathered at Amsterdam Avenue in New York last week on a morning when her favorite city was bathed in brilliant sunlight. As can be imagined by anyone who has read any of Laurie's books, a large hall was required for this assembly; it was filled to overflowing. What is far more difficult to imagine is the occasion: The place was the Riverside Memorial Chapel and the event was Laurie's funeral.

Even now, more than a week after her death, this loss remains incomprehensible to those of us so privileged as to have known and loved her. She was, when she failed to wake from slumber on the morning of October 24, a mere forty-eight years of age and, so far as anyone knew, in vigorous health. She had recently completed two manuscripts—her ninth and tenth books—and had seen them on their way to her publisher. She had been, when last we talked, as sassy and ebullient and affectionate as ever, full of chatter about books and authors and, most particularly, about her beloved young daughter, Rosa.

Small wonder then that those of us who came to the Riverside had upon our faces stunned, bewildered looks. Never have I been in a room so saturated with shock and grief. A couple of days earlier one of Laurie's friends, trying to find comfort in the unacceptable, had said that hers had been "a merciful death," because it had come without warning or pain, and perhaps this is true; but none of us was having any of that on Tuesday morning. Laurie had been taken away from us for no good or explicable reason and all we wanted was to have her back, no questions asked.

What a joy she was! On the train to and from New York I re-read some of her stories, rejoicing once again in the piercing wit, terrifying wisdom and bottomless human sympathy with which every page of them is suffused. She was, as her kind and gentle husband, Juris Jurjevics, said at her funeral service, a master of the "comedy of manners"; the intensely loyal readership she accumulated over the years was testimony enough to the enduring pleasures such comedies afford.

Laurie knew that the line between joy and sorrow can be so fine as to be indistinguishable, but she set herself on the side of the angels. Her books had titles like *Family Happiness* and *Happy All the Time*. There wasn't an ounce of manipulative or false sentiment in them, but they celebrated those things in life that lift and gladden the heart. Like her heroine Polly Demarest in *Family Happiness*—"heroine" most certainly is the word—Laurie "believed that all people unless impeded wanted family, needed family, that family was what life was for," because:

> After all, family life was the mortar that kept the bricks together; the pitch that made the basket watertight; the chinking that kept out the wind and the weather. It was life itself, without an inch to spare. A person immersed in the realities of family life did not stop to ponder the meaning of life: that person was *in* life, up to his or her neck and beyond. The family was the beginning, the future, and the past. It protected the weak and the strong. It brought the like-minded together and gave the unalike a common cause. It gave shelter and hope.

Laurie's own family, as Juris reminded us at the service, had come to this country eleven generations ago, a fact of which she was deeply proud. Like Polly Demarest's, her people "were of old, old Jewish families, the sort that are more identifiably old American than Jewish." But however much pride and love she may have fastened on her forebears, her real family was in the tiny apartment on West 20th Street that she shared with Juris and

Rosa and in the vast extended circle of friends upon whom she lavished attentions that were sometimes prickly, sometimes motherly, sometimes jocular, always loving.

She was born to be a mother, yet she waited nearly forty years to become one. When at last she did, she was consumed by it. "Our darling is home with us," she told me a month after Rosa's birth in the spring of 1984. "We are both a little sleep deprived but it is heaven to have our critter home with us." A year later: "She is *extremely* chatty and quite amazingly gorgeous which you are not supposed to say about your child but it is true." A few weeks later she sent a picture, which ever since has hung on the bulletin board above my desk; it shows Rosa in the arms of her mother, upon whose face is the look of perfect happiness.

It is a pretty face, though not a beautiful one; Laurie's real beauty lay in deeper places. She was short in stature and brisk in manner: "I love to shove around people who are older, taller, more distinguished and better educated than me." She had opinions the way rabbits have bunnies. Once, after subjecting me to two pages of heated remonstrance on literary matters, she drew a box across the middle of the page, in it wrote: "In my opinion," and then added: "I feel I should wear this embroidered on all my clothes."

Yet as liberally as she dispensed these opinions—she made a couple of cameo appearances in my columns as "my friend the ferociously opinionated novelist"—she did so without, at least to my knowledge, ever giving offense. Indeed, at the service last week every mention of her exuberant combativeness was greeted with wistful laughter. One of the qualities people so adored about her was the utter honesty with which she presented herself to the world; she loved to talk and to write, and she assumed that it was quite impossible to do either without letting the inner self come to the fore.

Not only that, but she got as good as she gave. Once, after reading her novel *Goodbye Without Leaving* in galley proofs, I wrote her a letter containing a somewhat lukewarm assessment of it. I heard nothing in return. This worried me, and I told her so. In reply she said my original letter no doubt had gotten lost in a pile of mail and then let the inner self have its say: "What I want in this world is some smart and decent criticism not adulation. What kind of girl do you take me for, anyway."

I never really told her what kind of girl I took her for, but I like to think she knew. She had a heart as big as the world; maybe it was too big, because it was her heart that killed her. It was big enough to take in not merely her family and her friends and her work, but those she scarcely knew. When homeless people started crowding the sidewalks of New York, she marched off to the Olivieri Center for Homeless Women and cooked their meals, cooking being yet another marvelous thing at which she was spectacularly gifted. When she and Juris enrolled Rosa at the City and Country School, she became its ardent if impecunious supporter: If she thought something was good enough to believe in, she assumed it was good enough to work for as well.

Her death is a terrible, insupportable loss. She should have lived at least another three decades: watching Rosa grow into womanhood, giving support and sustenance to her friends, writing a dozen more books. But fate, random and cruel as it can be, has chosen otherwise. So let us be grateful then, those who knew her and those who did not, that she left us her books, and let us be grateful all the more that by some miracle she was granted the time to leave us two as yet unseen. Through those books, she lives.

A banal sentiment, but true. The libraries of the world are filled with the living testaments of countless thousands long since gone. Laurie was proud, one of her friends said at the service, that all of her books are still in print; this is because Laurie knew that those books were her lasting presence in the world. They are her legacy and they are our consolation. Right now, though, that consolation is not enough. Dear girl, dear friend, the world is too much smaller without you.

PETER TAYLOR

୰

November 7, 1994

Three decades ago the name of Peter Taylor was as unknown to me as it was to all save a handful of Americans. Yet in the fall of 1964, as I set up residence in the Piedmont North Carolina city of Greensboro, it seemed that everyone talked about nothing except Taylor. What was going on? Had I stumbled across some quaint tribal form of author-worship? Who was this man and why were all these nice North Carolinians so mad about him?

Taylor, I learned over the ensuing months, had taught for a time at the University of North Carolina at Greensboro, formerly the Women's College of North Carolina. He was a friend of Randall Jarrell, who had lured him there and whom I had met briefly before his sudden and bizarre death. He was also the brother-in-law of James Ross, a splendid reporter on the Greensboro paper as well as a lapsed novelist, who in time became my close friend.

Eventually Taylor himself came to Greensboro, and part of the mystery began to clear. He proved to be a man of consummate charm and unceasing interest in the lives and minds of other human beings. He was two decades my senior but displayed, on the several social occasions when we met, nothing except a genuine egalitarian affinity for someone whom he apparently regarded as like-minded. To say that we became friends would press the truth for we saw each other insufficiently, but we were friendly acquaintances who held each other in mutual regard.

So it was at last that, pressed forward by my liking for the man, I began to read his work. It is no exaggeration to say that I was left stunned and exhilarated. Then as ever after, my admiration for Taylor the writer was almost entirely unrelated to my liking for Taylor the man. Here, simply, was a writer whose world was not my own and whose narrative voice possessed an elegance to which I could never hope to aspire, yet who spoke to my innermost self with a depth of feeling and psychological insight that I had never before encountered. I realized that I had found in Taylor what every reader longs for: my own writer.

Any other reader thus blessed will understand why it was that, when several telephone calls last Thursday brought the news of Peter's death, the world at once seemed a smaller place. At the death of a great artist—for that is what Peter Taylor most indisputably was—we are consoled by the enduring presence of the work and bereft at the certain knowledge that there will be no more of it beyond whatever posthumous snippets can be cobbled together to appease the faithful. Even though as I write these words I have before me a stack of Peter's books that will console and gladden me to the end of my own life, it is this sense of loss that permeates the moment.

In this instance the sense of loss is compounded by personal considerations. Though Peter and I had fallen out of touch over the past decade, in the way that people do when they do not know each other really well and no longer have occasion to see each other, it remains that the man as well as the writer was a vivid presence in my life and it is the man whom I now mourn. The writer can return at any moment when I open one of his books, but the man is gone forever.

As much as anything else, Peter will be missed by those so privileged as to have known him for the utter brilliance of his talk. This will come as no surprise to his readers, for his stories and novels are in fact highly literary conversations, but to encounter it in life was a delight and something of a miracle. Everything about Peter's conversation was animated: his voice, his hands, his amazingly expressive face. He loved to listen to stories and he loved to tell them. In his pronunciation the word emerged as *stOHry*; speaking the word he often lingered over it, stretching it out, savoring the pleasures and possibilities that lay ahead in the telling.

As a boy Peter had heard stories on porches in Nashville and in parlors in Memphis. They became the raw material out of which his work emerged. It is important to an understanding of the writer as well as the man that although these stories were autobiographical in both the familial and the communal sense, he refabricated and retold them with not an ounce of the solipsism so common in American literary fiction. Certain male characters in Peter's fiction have qualities that I suspect Peter sensed in himself, but his real interest lay in the lives of others.

It is inconceivable to me that Peter would be offended by the observation that he was more than incidentally a gossip. If anything he would have laughed and remarked self-deprecatingly about his fascination with the linen, soiled and otherwise, of others. But though he could be tough indeed when it came to their failings, he was far too aware of the inherent fallibility of humankind to pass judgment or assume moral superiority. His interest was kind rather than censorious; human faults were to be understood, even liked, rather than mocked or vilified.

As much as he loved human beings, he loved human habitations almost equally. Precisely how many houses he and his wife, Eleanor Ross Taylor, owned and occasionally inhabited during their long and fruitful marriage, I could not possibly guess; Eleanor herself no doubt would have to do research in order to provide the answer. Suffice it to say that they were numerous and far-flung, though mostly in Tennessee, North Carolina, Florida and Virginia. The last time I asked how many houses they owned at the moment they paused, consulted each other, and said seven, or so at least they thought. They bought, rehabilitated and sold houses for the sheer pleasure of it; this may have been an eccentric domesticity, but it was of a piece with the domestic themes that are the very core of Peter's writing.

Peter's kindness and abiding concern for others, combined with his long service in various places as teacher, compounded the domesticity of his own household with that of a large and passionately loyal following. He was loved widely and well. Some of those to whom he was mentor went on to accomplished writing careers of their own, while others merely cherished the personal acquaintance they had been given with literary genius; but all are bound by their devotion and gratitude to this remarkable man.

Never having been Peter's student and having an innate incapacity to become another man's acolyte, I was not one of these, though I would have been honored to have been. But in my files I find several letters from Peter, written in the late 1970s in response to my own first book. Not merely was he kind and generous to me; he also had read the book with real care, and had responded to it in ways that only the most sensitive of readers could. Those letters, I now realize, are the nearest I ever came to intimacy with Peter, and I treasure them as my private relics of him.

CALDER WILLINGHAM

⌇∽∽⌇

February 27, 1995

"**Y**ou patronizing nitwit": Thus began a letter I received two decades ago; it continued in this vein all the way to its end some seventy-five lines later. It was, unsurprisingly, an angry author's response to my review of one of his books. What may come as more of a surprise is that I welcomed the letter and the brief but intense correspondence that it initiated.

Its author was Calder Willingham, whose *The Big Nickel* I had treated coolly some months earlier in *The New Republic*. After praising Willingham as "one of the most skilled, observant and purely funny satirists of the postwar generation," I wrote that "*The Big Nickel* is barely coherent structurally, its characters sustain only marginal interest, and its conclusion is oddly sentimental," though I did find space to quote two paragraphs from a hilarious sexual encounter that was Willingham at his best.

Now Willingham is dead, of cancer at age seventy-two, which seems far too soon in this age of advanced medical mumbo-jumbo. As it turns out *The Big Nickel* apparently was his last novel, a sad final bow for the man who had written such distinctive books as *End as a Man*, *Natural Child*, *Eternal Fire*, *Geraldine Bradshaw*, *Providence Island* and, best of all, *Rambling Rose*. Precisely why Willingham was essentially silent for the last two decades of his life, save primarily for his delicious screenplay for the delicious film of *Rambling Rose*, is a mystery, but not, I think, one beyond solution.

Whatever its shortcomings, *The Big Nickel* was, I wrote, a

novel about "a solid, important theme," one that reverberates through the history of American letters: "early success and the burdens it imposes on American writers." Though Willingham seems not to have been an autobiographical novelist in the received sense of the term, there can be little doubt that in treating this theme he cut close to the bone. "Success is always dangerous," Willingham said according to his obituary last week in the *New York Times*, "and early success is deadly. What I went through writing my second book shouldn't happen to a dog."

The Big Nickel was Willingham's attempt to come to terms with the pain of writing *To Eat a Peach* after the prodigious success in the early 1950s of *End as a Man*, which was a best-seller, then a successful Broadway play, then (retitled *The Strange One*) a film, both of the latter starring Ben Gazzara. His success as playwright and screenwriter led Willingham to Hollywood, where his record bordered on the amazing: As well as *Rambling Rose*, achievement enough for anyone else, he wrote *Paths of Glory*, *One-Eyed Jack* and *Little Big Man*, and in the mid-1960s he turned a minor novel by an unknown writer named Charles Webb into *The Graduate*.

"I go to Hollywood purely for the money," Willingham said once, but it surely was more complicated than that. Whether his experience in the movies encouraged him in the more lurid and overwrought aspects of his fiction is impossible to say, but there can be no question that he explored them with passion and humor. The humor was usually scanted by the critics—"I bother critics," he said. "They can't seem to fit me into a neat little category"—but the passion attracted readers, who bought paperback copies of his novels by the hundreds of thousands.

Which leads us back to the beginning. Responding to the letter quoted briefly above, I wrote: "It must be almost as painful to be commercially successful and critically neglected as it is to be critically successful and commercially neglected." To this and what else I wrote, Willingham replied with an extraordinary document (certainly I have never received another even remotely like it), a sixteen-page single-spaced letter *plus* cover letter as well as a six-page defense of the fiction of Erskine Caldwell, which he thought superior to that of William Faulkner.

Willingham clearly regarded this missive as his statement of literary principles and his *apologia pro vita sua*. He said he hoped to publish it, along with his original letter and my reply thereto, in a collection of essays that he was in the process, or so at least he said, of assembling. Since that book is as yet unpublished, I would not presume to quote from this massive letter, but I have no doubt that one would look long and hard to find a more ardent expression of the misunderstood artist's hurt and anger. In every sense of the phrase, it is a *cri de coeur*.

Willingham took great pride in his work, as well he should have, because much of it is wonderful. Unfortunately his pride got all mixed up with defensiveness, and he made claims for his work that simply are not sustainable. But in what seems to me his essential point—that he had been made to pay in critical regard for his commercial success—he was absolutely correct.

The American literary community, whose approval Willingham sought even as he ridiculed it, cannot abide what William James so famously called "the bitch goddess SUCCESS." This disdain is fraught with hypocrisy for it is disdain born of envy, but that makes it no less painful for its victims. Willingham, who was fearlessly uncompromising in writing what he wanted rather than what literary fashion dictated, was one of these.

Whether this is the explanation for his marked decline in productivity after *The Big Nickel* probably was known only to him. A more mundane explanation may well be that having earned quite considerable fruits from his success, Willingham simply lost much of his drive; the same has happened to others thus blessed by fortune, and there is no shame in it.

My own judgment, for such pennies as it is worth, is that Willingham merely wanted what all of us want, both success and respect, and that it angered him beyond measure when the best he could do did not reap the latter as well as the former. His obituarist at the *Times* wrote that "many critics thought he failed to develop his early potential," but in that as in so much else they were wrong. He developed it all right, just not in the directions they demanded. At least a half-dozen of his books will be around for a long time, and *Rambling Rose* may well be with us forever.

He wrote brilliantly evocative prose, he could make a reader laugh out loud, his plots moved faster than Citation and he had interesting things to say. A body of work about which all this can be said is a legacy that only the rarest writers are permitted to leave.

J. Anthony Lukas

ᦞᦞ

June 9, 1997

On Thursday of last week my old friend J. Anthony Lukas—dear, beloved, incandescent Tony—died by his own hand. People who did not know Tony and who read news accounts of his death presumably assume that he killed himself because he feared that his forthcoming book, *Big Trouble*, was not—or would not be regarded as—up to the impossibly high standards set by his masterpiece, *Common Ground*. Perhaps. But that, however true it may be, is only part of Tony's heartbreaking story.

Tony was at once the happiest and the saddest man I have ever known. His energy and his enthusiasm were limitless; he loved many people and many things, with a boyishness that, in his six and a half decades, never deserted him. Yet for all his zest, for all his accomplishments, for all the praise and prizes that came his way, he was susceptible to spells of bleakness before which he was, in the end, helpless.

These had their roots in familiar sources: his innate self and his childhood experience. He was born in 1932. His early years seem to have been happy. His father was a prosperous New York lawyer, his mother a former actress. They and their two sons lived in Westchester County, on six acres that once had been farmland. He wrote about this a few years ago in a piece called "Surrogate Family," for a collection of baseball reminiscences by various writers called *Birth of a Fan*. It is a lovely essay, and an uncharacteristic one, for Tony was not comfortable with himself as subject. Yet he reached back into his memory and wrote:

Beautiful and talented as she was, my mother was a manic-depressive. Shortly after my birth, she tried to kill herself. On several occasions, she was confined for weeks to a mental hospital. Tortured by her illness and by his own self-doubts, my father drank too much. And he incubated the tuberculosis which emerged full-blown in 1941 shortly after my mother succeeded in killing herself.

Ever thereafter Tony longed for "a realm which made more sense than this one, a place in which beauty and virtue and talent were rewarded not by pain and death, but by the love and approbation they deserved," a realm he found in baseball. Writing this, Tony told me, had helped him come to terms with his mother's suicide. So he said. He may have believed it as well. But her death was at the core of his being, and the fear that it prefigured his own haunted all of his days.

This is why, when another cherished friend called with the terrible news, my shock and grief were alleviated, if that is the word for it, by a sense of grim inevitability. But the timing was all wrong. This was not the hour for Tony to die. His apprehension to the contrary notwithstanding, *Big Trouble* is a splendid book, a work of serious popular history that can stand confidently beside *Common Ground*; surely reviewers will confirm this, as will readers. Not merely that, but Tony had found a spectacular subject for his next book—New York City during the Civil War—and had swung into it with his customary passion.

No, during the three decades of our friendship the time when Tony seemed most vulnerable to his ghosts and demons was not now but a decade ago. *Common Ground* was published in 1985, received extravagant reviews, sold exceptionally well considering that it was a long, complex and pessimistic account of racial discord in America, and swept all the major literary prizes. Tony, who had a large but uncommonly tender ego, was thrilled with his success, yet even as he rejoiced in it, he saw the cloud on the horizon: He had to find another subject for another book, and he was terrified—no other word will do—that neither the subject nor the book he would make of it could meet the expectations *Common Ground* had aroused among its many devoted admirers.

For what seemed forever Tony brooded. To my knowledge he was not manic-depressive, but the state into which he descended can only be called depression. For hour upon hour—over the phone, at his house on Long Island, at mine in Baltimore, at a hotel room in Manhattan—we hashed and rehashed potential subjects, some of which seemed entirely feasible, all of which Tony discarded for one reason or another. He thought seriously, for example, about finding a dramatic malpractice case and following it through, using it as a device for depicting the war between two of the most venerable professions, medicine and the law; but he was squeamish, and feared he could not face up to the blood and suffering he might encounter.

It was during these long years that Tony seemed most likely to snap, yet he fought through. There can be no question that he was able to do so because, in his domestic if not his writing life, he had achieved happiness. At about the time *Common Ground* was published he married Linda Healey, a gifted and respected book editor then working at W.W. Norton. He ended a long succession of bachelor flats and bought, with Linda, an apartment on the Upper West Side, then a small house in Sag Harbor to which they retreated—in the company of their boisterous Norfolk terrier, Steunenberg—each weekend and at every other available moment.

Before Linda and domesticity, Tony's pleasures had been, like so much else about him, boyish. He was an accomplished pinball player whose feats were once written up in the *New Yorker*. He loved the music of his youth, the jazz of the golden age, the 1950s: Miles Davis, Erroll Garner, Dave Brubeck, John Coltrane. The Chesapeake Bay did not manufacture enough blue crabs to satisfy his appetite; he could spend hours bashing his way through bushels, crooning his approval of each morsel. Baseball was an enduring passion; he belonged to what he believed was the original Rotisserie League, as co-owner of a team called the Palukas, in which high responsibility he called me each March for a player-by-player analysis of the Baltimore Orioles' lineup, looking for potential Palukas.

Above all else in those bachelor days, Tony loved newspapers: not the media, *newspapers*. The work of his maturity rises far higher, but at heart he was always a gumshoe reporter racing toward deadline. Tony burrowing into a pile of newspapers was a Talmudic scholar; he especially loved visiting us in Baltimore, because there he could read the *Sun*, the first paper for which he worked, for which he retained a deep, nostalgic affection, and because he adored Baltimore itself. His feelings about the *New York Times*, where he established his reputation in the 1960s, were more complex; he was proud to have worked there, knew what it had meant to his career, reveled in gossip about its byzantine intrigues, but resented its restrictions on his coverage of the trial of the Chicago Seven in 1969 and 1970, resentment that ultimately led to his disembarkation from the mother ship.

None of these enthusiasms faded over the years; they simply were joined by others, after Linda entered his life. Furnishing the Sag Harbor house made him a passionate devotee of the American country style, so he spent countless hours—not to mention dollars—in the pricy antique shops of the Hamptons. Utterly maladroit in all matters mechanical—the house came with a pool, and for years Tony insisted on having a service do even the simplest of maintenance chores—he found his metier in the garden, where he worked contentedly for hours, coming in at cocktail time to regale his guests with tales of his plants and his lawn and his grand horticultural ambitions.

He looked for all the world like a happy man, but with Tony one never knew. Being his friend was infinitely rewarding, but rarely easy. We met in the fall of 1968 at Harvard, at the beginning of the academic year as fellows in journalism. It may seem strange that a strong bond was established between Tony, the newshound, and me, the editorialist (as I was then) and reviewer, but there's no accounting for friendship. That is what we had for nearly 30 years, with the exception of a hiatus in the 1970s following my rash decision to review one of his early books in a national publication; I admired Tony's reporting but took gentle exception to his interpretation of it, learning in the process that (a) Tony was no glutton for punishment and (b) one should never, ever review one's friends' books.

of whom we selected by reaching under a bush and pulling out whatever came first. To be sure the nice one turned out to have a nervous disease and was dead within a month while the nasty one had an incurable personality disorder, but so what? We'd done it the old-fashioned way, just the way Tom Sawyer and Becky Thatcher would have done it.

Eventually we ended up with a fine kitten who turned into a prodigious cat, but last winter cancer and heart trouble and God knows what else descended upon him all at once, and one evening he just couldn't stand up any more. We were heartbroken. The vet said we could probably find a replacement at one of the local animal shelters, information we received with a skepticism born of hard experience: The brown puppy we'd gotten from an animal shelter a dozen years before had died in my wife's arms three hours after we'd brought him home.

Still, after dawdling for nine months we went to the animal shelter anyway. Have you been there lately? It's a whole new ball-game. Twelve years ago we walked in, picked out a puppy, wrote a check for $15, and left. In the late summer of 1991 we went to the Humane Society of Baltimore County, picked out two kittens, said, "We'll take those home with us," and were told, "You'll take them home three days from now, after we've checked you out."

Turns out it's easier to get into St. Alban's or the Cosmos Club than to get a tiny feline time bomb from the 1990s version of the animal shelter. The animal-rights people have taken over, or maybe it's their first or second cousins. Whoever they are, they're sure of one thing: If you want one of their animals, you'd better be a combination of Roger Caras and Joy Adamson.

How do they find out? They call your veterinarian, to ask if you bring in your animals for regular checkups and routinely shell out $90 apiece for dental work; if you don't have a vet they probably ask your dentist if you floss. Not merely that, they insist on a character reference; our next-door neighbor, to whom we turned for this kindness, told us they kept her on the phone for nearly half an hour. Later we learned that in some jurisdictions, the animal shelter actually sends someone to check out your house, like the Internal Revenue Service doing an on-premises audit.

Want a male kitten? You can't take it home until it's old enough to be neutered, which means that if you pick out a two-month-old mouser, it has to stay in Kitty Purgatory for three months before you can take it home. Want to keep your kittens indoors and, for the sake of your furniture and clothes, have them de-clawed? You have to sit through a long lecture about how this deprives them of their basic animal rights, which leaves you feeling so guilty that (a) you let all your furniture and clothes go to hell or (b) you sneak out at night to some guy who pulls the claws out with a wire coat hanger.

We passed all the tests—heaven knows how—and three days after selecting our two young ladies we drove out to get them. After much disputation and consultation with outside authorities we had decided to name them Eudora and Vita, but someone at the Humane Society should have told us the truth: Their real names are Eva Peron and Margaret Thatcher.

So at least I have come to believe after a full month in their company. Why didn't the Humane Society tell us about this? Why didn't it remind us of what had long since been forgotten, to wit: If you want to raze your house, don't rent a bulldozer, just adopt a couple of kittens. As for being a newspaper columnist, forget it. Put one finger to the keyboard and *WHAM! BAM!* . . . There goes the neighborhood.

DON'T KNOCK

THE BLOCK

ᔕᕉᑌ

May 4, 1992

The Lord giveth and the Lord taketh away, and if for a moment you doubt that, come on over to Baltimore. Of late this most charming of cities has received a gift, the new baseball park at Camden Yards, the sheer exquisiteness of which has the local populace in a state bordering on ecstasy. But emotion of a quite different order will be stirred if, as seems likely, the city suffers a grievous deprivation only a few blocks away.

The city fathers and mothers have been urging it for years, always to no avail. Now they are on the verge of triumph. A bill before the City Council would prohibit what are euphemistically known as adult entertainment businesses in Baltimore's central business district as of July 1995, which in itself is a euphemistic way of saying that, assuming the bill passes, as of then The Block will be extinct.

Ah, The Block. To imagine Baltimore without The Block is scarcely to imagine Baltimore at all. For longer than even the most doddering Baltimorean can recall, The Block has stood, on East Baltimore Street between Gay and South Streets, as a living monument to the illicit pleasures of the flesh. Generations before the tame attractions of Harborplace lured Mr. and Mrs. America and their 2.5 children into downtown Baltimore, The Block was, as some anonymous editorialist for the *Baltimore Sun* put it (sniffily) last week, "an entertainment oasis for traveling salesmen, sailors and bachelor party revelers."

Some oasis! Some entertainment! Those polite words don't even hint at the radiant charms of The Block. Say instead that it is, in miniature, Sodom and Gomorrah multiplied by Times Square: a scruffy, disreputable, funky, racy strip of packaged passion right on the edge of the city's newly glamorized and distinctly sanitized downtown. As such it is of course anathema to the lawyers and stockbrokers and editorialists who work nearby and fancy themselves guardians of the city's morals. For years they have wanted to stamp it out; now, with all the world's eyes on Camden Yards and Harborplace and other downtown attractions, they seem to have acquired the impetus to have their way.

The bill that would obliterate The Block is, according to the *Sun*, "a timely legislative initiative" and "a step in the right direction," and perhaps indeed that is so. No doubt the gaudy lights of East Baltimore Street give offense to the eyes of tourists as they hasten up Gay Street en route to Interstate 83 and suburban points north; no doubt, too, The Block's shabby daytime mien—it looks as though the entire street has a hangover—will cause culture shock among future occupants of Commerce Place, a building now under construction nearby that is described reverently by the *Sun* as "a stately 30-story high-rise costing $90 million."

So The Block must go. It stands in the way of Progress and Uplift and Right-Thinking and The Civic Weal, not to mention The Almighty Dollar. It is smack in the middle of what the *Sun* calls "a desirable redevelopment area." As the *Sun* says: "Once the sleazy porno merchants leave, its existing buildings could easily accommodate a variety of badly needed retail shops, professional offices, restaurants and other service establishments."

Yes, indeed, that's what Baltimore needs: more retail chain stores, more lawyers' offices, more McDonalds and Burger Kings, more Kinko's Copies. Knock down The Block and build another street in Anywhere, U.S.A., so that all the nice people who come in to work and play from Hunt Valley and Glen Burnie will think they're in just another shopping center or theme park. Sounds good, doesn't it?

As a matter of fact, it doesn't. Baltimore without The Block sounds like just another stop in Monotony, the board game popular among city planners and other urban visionaries. However seedy The Block may be—and you'll get no argument on that score from this quarter—it is, beyond any doubt, a very real part of the complicated mix that has produced the place called Baltimore. If its glory days are well behind it, it still provides certain pleasures for certain people, and it still gives off an ambience that isn't to be found anywhere else in the city.

Precisely what goes on there is as much a mystery to me as it is to most if not all of you. Though I live less than five miles from The Block, I have not been there for more than two decades, long before I established residence in Baltimore. I visited it with a friend who cherishes memories of his journalistic apprenticeship in Baltimore and, late of an evening, proposed to refresh them. We drove over from Washington and presented ourselves at an establishment the name of which has long since fled my memory; it must have been the Dynasty Show Bar or, more likely, the Oasis Nite Club.

Whatever it was, it was something. The woman who was dancing—*dancing?*—at the center of attention had apparently forgotten to dress for work. To say that she left nothing to the imagination is to give new meaning to an old phrase. She was bored beyond description—so in time were we—and she went about her labors with an indifference so thick you could have sliced it up and carried a piece of it home, but there wasn't much doubt that this was the real thing.

An hour of it went a long way so far as I was concerned, but I'm not about to pretend that I didn't enjoy it. Nor did it seem to have any lasting or injurious effects; it was just a little taste of old Baltimore, one I remembered ever thereafter with no small amusement, as well as a conversation piece with which to regale visitors when, like the aforementioned motorists, we drove past The Block on our way home from the airport or the Inner Harbor.

What tales will we have to tell when The Block itself is but a memory? Will there be side-splitting anecdotes about "stately" Commerce Place and its thirty stories of mad passion? Somehow I doubt it. Baltimore without The Block simply will be less Baltimorean, just as Washington has been rather less its own true self since the prettification of the 14th Street porno corridor.

This isn't mere sentimentality about a lost past that wasn't half so wonderful as we like to think it was. A city without a tenderloin district is scarcely a city at all. The urge for porn—the urge for what the *Sun* airily dismisses as "go-go bars, peep shows and smut emporiums"—runs a good deal deeper in human nature than we like to admit, and cities have usually devised ways to accommodate it. By and large they have found it better to do so in constricted areas—Times Square, 14th Street, The Block, the Combat Zone in Boston—and thus to gain a measure of control over the crime that invariably follows it.

It is true that in the age of drugs this crime has gotten worse, but drugs really haven't much to do with the drive to demolish The Block. My friend the erstwhile apprentice reporter recalls writing about a similar drive fully three decades ago; then, as now, the real motive behind civic do-goodery was the profit allegedly to be made if only the rascals could be run off and "desirable redevelopment" undertaken.

What the do-gooders will never understand—it simply is not within their nature—is that no city can ever be made wholly "desirable." Bring human beings together in large numbers and what you get, along with high-rise lawyers' nests and waterfront theme parks, is vice. It's part of the package. Rub it out in one place and it simply resurfaces somewhere else. The prospect that it might do so next door to the anonymous editorialist of the *Sun* is delicious to contemplate but not, alas, likely to occur.

For Whom the Bell Rings

∽o∾

July 12, 1993

Back in my comics-reading days there was a feature called "There Oughta Be a Law!" the gist of which was precisely what its name suggests. There oughta be a law against people who put one car in two parking spaces; there oughta be a law against people who leave unattended carts in the grocery checkout line while they complete their purchases; there oughta be a law against people who wear Lycra Spandex tights over elephantine derrieres.

There oughta be a law, in other words, against people born and/or reared with an insufficient regard for the sensibilities and needs of others: an Anti-Lout Law, if you will. Should Congress at last enact such a law and the president sign it, more would be done for the public weal than has been done by all such laws before it, up to and including the Constitution of these United States.

Perhaps you have noticed that yearnings for such a law tend to become particularly ardent on weekday evenings at precisely the hour that you and yours have gathered at table for dinner. You have said a few words of blessing, if that is your wont; you have sliced the chicken or meted out the lasagna; you take a sip of water or wine, you lean back in your chair to open familial discussion of the day's events—and then it happens.

Can there be a sentient American in this last decade of the

second millennium A.D. who does not know what "it" is? Of course not, because "it" is the universal pestilence: the telephone. From sea to shining sea, the telephone now rings at dinner hour as surely as—and one hell of a lot more loudly than—the dinner bell itself once rang for Tom and Huck and Amy and Meg.

In America of the 1990s, never send to know for whom the bell rings; it rings for thee. So you rise from the table and hasten to the kitchen, full of hope that a relative is phoning with good news or that the state lottery, with its $100 million check, has at last tracked you down. In your heart, though, you know that no such luck awaits you. In your heart you know that lurking at the other end of the line is no kith or kin, no burst of good fortune, but the evil that afflicts us all.

It is called—with that genius for polysyllabic euphemism that distinguishes genus Americanus from the rest of homo sap— "telemarketing." It can be defined as high-pressure sales pitches of highly questionable honesty delivered via telephone by pushy pitchmen at the most inconvenient hours imaginable. Its distinguishing characteristics are implacable rudeness and utter irrelevance, i.e., no product or service has ever been sold by telephone solicitation for which any sane human being could have the slightest desire or use.

Six and a half years ago the question of telephonic harassment was first raised in this space. In the intervening period the harassment has increased exponentially, in large measure because of one cataclysmic event: the stock market crash of October 1987. The effects of that calamity touched almost all of us, but most particularly they touched the greedy young men who descended upon Wall Street during the 1980s in hopes of becoming Masters of the Universe.

Thanks to the crash, the greedy young men became needy young men. The accounts that had come tumbling into their laps during the Reaganite boom suddenly withered and died, leaving these feral capitalists to fend for themselves. This, as you most certainly do not need to be told, they commenced to do by becoming telemarketers, hawking the services of their houses of ill repute to innocents such as thee and me. They began plucking our names from the phone books and inflicting upon us their telephonic sales pitches: wheedling, whiny, insistent.

They know neither restraint nor shame. Usually they content themselves with phoning in late afternoon or early evening, managing with exquisite accuracy to assault their targets' ears at whatever moment is least convenient and congenial. Lately, their chutzpah has gone out of bounds. Last Wednesday, to cite an example that still strikes ghastly chords in memory, I was sitting around waiting for a Baltimore Orioles broadcast from Chicago that was scheduled to begin at 8:30. Precisely eleven minutes before the appointed hour the phone rang. Expecting to hear the voice of one of my sons, I picked up the receiver in a mood of pleasurable anticipation, a mood that instantly turned sour when a slimy male voice introduced itself as belonging to a representative of a brokerage firm.

It's nothing to be proud of, but there you have it: I went ballistic. Even the Wall Street sleazeball at the other end of the line must have shrunk in horror at the string of obscenities I hurled across time and space before crashing the receiver into its cradle in one last purgative explosion. All the irritation accumulated over nearly six years of gratuitous invasions of such privacy as I have managed to retain at last found furious expression in those few seconds of invective; rarely has dirty talk left me feeling so clean.

Rest assured, though, that a few moments of abuse will not keep this fellow from calling again, after he's made another tour through the telephone book and come full circle to the "Y" listings. Like another no less obnoxious creature of contemporary American life, the telemarketers just keep going, and going, and going, their determination undiscouraged by sales resistance, libel or slander. Neither snow, nor rain, nor heat, nor gloom of night stays these couriers from the swift completion of their appointed rounds. If anything, gloom of night now seems to be their preferred time of operation.

Precisely who succumbs to their siren calls is a mystery. Would you turn over your money to some bodiless voice that calls over the phone and asks for it? No, neither would I. But somewhere out there—in that vast obscurity beyond the city, where the dark fields of the republic roll on under the night—there must be a great tribe of the trusting and the gullible, its members huddled by their phones in eager expectation that soon they will ring and some nice man from New York will say: "Hello. This is Jason Goodlove from Trustme and Company. How would you like to send us another ten thousand dollars this evening?"

If it's not the stockbrokers it's the cops or the firemen or the disabled veterans or the home-remodeling specialists or the mentally retarded. Whether they're peddling good causes or bad products, the one certainty these days is that they're going to besiege you with an assault team of telemarketers. Some are aggressive, others passive aggressive, but whatever their style they're all sedulous invaders of privacy.

So there oughta be a law, right? The Supreme Court has opined that privacy is a right implicit in the Constitution, one so sweeping as to embrace just about every aspect of human behavior including a few that have nothing at all to do with privacy. In accordance with that principle, let's have a federal law prohibiting telemarketers from phoning people who don't want to hear their pitches, right?

Wrong. Quite apart from the somewhat shaky constitutional ground upon which the right to privacy still rests, it remains that such a restraint would almost certainly be, in some way, itself unconstitutional. No, the telemarketers are here to stay. You can fight them by letting the answering machine screen them into oblivion or you can scream at them to your heart's content, but they are an inescapable fact of late-twentieth-century American life. Death, taxes, telemarketers; by contrast with this last, the first two seem positively inviting.

UNCLE!

⌒◦⌒

February 14, 1994

It is as these words are written precisely two minutes before eight o'clock on the morning of Friday, the eleventh day of February in the Year of Our Lord 1994, and I am about to SCREAM. I am looking out the window and from what I can see I am about to be embalmed in ICE. I am trying to write a sensible thousand words for readers of the *Washington Post* about some matter of pressing public concern when the fact is that I am going CRAZY.

Whoa, son. Back off a little. Bring yourself down to earth. Think about something that amuses you. Think about, oh, Famous Newspaper Headlines of the Past. Think about when the stock market collapsed and some wit at Variety wrote: "WALL STREET LAYS AN EGG." Think about when New York City was sliding into ruin and the Ford administration declined to help and someone at the *New York Daily News* wrote: "FORD TO CITY: DROP DEAD."

I'm trying, I'm trying, but what I'm mainly thinking about is the winter of 1979, my first in the Mid-Atlantic after five in—O lost!—Miami. In January a snow fell on Baltimore such as had not been seen or remembered in many eons past. It amounted to more than two feet, it brought the city to a dead halt, and it produced my favorite headline of all headlines. It was written by some anonymous soul at the now-gone-and-by-me-still-mourned *Baltimore News American* and it read, in plaintive simplicity: "UNCLE!"

"UNCLE!"? Somehow that seems inadequate to what

we've endured these past seven weeks. "GREAT-GRAND-MOTHER!"? Maybe that's more like it: something so fearsome and distant and unconquerable as to shiver one's timbers, which is precisely what has been happening around here since Christmas Eve 1993, when the first of what weatherpeople call "frozen pre-cipitation" descended on the Mid-Atlantic. Since then the prob-lem hasn't been that the stuff has continued to fall without interruption—there was actually a ten-day break not so long ago—but that it has seemed that way. In spades.

There have been bigger snowfalls, by far. There has been thicker ice, though not much. There have even been, by the nar-rowest of margins, colder temperatures. But never within the memory of man or beast have there been all three in such endless, massive, MADDENING combinations.

Speaking of beasts. The cats are too stupid to know what's going on and in any event they can, if they are so inclined, do their Business indoors, or at least they can for a couple more days, because their reserve toiletries are now sprinkled all over the front sidewalk. But the dogs are smarter, and sadder, and they don't like any of this one single bit. The seven-year-old Norfolk terrier is entirely too dainty to do *her* Business on any surface save a leafy one, so she drags her servant half a mile until she finds a tree under which to perform her transaction. As for her companion, the fifteen-year-old dachshund, he is half deaf, two-thirds lame and totally blind; he just stands on the ice and shakes, his empty eyes pleading for someone to pick him up and put him back on his tuffet in the livingroom.

That's the sort of action a person gets in this kind of weather when he chooses to work at home. Fellow-workers envy him for not having to scrape off the car at 6:30 a.m. and then slide down to the train station, but on the other hand once they get to work, all they have to do is *work*. But for the home-office drone—the worker of tomorrow, so the futurologists tell us—duty multi-plies exponentially when the snow decides to conduct an ardent and ostentatious love affair with the sleet and the ice.

Take, for instance, the dogs; take them, please. Instead of just letting them out back, you have to dress up as if you were a contestant in the Winter Olympics and spend half an hour outdoors while they decide which frozen sprig of pachysandra to honor with their latest droppings. Driving half a mile to the neighborhood convenience store to pick up the *Washington Post*, normally a three-minute round-trip, becomes an heroic undertaking worthy of Peary or Byrd. Trying to make the front walk inviting for the mailman, should he condescend to drop by, involves marinating it in kitty litter and rock salt for three hours, then spending two hours whacking away at it with a shovel.

Ah yes, the mailman. He was otherwise occupied on Wednesday, when the ice decided to settle in. On Thursday he drove by, cast a disparaging glance and drove away, but later he returned and, seeing the newly cleared sidewalk, decided to disencumber himself of his precious load: four press releases, a plumber's bill, three catalogues, a half-dozen review copies (no keepers) and the *Sports Illustrated* swimsuit issue. I must be getting old. It didn't help at all.

No, these days everything hurts. Undoubtedly the best thing to do is to laugh at it, but you'd be amazed how rapidly that heh-heh-heh-hilarity turns into INSANITY. The cruellest blow was delivered at three o'clock this morning, when I awoke for the first of several dozen times. Eight different weatherpersons had told me on Thursday evening that what I'd hear at three o'clock Friday morning would be snow, so what did I hear? I heard SLEET, and it made me SOB.

Oh, those weatherpeople. In the best of times I'm a Weather Channel addict—I know what time to get the international weather, what time to watch the Weather Classroom, what time to check in with Jim Cantore and when to catch Jill Brown—but for the past six weeks my addiction has reached a crescendo such as can be cured only at the Betty Ford Center. The Weather Channel stays on round the clock, bringing minute-by-minute radar and Five-Day Business Planners and, best of all, the particular and peculiar argot of the Weather Channel, to wit: "This latest in a series of winter weather events" and "a big dome of Arctic air" and—EEEAGH!!—"just be patient a while longer."

Well, I'd really like to stick around and give you the full

benefit of my deepest thoughts on Bosnia and Whitewater and all the other great issues of the day—chief among them being, "Can Michael Jordan hit the curveball?"—but more pressing matters beckon. Looking out the window I can see the limbs of the big old elm bending in an ever more stately fashion. That long thick one now looks to be about six inches from the power line. I'd better zip this into the modem before we lose our elec

ON THE GULF COURSE

〜◦〜

June 19, 1995

In Rochester last week on a lit'ry gumshoeing mission, I found myself with time to kill between visits to the rare-book room at the University of Rochester's library. This is a familiar problem for the nation's road warriors, those men and women to whom the interstates and the friendly skies are home sweet home, but to a domestic creature whose universe ordinarily is a quarter-acre lot, this was a new and daunting challenge.

Thank heavens, then, for television. Not merely did it provide innumerable baseball games, all dull beyond imagination and thus excellent soporifics, but it offered the bizarre spectacle of the sachems of the militia "movement" testifying to a committee of the United States Senate. Surely the most bizarre of these was Norman Olson, of Michigan, duded up in his camouflage and looking for all the world like Donald Sutherland in one of that actor's more outre films.

Television also provided the Weather Channel, which was of only marginal interest because the weather in upstate New York last week was ethereal, but this did not prevent me from wasting plenty of time staring at its radar pictures and West Coast rain reports. More about that in a moment. First it is necessary to report that while staring at the TV early in my stay, I looked up, glanced out the motel window and realized, after several minutes' bewildered speculation, that I had landed amidst the highest priestesses of golf.

Golf is not a matter of interest to me. Some of my best

friends and even a few of my most treasured relatives play the game, but in my considered opinion it ranks somewhere up there with camouflaged militiamen in the idiocy department. Still, there I was, stuck for an entire week at a motel that had transformed itself, for the same week, into home sweet home for members of the road show known as the Ladies' Professional Golf Association tour.

The presence of these fetching creatures in surroundings so intimate as these was immensely interesting, as no doubt you can imagine, and not merely because, though golf may not be appealing, ladies are. It was especially interesting because of the comments allegedly made by a television gentleman a few weeks back to the effect that women's golf has no following because too many of those who play it are of the lesbian persuasion and, beyond that, because anyone of the female sex is limited in her golf swing by certain natural appendages that gentlemen ordinarily find much to their liking.

Being neither a golfer nor a sports consultant, I am unable to report with anything approximating authority on my findings in regard to the second of these charges, though this was not for lack of looking. But as to the first, it must be reported that if the ladies' golf tour is populated by the sisters of Sappho, those in residence at my inn were mighty peculiar ones. Almost all had children in tow. I heard much poolside chatter about infant formulae and babysitting difficulties, saw much romping not merely with children but also with male types who appeared to be companions and may even have been husbands.

In an attempt to maintain a conspiratorial mood I imagined that these children and men had been hired by the LPGA ("L" as in "Lesbian"?) to present a scene of sham hetero domesticity for the delectation of the good burghers of Rochester, but if that was the case all concerned should receive Lifetime Achievement Awards from the American Academy of Motion Picture Arts and Sciences. They put on one hell of a show.

It was while watching said show that I happened to overhear, in the background, the steady hum-chatter-hum of the Weather Channel, with its customary reports on occluded fronts and stationary low pressure systems. At thirteen minutes before the hour talk turned, as it always does this time of year, to the tropics and the various weather antics therein, antics that weather people love the way news people love disasters natural or otherwise. Talk of the tropics led to the Gulf of Mexico, wherein has been cooked up not merely many a storm but many a killer hurricane as well.

Except that at the Weather Channel nobody talks about "the Gulf of Mexico." They talk about "the Golf of Mexico." You may have thought that at meteorology school they teach the aspiring weather persons about the aforementioned occluded fronts and stationary low pressure systems, but you thought wrong. The entire four years of weather school are spent learning that, contrary to everything Mom and Dad tried to teach you, "gulf" is pronounced "golf."

This is confusing in the best of circumstances. There you are with your coffee and your newspaper, trying to get the day off to a happy start, and in the background someone is talking about "a storm brewing in the Golf of Mexico." The person from the Weather Channel is trying to get you to imagine howling winds and stormy seas, but the only picture those words conjure up is of Jack Nicklaus in a sombrero or Nancy Lopez in a serape.

Speaking of whom, she is the only lady golfer whose name means anything to me, and there she was at my very own motel, shepherding children this way and that, chauffeuring them and herself in a "courtesy" car provided by a friendly local Buick dealer. She looked like a nice lady. It was tempting indeed to ask her about the television gentleman's alleged Major Charges against ladies' golf, but by this point I was so addled that I wouldn't have known how to frame that question or any other. "How's your gulf game this week?" "How's the weather in the Golf of Rochester today?" "Is ladies' gulf suffering from a credibility golf?"

So I just sat there, tongue-tied, while another nice lady, Cheryl Lemke, talked on the Weather Channel about "the Golf of Mexico" and about various weather systems "draped" this way and that across the continental U.S. of A., a phrase that invariably calls to my twisted mind not the image of weather systems sprawled across the country but that of a fetching female creature recumbent upon a bed of roses with a gossamer thingie "draped" across all those parts that do so much to hamper her gulf swing.

Tongue-tied and imagery-perverse, I searched desperately for something, anything, to restore me to normality. Knowing that there's nothing more normal, more apple pie, more all-American, than *USA Today*, I reached for the copy I'd picked up in the lobby. Talk about all-American! The first words I read were from a new "song" by Michael Jackson: "I'm taking no s—-!"

Gulf, anyone?

CALL ME . . . JOHANNA?

∽◦∾

October 9, 1995

"**U**h . . ." The woman behind the counter looked in bewilderment at the document in her hand." "Johanna?" she asked, peering over her eyeglasses at the handful of people facing her. Nobody budged. "Joanna?" she tried, but still no one stirred, so she beckoned to the woman at the adjoining desk in a "Driver License Renewal Express Office" of the Maryland Motor Vehicle Administration.

The second woman seized command at once. "Jonathan!" she proclaimed at once. "Jonathan!" she cried out to the throng. "Jonathan, come get your license!" So that is what I did, uttering not a word of protest, shuffling to the head of the line to take possession of the worst portrait in the history of photography and then fleeing the premises.

What I should have done . . . ah, but no one does what he or she should do any more. No one protests. No one says, "Call me mister" or "Call me madam." Instead everyone capitulates to the now all-pervasive abandonment not merely of old-fashioned formal honorifics but of surnames themselves. In the decade since the subject was last raised in this space, the battle has been lost and unconditional surrender has been declared in the war itself.

Ten years ago I wrote that "to insist on a measure of formality in your dealings with persons you do not know is to mark yourself as a snob, a fuddy-duddy encrusted with the barnacles of Victorian reticence," that "to address strangers by honorifics, and to expect that they in turn address you similarly, is now regarded as strictly antisocial behavior." That was 1985. Now, in 1995, simple, mannerly formality is so alien to the common experience of most Americans that its occasional appearance is cause for comment, if not contempt.

Precisely how and why this came to pass is one of America's unfathomable mysteries, like Twinkies and grunge, but it seems reasonable to assume that it is yet another byproduct of the 1960s and their let-it-all-hang-out culture. Giving the devil her due, let's assume that it began as a well-intentioned effort to narrow the distance between people by making them more easily approachable. But if that's how it began, it has ended in an institutionalized informality that is every bit as rigid as the institutionalized formality it replaced.

Do business with almost anyone in America now and chances are you will immediately be addressed by your first name. The other day I called a tire shop to make an appointment. "Name?" the man at the other end asked. "Jon Yardley," I replied. "Okay, Jon," he said, "see you at eleven tomorrow morning." The sleazeballs who call several times a day from Wall Street brokerages invariably open their pitch with, "Hello, Jonathan, this is Jason from . . ."

Not long ago a man called to request my assistance in a project he had underway. He called me "Jonathan" from the outset but I insisted on calling him "Mister." When finally we appeared together in the same room I found an excuse to mention my strong aversion to instant intimacy; so he called me "Mister" once, then immediately lapsed back into "Jonathan" for the duration.

Sometimes the urge to protest becomes irresistible, but it does absolutely no good. A while back I asked a woman who called me "Jonathan" if we'd ever actually met. She acknowledged that we had not. On what authority, then, did she have the effrontery to call me by my first name? She was offended and furious. In questioning the prevailing social norm I had somehow managed to deliver a personal insult to her. The conversation ended in a mutual huff.

An occasional hazard of my line of work is phone calls from

youthful publicists at New York publishing houses. A quarter-century ago, when they and I were the same age, they called me "Mister" until we had met and become friends. Now, when I am three decades their senior, they call me "Jonathan" from the first call. The next one to call me "Mister" might actually find his or her book reviewed, out of sheer gratitude and amazement.

It isn't just the business world where artificial intimacy prevails, it's the private world as well. Young children call me by my first name, and I silently countenance it out of affection for their parents; I learned my lesson years ago when I asked a child to call me "Mr. Yardley" and was not-so-silently scorned by one of her parents for doing so. That the eight-year-old next door actually calls me "Mister" is one of the miracles of the age, and I blink in wonder whenever I hear her say it, but doubtless she'll learn better when she becomes a member of what is known, incredibly enough, as adult society.

Grumble, grumble, groan, groan. None of it will get me anywhere and all of it merely confirms what I know all too well, i.e., that I'm an old crank. So rather than grumble and groan any further, I propose that we all unite to take this social movement to its logical conclusions, each and every one of them. Away with honorifics, away with them all! Away not merely with mister and mistress, madam and miz, but also with señor and señora, signore and signora, memsahib and mem, shri and sri—not to mention effendi, citoyen and tovarich! No more Mr. Nice Guy? No! No more Mr. and no more Guy.

First we go to work on the journalistic holdouts, the *New York Times*, the *Wall Street Journal* and the *Baltimore Sun*, which with a certain endearing stuffiness insist on using the honorifics everywhere except for convicted criminals and on the sports pages, thus producing the odd phenomenon in which "Ripken" becomes "Mr. Ripken" when he is front page news. Away with it all! Not merely away with honorifics, but with surnames as well. Inasmuch as our highest national leaders long ago went halfway informal, let's now go all the way:

> Bill informed Congress yesterday that he supported reforms of the welfare system devised by Pat and endorsed

by Al but opposed by Bob and Phil. Barbara immediately expressed support for this position; Carol said she would think about it; Nancy said she was definitely against it. Pat angrily denounced it as socialistic and Pat said he would pray about it on television. Jimmy and Jerry disagreed as usual, while Ron and George had not been heard from as this newspaper went to press. Run, Spot, run.

Honorifics, surnames—they're all gone. No more presidents, no more reverends, no more senators, no more popes, no more saints. Nobody is sacred now, not even that highest priest of American sport, Neon Deion. Just call him Neon.

The Breaking News

‿◦◦‿

July 8, 1996

The shucks-'n'-nubbins school of journalism is hogwash through and through, but that doesn't prevent the occasional journalist from taking a stab at it. Its essential conceit is that a big-city media type can slip into a pair of worn denim coveralls, stick a hay straw between his teeth and, thus disguised, somehow tap into the Voice of the People. The truth is that you can take the journalist out of the city but you can't take the city out of the journalist, especially a journalist of the big-city, big-foot variety.

But the temptations of shucks-'n'-nubbins are considerable, even to one who has spent a lifetime doggedly resisting them. For a week I and my laptop have been on duty on the western bank of the North East River in northeastern Maryland—got that straight?—which is just about as far as one can go in that direction and still be more or less within striking range of the *Washington Post*. I have to drive eight miles to get it, at the 7–11 in Havre de Grace, but it's worth every inch of the trek to stay up to speed on such cardiac-arresting matters as (a) Is Boris Yeltsin live or embalmed? (b) Is what we have here the "old" Bob Dole or the "new" Bob Dole? and (c) Whither Saudi Arabia?

I mean, guys, get off it. Does anybody out there really care? Is Washington out of touch or is Washington out of touch? Is there a soul within shouting distance of sanity who actually thinks it matters whether (this is what some *Baltimore Sun* editorialist was stewed about last Friday) Turkey is more Islamic or less Islamic? Let Turkey worry about Turkey is what I say, and let me worry about . . .

Well, for starters I am worried about crabs. The *Cecil Whig* is worried about crabs. The Cecil What? No, this is not a joke. The *Whig* is the only daily newspaper published in Cecil County—five days counts as a week in Cecil County—and a copy awaits me each weekday morning in a bright yellow plastic tube hard by the garage. The *Whig* was founded in August 1841, as an organ of the Whig party; two years later its founding editor shot and killed a leading Democrat of the county, but after this moment of glory, according to George Johnston's history of the county, he "lived long enough to win the respect and esteem of many of those who were once his bitterest enemies."

The *Whig* itself has lived long enough to outlast its founder, the innumerable controversies in which he was engaged, and the party whose name he gave to his newspaper. This last is unfortunate. The *Whig* party in this country emerged in large measure as the instrument of two great men, Henry Clay and Daniel Webster, in opposition to one scoundrel, Andrew Jackson. The first time it won the White House, in 1840, with the ticket of William Henry Harrison and John Tyler, it did so under the slogan, "Log Cabin and Hard Cider," which seems to me an entirely agreeable combination, especially for the western bank of the North East River. In any event I am a closet Whig at heart, and I emerge from that closet each morning when the *Whig* arrives.

Last Friday it did so with the obligatory front-page Fourth of July photo feature about cute children, fireworks and Old Glory. Ho hum. The real news was elsewhere on the same page: a lead story recounting the woes of a North East (compounding the confusion, North East is a town as well as a river as well as a direction on the compass) restaurateur whose off-track-betting parlor is taking a beating from the slots in Delaware; a parking "nightmare" in Chesapeake City, where a new restaurant has "added to the town's parking difficulties"; and, across the bottom of the page, a piece lamenting that "everyone wants crabs and nobody has them."

The Fourth of July holiday is one of the great crab-eating

occasions of the crab season, but this year crabs are as scarce as hens' teeth. "The harsh winter, a wet spring and hungry rockfish have taken their toll," the *Whig* reported, with the result that crab supplies are low and crab prices are high. Buddy's Seafood Crab Shack in Perryville could have sold 100 bushels on the Fourth, expected to get 24 bushels, but wound up with only 14, which were gone by mid-afternoon. The Crab Shack in Chesapeake City was getting $120 a bushel; a restaurateur in Elkton reported prices as high as $130, $35 higher than a year ago.

Now, not to slip into the denim coveralls or anything like that, but doesn't the crab shortage in the Chesapeake Bay strike you as just a tiny bit more interesting, not to mention important, than whether Boris Yeltsin is or is not just a great big ventriloquist's dummy being manipulated from behind the curtain by Aleksandr Solzhenitsyn? If you decide to have dinner at the Bayard House in Chesapeake City on Saturday night—sounds good to me—your inability to find a parking place is going to seem a whole lot more important to you than whether Bob Dole is just a great big ventriloquist's dummy being manipulated by the ghost of Richard Nixon.

Among other noteworthy matters with which the *Whig* was preoccupied last week were the fireworks show in—here we go again—North East; it was cancelled because the organizers never managed to get organized, leaving North East officialdom to squabble over who was at fault. In Elkton the cable company is up in arms because some of Cecil County's sneakier citizens—5 to 10 per cent all told, a tribute to local resourcefulness—have figured out how to tap illegally into cable lines. In yet another dispatch from that seething hotbed of newsworthiness, a teenager from North East and his mother were nabbed by town police in what looked for all the world like illegal possession of firearms; maybe they should have run the fireworks show.

From time to time I find myself snickering at the *Whig* because its news diet consists primarily of auto accidents, minor break-ins involving the theft of chainsaws, and county commissioners denying conflicts of interest. But think about it. If you have the misfortune to be in an auto accident or to be a witness to one, it is the most important thing in the world to you that day. In the *Washington Post* or the *Baltimore Sun* or—hah!—the *New York Times*, the only way an auto accident makes the paper is if it kills off a president, a movie star or a truckful of illegal immigrants. In the *Cecil Whig*, by contrast, all you have to do to get your picture in the paper—your car's, too—is to rub up against someone else's fender on Main Street in North East. That's news, folks, and that's the *Whig*, and that ain't shucks-'n'-nubbins.

BOTTOMS UP

∽०∾

November 3, 1997

From readers too numerous to count have come phone calls, e-mail and letters, all expressing surprise, delight and pride at my recent appointment—after years of supplication and prayer —as official "shot-and-beer guy" of the *Washington Post*. This, I well know, is a large honor and a grave responsibility. An official shot-and-beer guy must pour the best shots and drink the best beer. This is why, in hopes of improving my performance, I have been seeking expert advice.

Actually—"in point of fact," as we pointy-heads like to say—I am not a shot kind of guy at all. In my extraordinarily foolish youth I consumed so much of what goes into shot glasses that a couple of decades ago I quit hard stuff altogether. Except for a ritual glass of bourbon each Christmas Eve, after the rest of the household has gone to bed and I have done my Santa Claus duties, I no longer hang around with John Barleycorn. In the boozy words of my fellow Chapel Hill alumnus Thomas Wolfe: "O lost, and by the wind grieved, ghost, come back again."

Into the bargain I am not, if the truth be laid out like a wino etherized on a table, all that much of a beer guy, either, though for a while I certainly was. In my salad days—which took place long before salad became an obsession of the power-luncheon crowd—I hung out at a subterranean place in Chapel Hill called the Tempo Room, drinking beer by the pitcher, listening to Miles Davis and Duke Ellington and Gerry Mulligan and Erroll Garner

285

(in those days college-town bars played good music) and generally misbehaving.

Since then I have corked the keg. My beverage of choice is cheap but tasty red wine, a step or two above what the Brits call plonk—one of the language's great words, by the way—at an absolute maximum of $8 per bottle, $5 being my preference; buy it at case prices and you'll get something not bad, often remarkably good. Beer is now only an occasional hot-weather treat, though a supply is always maintained for my sons, who politely claim that good old Bud is just fine but whose eyes light up when they spot a six-pack of Sam Adams in the fridge.

Which leads, admittedly in a most circuitous fashion, to the real topic of this morning's disquisition. Attending to my shot-and-beer duties, I jumped with joy the other day when the mail yielded a review copy of *The Beer Essentials: The Spirit Journal Guide to Over 650 of the World's Better Beers*, by one F. Paul Pacult. Here, it seemed, was just what I needed. In the past I had been a faithful reader of *The Simon & Schuster Pocket Guide to Beer*, by Michael Jackson—no, not *that* Michael Jackson—but my copy is more than a decade old and, though still readable and witty, out of date. F. Paul Pacult, I was confident, would be my new guide through the world of beer, his *The Beer Essentials* my vade mecum.

Then I started to read *The Beer Essentials*. I soon discovered that the prose of wine criticism—the worst prose this side of academic lit-crit—has now found its way into beer criticism. *Beer criticism?* Isn't that an oxymoron? Certainly it used to be. Nobody bothered to *criticize* beer, except perhaps in language unprintable in a family newspaper but having to do with equine emissions; guys just bellied up to the bar and drank it, like—note the shot-and-beer-guy misuse of "like"—beer guys generally do.

But that was yesterday. Beer guys who once made sport of wine snobs and their sommeliers now must genuflect before the dicta of F. Paul Pacult. Back in the old days the beer guys would have snickered at F. Paul, mocking him for putting his middle initial in the wrong place, but now he is their high priest, and it is at his altar that they must worship.

If, that is, they can figure out what in hell (shot-and-beer-guy lingo) he is talking about. If you take a dive into F. Paul's prose you'd better have on your Mae West, because if you don't you're going to sink like a rock. Here, chosen—I swear!—utterly at random, is his appraisal of something called Mamba Malt Liquor:

> Sturdy-looking, 14-carat-gold hue, eggshell foam, very good head retention; the nose is zesty, assertive and estery—I think of yellow tropical fruit when smelling this appealing malt liquor from Africa's west coast—the last two nosings highlight both malt and fruit—a good, happy, snappy bouquet; in the mouth, the malt makes a strong play at entry, then in midpalate a succulently sweet, bread-dough flavor dominates; the finish is quite sweet, almost sugary, and very extended.

Wow. Sommelier, bring me a Miller Lite, but go easy on the nose, not to mention the ester. *(Ester?)* Actually, bring me almost anything but Miller Lite: "Very pale straw color, moderately foamy head, no head retention; the embarrassingly bland, salty, tanky, almost nonexistent nose is a total loser; on palate, it's neutral, virtually devoid of taste; the finish is hard, tinny, mere skin and bones. . . ."

No . . . head . . . retention. When F. Paul whips out the stiletto, it's time to read the last rites. But on the other hand, when he plants a kiss—as he does on Pilsner Urquell, "a perfect beer"—it's as wet as the French Quarter on Saturday night:

> the dry nose is the deepest, most profound and most layered of any of the world's golden lagers—the fragrant bouquet is so supple, round, voluminous and evolved that you can almost chew it—the complex network of aromas, including dry, flowery Zatec hops, lightly toasted malt, corn husk, brown rice and kid-leather gloves, keeps the olfactory sense focused and thoroughly entertained through all four nosings. . . .

Kid-leather gloves? If that doesn't send the shot-and-beer guys down to Murphy's Bar & Grill, what in the name of Jimmy

Breslin will? They can belly up to the bar and slurp kid leather. Then, as the high starts to escalate, they can switch to Lakefront Brewery Cream City Pale Ale ("aromas of sweet cereal, cocoa, grain husk and Butterfinger candy bars"); from there they can stagger along to Catamount Bock ("ripe banana, guava and honey"); come midnight, if they haven't already puddled out on the floor, they'll at last be ready for Thomas Hardy's Ale, which offers not merely "dried roses, sweet licorice and molasses," not merely "charcoal, cola and nuts," not merely "licorice, herbal finish" but—brace yourself—"endless road tar."

As the late John Denver doubtless would have put it: Thank *God* I'm a shot-and-beer guy.

A Modest Proposal

∾

December 15, 1997

From Hollywood, where all things can and sooner or later do happen, a couple of interesting developments have been reported. The issues these raise may seem unrelated to the insufficiently nimble, but to this department they look as interconnected as salt and pepper. That being the case, herewith a modest proposal by which the twain shall meet.

The first was noted last week in the *New York Times*, as indeed was the second, leaving one to ponder the vast hole that would be left in our lives should this most venerable and respected of news organs suddenly decide to stop reporting on the doings of the rich, the famous and the bubble-headed. The story had to do with something called a "Brad Pitt." My immediate thought upon encountering this phrase was that someone had at last met one of humanity's great unfulfilled needs by inventing a repository for used finishing nails, but it turned out that I was wrong. "Brad Pitt" is a laborer in motion pictures—a "cinemactor," to use a coinage that any connoisseur of *Time* magazine prose will fondly recall—and thus a person who has far more money than he deserves or needs.

What to do with it all? This question may never cross the mind of thee or me, but it is a quotidian worry for the high and mighty of our land: Stockbrokers, professional basketball players, movie stars. Some buy houses in the Hamptons, then raze them and erect even bigger and indescribably more gaudy ones in their place. Some, not patient with the tortoise-like pace of nature, import full-grown trees to line the drives to their estates, as that avatar of cinematic profundity, Steven Spielberg, did some years ago. Yet others fill their garages with German and Italian driving machines so costly as to leave the minds of poor ordinary mortals spinning in bewilderment.

But some—and this is where "Brad Pitt" enters the story—lavish lordly gifts upon those whom they most love, who are in position to do them the most useful favors. In the case of "Brad Pitt" the object of his affections is one Alan J. Pakula, a director of the cinema in whose vineyards the cinemactor not long ago toiled. When the project was at last completed "Brad Pitt" felt it necessary to express his gratitude and affection in material form, so he betook himself to a (!) bookshop and purchased, for Pakula, a (!) book.

Ah, but not just any old book. A very, very expensive book—"worth from $2,000 to $5,000," according to the *Times*—and, into the bargain, a very, very, *very* unreadable book: a first edition of *Finnegans Wake*, by James Joyce. It's the thought that counts, leaving us to ponder exactly what thoughts lay behind the purchase by a movie actor—who probably runs his finger along the page as he struggles though the comics—of a book that can paralyze tenured professors of semiotics, deconstruction and other lunacies.

Whatever those thoughts may be, apparently they are now pandemic among La La Land glitterati, for the *Times* reports that "expensive, first-edition volumes of classic works of literature are hot properties in Hollywood," purchased "for prices ranging from $500 to $45,000, [as] gifts—from actor to director, from agent to client." Gift-giving being how brown-nosing gets done in Hollywood, first editions are flying this way and that, purchased not merely by "Brad Pitt" but also by something called "Johnny Depp," the very name of which conjures up visions of Shakespeare and Ruskin, Euripides and Racine.

Yet because Hollywood is indeed a wondrous strange place, a mere stone's throw from the scene of this ostentatious generosity is one of piteous deprivation. As the *Times* also reported, Hollywood Memorial Park Cemetery, where "the ghosts of the great ones linger: Cecil B. DeMille, Tyrone Power, Rudolph Valentino, Douglas Fairbanks Sr.," went bankrupt two years ago and was allowed to fall into grievous disrepair. Last month "the only bidder at a public auction . . . offered just over half the $500,000 asking price of the bank that holds the mortgage, and a court-appointed trustee sought permission to padlock the gates and abandon the graves to the fates."

Well, salvation subsequently rode to the rescue in the form of Callanan Mortuary, a funeral home "whose owners vowed to take good care of the legacy." This will come as a vast relief to all who cherish the grand tradition of Hollywood morbidity as epitomized by Evelyn Waugh in *The Loved One*—a novel that Hollywood, true to character, eventually bowdlerized and trivialized in the movie version. But as a ranking manager of Callanan Mortuary told the *Times*, "This [cemetery] has years of deferred maintenance," which raises doubts—at least in this suspicious mind—about whether Callanan will have, over the long haul, the way as well as the will to keep the cemetery spruce.

But there is, as perhaps you yourself have concluded, an obvious and potentially lucrative solution to the problem. If rare-book dealers in Hollywood—I know, I know, it *does* have the ring of oxymoron—can make a killing off dead authors, why can't Callanan Mortuary underwrite the restoration of Hollywood's most famous cemetery by selling off dead movie stars?

Here's the way it would work. Right now, once a movie is finished and the star wants to express gratitude to the director—not to mention stay in his good graces with an eye to other projects down the line—she hands him a slender volume and says, "Here, darling, especially for you, a first edition of *Leaves of Grass*." This being Hollywood, the only imaginable response is, "Hunnnh?" To put it bluntly: an utterly inappropriate tribute.

But now, for those who care enough to give the very best, the gift that keeps on giving is at last available. Our grateful star can venture down to Rodeo Drive and get Gucci or Pucci to gift-wrap her special expression of gratitude. When the lucky recipient unwraps his tiny box he will find inside a tasteful model of a Callanan Mortuary hearse. Opening the rear doors, he will behold a teeny weeny coffin, and inside that he will find an engraved card announcing that he is now the proud owner of Cecil B. De-Mille.

A hundred grand seems about right for so sumptuous a gift. Sell off DeMille and Power and Valentino and Fairbanks—not to mention Janet Gaynor, Joan Hackett and Peter Finch—and the cemetery's well-being will be assured unto the next millennium. In time whole new universes of meaning will accrue to a phrase already much cherished out yonder: It is to die for.

COUNTRY BOY

❦

December 22, 1997

Here sit I, on the west bank of the North East River, watching the days of summer dwindle down to a precious few. It's a perfect spot for such idle business, this tiny place called Sand Cove, on a spit of land at the head of the Bay called Carpenter's Point, in Cecil County, in northeasternmost Maryland, just a few minutes' drive from North East.

The town, not the river. The North East River is right at my feet; every once in a while, when a fair- to medium-sized storm pushes up the bay, the river invades the yard, moving decorative lumber this way and that and, in one of the hurricane leftovers we were treated to last year, completely washing away the little raised garden.

The vagaries of the river inspired me to do something about that garden, so last spring I dug more than a dozen three-foot postholes, filled each with a 4"x4"x4' treated post sunk in concrete and bolted two dozen 4"x4"x8' posts to them. Then I went to bed for about a week. By the time I stumbled back into action the rest of the family had filled the new hurricane-proof bed with topsoil, treated it to a big drink of fertilizer and planted it with tomatoes, peppers, basil, parsley and cucumbers.

All of which were quite spectacular in August, but now we're well toward the end of September and the plants too are dwindling down. The cukes, of the pickling variety, have long since come and gone, but the basil and parsley and peppers remain hardy. It's the tomatoes I worry about, mainly because it's the tomatoes I like the most. In the heat of August they thrive, bursting with moist sweetness—or should that be sweet moistness?—but they didn't care for the cold snap that passed through a couple of weeks ago, and expressed their dissatisfaction by slowing the ripening process just about to a halt. Last week's warm spell helped matters, but it's going to take some artful slicing and dicing to make a tasty sauce out of the dozen or so pinkish-red ones now sitting on the kitchen counter.

Those rebellious tomatoes are one sign that fall is here. Another is the kids standing by the side of the road at seven of a weekday morning, waiting for the school bus. All summer I made the fifteen-mile roundtrip newspaper run to North East—the town, not the river—with nobody else on the road except the occasional pickup or construction truck, but suddenly a few weeks ago the kids were there, and the buses, and it became necessary to reconfigure the morning schedule in order to avoid getting stuck behind one—or more—of the buses.

So now I get up at six, walk the dogs, and get back from the paper run in time to see the early-autumn sunrise. This morning's was spectacular. The sun rose over the east bank of the North East River, slowly coming over the hills of Elk Neck, at first casting a pink glow through the low, thin clouds, then bursting into view, a bright orange ball announcing the arrival of the day.

This morning it was cool, in the low 50s, and for a couple of minutes the sun pulled moisture from the river, leaving the few boats still moored there floating in a mist. Few boats, that is, because most of the summer trade has packed up and gone home. Cecil County may not seem much of a resort to the rest of Maryland, but tell that to Pennsylvania, which sends so many of its folk down here in the warm months that the vessels moored or docked in the county's many miles of waterway are known, locally, as "the Pennsylvania Navy." Sometimes to break the monotony of my daily walk I count license tags from the two states; it's not uncommon for Pennsylvania to outnumber Maryland by two to one.

This is the way most Cecil Countians seem to like it. They prefer income derived from what passes for tourism to income derived from business and industry. To call this conservation would be to abuse the word, since the visitors bring campers and propane tanks and thunderous outboards and sewage in many varieties, but since Cecil Countians have their own ample supplies of all the above, they assume that this is the natural way of things, and they aim to keep it that way.

This is why the county is having a great argument about its future. The local powers that be have it in mind to lay a pipeline to bring fresh water in from the Susquehanna, the magnificent river that forms the county's western border. The powers that be include the editors of the *Cecil Whig*, who last week advised their readers that such a pipeline would benefit not just "a few landholders" but all of us: "Abundant water, along with gas and sewer service promised through other planned pipelines, will attract the kind of business development that ultimately will benefit all countians through employment and lower property tax rates."

Maybe so, maybe not. As a city boy not entirely immune to the big-picture thumbsucking that passes for thought in Washington, I suspect that the *Whig* and the Chamber of Commerce and the resident movers and shakers are right, but as a part-time resident of Sand Cove I tend to nod in sympathy at all the antipipeline placards with which roads hereabout are littered. Cecil Countians seem perfectly content to drive a few miles into Delaware to find employment, if that means returning to a home sweet home of RVs, Jet-Skis and Webers. In a world where everything is growing too fast and too chaotically, the preference of what may well be a majority of Cecil Countians for these bits and pieces of the American dream is, in its fashion, admirable.

How all this pipeline business plays out may well be determined during the winter, though the issue has alternately percolated and marinated for so long that it may never be resolved. But if winter is the hour of decision, I probably won't be around to learn the outcome. It's not that I'm a fair-weather resident of the county—the river can be even lovelier in cold weather, especially if it freezes over in what seems mid-motion—but that this little house, originally not much more than a fishing cabin, can't keep me and my bones as warm as we like. A couple of years ago I spent the two longest days of my life on my back in the three-foot dirt crawl space, shoving thick pads of insulation between the joists and securing them with chicken wire, but cool January breezes still make their way through my toes. In a few weeks I'll drain the pipes, put the *Whig* on home-delivery hold and head back to the city for the cold spell. With visions of spring and the river dancing in my head.

ABOUT THE AUTHOR

⚬⚬⚬

JONATHAN YARDLEY is the book critic and a columnist for the *Washington Post*. He was a Nieman Fellow in Journalism at Harvard University in 1968–69 and was awarded the Pulitzer Prize for Distinguished Criticism in 1981. This is his sixth book. In 1998 he moved from Baltimore to Washington, where he lives with Marie Arana-Ward.